REUNION

*A Year in Letters
Between a Birthmother
and the Daughter
She Couldn't Keep*

KATIE HERN AND ELLEN McGARRY CARLSON

Cover design by Trina Stahl
Text design by Alison Rogalsky

Library of Congress Cataloging-in-Publication Data
Hern, Katie, 1969–
Reunion : a year in letters between a birthmother and the daughter she couldn't keep / Katie Hern and Ellen McGarry Carlson
Includes bibliographical references.
1. Hern, Katie, 1969—Correspondence. 2. Carlson, Ellen McGarry, 1948—Correspondence. 3. Birthmothers—United States—Correspondence.
4. Adoptees—United States—Correspondence. 5. Mothers and daughters—United States—Correspondence.
I. Carlson, Ellen McGarry, 1948–   . II. Title.
HQ755.85.H475   1999   306.874'3—dc21   99-38720
ISBN 1-58005-030-1

Printed in Canada

First printing, November 1999

10   9   8   7   6   5   4   3   2   1

Distributed to the trade by Publishers Group West
In Canada: Publishers Group West Canada, Toronto, Ontario
In the U.K. and Europe: Airlift Book Distributors, Middlesex, England
In Australia: Banyan Tree Book Distributors, Kent Town, South Australia

With love, to all our families

Acknowledgments

We would both like to thank the many colleagues, friends and family members who encouraged us to publish these letters and supported us along the way. In particular, we want to acknowledge Frank Free at the National Writer's Union and writer Cynthia Lamb for their helpful advice about book contracts; publisher Faith Conlon for her compassionate editing style; and all the great women at Seal Press for their commitment to the project.

Katie appreciates the ongoing support of her weekly writing group (Ann Aubin, Alissa Blackman, Matthew Davison, Sue Libby and Mary Michael Wagner), as well as her fellow writing teacher Laura Ann Kay. She'd also like to thank her parents, Mary and David Hern, for a lifetime of love and support; her sister Theresa for encouraging this book despite its occasionally unflattering depictions of her; her brother Matt for his kind, gentle spirit; and Cara, for so much love and good humor.

Ellen would like to thank the many English professors at the University of Massachusetts at Lowell who encouraged and promoted her efforts, especially Marlowe Miller for her enthusiastic early reading; her sister Ann for her open and generous heart; Gus and Jack for unselfishly giving up so much mommy-time; and John for his support, wise counsel and enduring love.

Authors' Note

The letters in this book have been edited for length, coherence and style; additionally, some names and identifying details have been changed to protect the privacy of those involved. But aside from these minor changes, the letters are as originally written.

REUNION

February 1996

✦

Dear Ellen,

I'm the grown-up version of the daughter you gave up for adoption in 1969. My name is Kathleen—Kathleen Mary Hern—and most people call me Katie.

So, uh . . . hello.

I know that Catholic Charities told you I received your name and address, so at least this letter won't come as a complete shock. I'm writing because over the past year I've become gradually more curious about my genes and the people I came from, and I've realized that you are probably curious about what happened to me as well.

Some kids feel abandoned and hurt by having been given up for adoption, but I've never been one of them. I've known I was adopted for as long as I've known anything, and it has always felt completely natural to me. Growing up, whenever I mentioned being adopted to new friends, I'd always assure them, "It's not like an afterschool special on ABC. I'm not traumatized or anything."

My parents took me home with them when I was six days old. I grew up in Brockton, Massachusetts, and I have a brother and sister, both older and also adopted. My father is a dentist and my mother an elementary school teacher who stayed at home with us until I was in fifth or sixth grade. I'm not sure why they couldn't have children themselves; it's an Irish Catholic household, so conversations about sex and reproduction weren't exactly free flowing.

My father called me "the world's best person" throughout my childhood, and one of my mother's fondest names for me is still "my six-day-old baby girl." Our house was filled with goodhearted sarcasm and limitless encouragement. My parents sent me to a Catholic girls' school for grades seven through twelve, and I got a scholarship to NYU. I studied journalism there and worked during vacations as a reporter at local newspapers. After graduating, I went to Ohio for a master's degree in American culture studies, and I taught first-year composition classes for the two years I was there.

Now I live in San Francisco, teaching writing at a small university (John F. Kennedy University), doing a bit of journalism here and there and writing short stories that I perform in local theaters and coffeehouses. My brother moved out to San Francisco this spring, and it's the first time we've lived in the same city since he went away to college when I was fifteen. It has been wonderful spending leisurely time with him and becoming the kind of good friends it was impossible to be when we were younger and lived so far apart.

I'm gay, with a wonderful partner named Cara, and my parents have recovered from the shock. I came out to them last spring, and my father's first response was, "When you were young, I told you that you were the world's best person. I want you to know that nothing's changed that." My mother took it a bit hard at first, but it didn't take long for her to resume the westward shipments of her special chocolate zucchini cake and Kahlua brownies.

I hope this letter isn't too disruptive for you. I decided to write rather than call because it seemed less invasive and out-of-the-blue. And, since this is new terrain for me, I wasn't quite ready for a phone call.

I've been reading some stories in which birthmothers describe their experiences of giving a child up for adoption, and I know that it was probably very difficult to be an unmarried Catholic twenty-year-old having a baby in the late sixties. I imagine it's also been hard for you to know nothing about what happened to me all these years. Part of the reason I'm writing is that I want you to know that I've led a wonderful life, and I'm deeply grateful to you for giving it to me.

I'm also contacting you because I'd like to find out about you and the life you've led. The report from Catholic Charities was very clinical and gave me no real sense of what you're like as a person.

On a more practical level, I want to know what runs in the genes that I should be looking out for. I've got bunions, gums that show when I smile, and a liberal dose of premature gray hair, so those are apparently part of the makeup. And, judging from the Catholic Charities report, I'd say the god-awful pilonidal cyst I had two years ago was probably genetic as well.

I don't know what level of contact you'd like to have with me, but if you are interested, I'd be thrilled to receive a letter telling me about yourself and what it was like giving me up for adoption. And I'd love to see a photo of you. I'm also interested in anything you might be able to tell me about my biological father, along with a photo if possible. Then maybe sometime down the line we could talk on the phone.

I'm enclosing a photo of myself, along with my work address. I'm in the middle of looking for a new place to live, so my home address will be changing between now and March 1. I hope to hear from you soon.

Katie

February 12, 1996

Dear Katie,

I ripped your letter open, realizing from the return address that it was you. I grinned all the way through. I am absolutely thrilled to hear from you and so pleased to meet you again!

I am happy to know that you are a well-adjusted and well-educated young woman with a fulfilling career, the product of a wonderful home and loving parents. I can hardly find the words to express how grateful I am. Your parents sound marvelous.

You look very much like your biological father, with a smidge of me. You have my dark hair and brown eyes, possibly my nose. You have your father's high cheekbones, eyebrows, perhaps his straight hair? You wear glasses like he did. (Does?) And you have the biggest, most beautiful smile I have ever seen.

I am finding it really difficult to write an intelligent, cohesive letter. So many feelings are surging about. I usually write much more eloquently than I speak, but you would not know it from this letter. I've decided to write this just as I think it, rather than letting my stern inner critic, Sister Mary Misconception, screw around with it. Feel free to edit as you go along.

I am a student at the University of Massachusetts at Lowell pursuing a major in English (writing concentration—what a coincidence!) and a minor in business management. I started out as a business major, but I detested calculus (three semesters were required) and decided to go with what I love. I have always been an obsessive reader and hope that my love for words can be translated into a lucrative career of some sort, so I can put the kids through college.

I suppose that right now I can primarily be defined as a wife and mother. My sons are Jack, age nine, and Gus, age seven. My husband of ten years is a big, blond Viking named John, a systems engineer in computers, with his M.B.A. We met twelve years ago when I was director of placement for a computer school and he was a student. I got him his first job in computers and he was so grateful, he married me. We have a terrific marriage and our kids are happy, wonderful, talented—very possibly geniuses. Jack has a scientific bent, loves to build and noodle on computers. Gus is very creative and artistic. I have stayed at home with them since Jack was born.

I worked for eighteen years before having my boys. I was a claims adjuster in property and casualty insurance before working at the computer school. At the age of twenty-three, I married a man thirteen years older. That marriage ended in divorce after seven years because he preferred tall, thin, supermodel types to short, pudgy types like me. Luckily, my current husband sees me as a Rubenesque goddess.

Regarding your genes, there is nothing particularly awful for you to be worried about, as far as I know. For me, the most odious gene is the one passed down from my father's side. He was thin but his father was corpulent and so was one of my aunts. I have fought fat all my life, at one point dieting down to a size three to please my first husband. I like to say, "I used to be a size three," but that is a gross exaggeration based on the fact that I was that size only for the six months that I ate nothing but an apple and six Cheerios a day. You can also blame the gray hair on me. I have paddle feet but no bunions, yet I suppose you also have to blame the bunion gene on my side of the family, since my sisters have them.

What a fascinating life you lead! I love the fact that you are a writer and performer. What kinds of things do you perform? I only wish your performance venues were closer to home so I could see and hear them. I bet your parents wish the same thing. It must be hard for them to have their children living so far away. Does your sister live away from Massachusetts too?

I told my older sister about your letter, and she is nearly as thrilled as I to know that you have contacted me. My husband feels the same way. I haven't told my children because I feel they are a bit young to understand.

About a year after Gus was born, I contacted Catholic Charities to open up my file to you, and I tried to obtain some information about you. They shut me right off, but I did eventually get your name and the address where you grew up. I attended a couple of meetings of a search support group, and I even made two expeditions down to Brockton in the delusional hope that I might catch a glimpse of you. You see, I had thought about you for so long, and I knew you were finally of an age when contact might be feasible. But I eventually decided that I could not intrude on either you or your family, and that I would just have to trust what Catholic Charities told me: that you were a member of a fine family and doing well. I always harbored the hope that you would seek me out someday, if only to find your genetic background. When they finally called me this year on January 2, I couldn't believe my good fortune!

I started to write about what it was like for me to give you up for adoption, but I've decided to keep our first contact light, so as not to overwhelm you in an emotional drenching. The last thing I want to do is put you off. In the interest of getting this to you right away, I am going to limit myself to a short letter here. I want to tell you everything you want to know, and I love the letter format because it allows us to get comfortable with each other. I think I would babble with nervousness over the phone. Please write back to me as soon as you can. I want to hear so much more about your life—an extensive bio.

With much fondness and affection,
Ellen

Dear Ellen,

I think you broke some kind of record with your turnaround time for that letter. I received it Thursday, having only mailed your letter the Saturday before.

It was wonderful to hear from you and to see the photos of you and your kids. Gus and Jack are adorable, and I was stunned by how much of myself I can see in your face. Aside from my more generous set of gums, we've got basically the same lower face. If I cover the top of the photo, anybody could mistake it for a picture of me. The tips of our noses seem different, but, like yours, my cheeks bunch up along the sides of my nose when I smile. And our hair is the same color, though mine is straight as thread.

Someone who looks like me . . . it's amazing. In my family, with each of the kids adopted from a different family, nobody looks even remotely like anybody else. I've got fair skin and freckles that come and go with the sun. I'm 5'6", with a big frame and a decent helping of both flesh and muscle on it. My brother Matthew's metabolism is so fast he even relaxes at an accelerated pace. He's 5'10" and weighs about 131 pounds, including winter clothes and boots. Unlike me, he has olive skin, a narrow face and a curved, Mediterranean-looking nose. My sister Theresa is short and shaped like an Earth Mother sculpture. Her skin is pale but unfreckled, and her hair is an enormous bush of tight, tight curls, which she likes to dye orange.

You asked about Theresa in your letter, noticing, no doubt, that I hadn't really discussed her. She lives in Los Angeles with her husband and son (Georgie, age seven, who is great). I don't see her that much, and it isn't only because L.A. is a seven-hour drive away. She's manic-depressive and exhausting to be around, and she's been that way for her whole life.

I read my girlfriend Cara your letter, and she said she could hear in you a lot of the same qualities that I have—a similar sense of humor, a bent for self-deprecation and an overall grounded-ness. I've always been skeptical when people attribute personality traits to biology, solidly planting myself on the nurture side of the nature-nurture debate. But I have a feeling that getting to know you is going to push me more toward the middle of that debate.

I was interested to hear that you'd already known my name and my parents' address. Where did you get them? Did someone at Catholic Charities relent, or was it through that search support group you went to? Even though it must have been a hard decision, you were probably right not to have tried to contact me before this. Until this year, I hadn't really thought that much about being adopted. In fact, the whole concept of a biological family was amorphous to me—I'd never envisioned real people leading real lives. Until I read the book *Within Me, Without Me* by Sue Wells, it hadn't even occurred to me that you might be wishing for contact. At any rate, if I had suddenly met you during that time, it probably would have been pretty disorienting for me. Now, though, after thinking about it for at least six months, I'm thrilled to be able to get to know you.

I haven't told my parents yet that we've been in contact. I probably will soon, but it's a delicate matter. They were always very open with us about our being adopted, but beyond that we haven't talked about it much. And my sister has already set a negative precedent. When she was a teenager, she and my mother went to Catholic Charities to look at her files. She learned that her birthmother had named her Courette. Not long after, Theresa started calling herself Courette and eventually had her name legally changed to Courette Kareen—Kareen because it sounded good with Courette and seemed an appropriate name for the rock star she imagined she'd become. The way I see it—and I suspect my parents see it this way as well—the name change was symbolic of her rejection of our family and of my parents specifically. Anyway, because seeking out birth information has taken on such painful rejection connotations in the Hern house, I need to introduce the news gently.

You asked for an extensive bio. For this letter I'll limit myself to what I've written here. In the future I'll try to flesh out my earlier life for you in bits and pieces. Have you ever read Anne Lamott's great book, *Bird by Bird: Some Instructions on Writing and Life?* In it she recommends that to avoid becoming overwhelmed by their material, writers should imagine one-inch picture frames. At any given time, she says, you should write only what can fit within that frame. What I'll try to do in future letters is give you some one-inch picture frames from the past. Is there anything in particular you'd like to hear about? If you're interested, I could also send you some color copies of photos of me growing up.

I think that's enough for this time. I have no idea how long I've been sitting in front of this computer, but it's dark now and I started pretty early in the afternoon. I look forward to hearing from you again, with more about your life. I'd love to see some of what you've written, if you're willing to show it. People get paranoid about showing their writing to me since I'm a writing teacher, but I promise I won't read with a red pen.

Until then,
Katie

February 28, 1996

Dear Katie,

In reading your latest letter, I had the sensation that I was falling in love. Please don't freak at my effusiveness, but I couldn't wait to absorb every word and nuance. It was like eating chocolate, something wonderfully delicious and a very heady experience. All I can say is that I am so happy to know you and so proud of you.

Funny you should mention *Bird by Bird.* My essay-writing professor is hooked on it and reads us passages all the time. One of her very first readings was the one-inch frame bit. I cannot claim to be a writer, only a student who aspires to write. I have only been a writing major since January, having been encouraged to try by a literature professor and by a political science professor who wanted me to publish a paper I had written on affirmative action. My focus in my younger days was always art. I had been told that this was where my talent lay and had won some small awards. Yet, back then, I was a meek, shy, trying-to-be-invisible middle child with no self-esteem. I never felt that my stuff was good enough, or creative enough, or that I could compete with anyone else.

Funny also that Cara said she could hear you in my letter. Those were John's exact words too. I only wish I had a tenth of your talent for expressing yourself.

Regarding my already having known your name: when the

officious, extremely unsympathetic social worker I had contacted at Catholic Charities turned down my request for information, I got pissed, to put it quite bluntly. She acted like I was some bug to be swept aside and made me feel ashamed for violating the laws of the church all over again. But I'd had enough of that when I was twenty and for some years after, so I was not going to be cowed into submission. I contacted a group headed by an adoptee who was only too happy to do some detective work, and within months I had your name and address. I then tried to find your picture in Brockton High's yearbooks, but to no avail. Then I thought a good Catholic family would probably send their children to Catholic schools, so I figured maybe you had attended Cardinal Spellman. (Is that the name of the high school in Brockton? I can't remember.) But it all came to a standstill because I am the world's worst liar and can't fabricate a good alibi to save my life. I couldn't figure out how I might get that school to give me a picture from a yearbook if I didn't even know whether you had attended or what year you had graduated. So I'm glad you approve of the decision I eventually arrived at: to wait until you contacted me. That decision seems doubly fortuitous now because of Theresa's negative experience.

I'm sure you saw in the Catholic Charities file that I named you Sarah Elizabeth, but after getting to know you this far, that name seems totally inappropriate. You are most definitely Katie. You know, the very act of naming you after you were born seemed inappropriate to me back then. I knew you were not mine, and I had known that almost from your conception. Your biological father, Doug, and I had been dating about three years, off and on. It's hard for me to remember this period of my life—it's the long-buried past that I have squashed down, so the details are difficult to dredge up. It seems to me I really loved him, yet when he went to Vietnam

I could not maintain the long-distance relationship. I started dating another fellow and my letters to Doug diminished to few and far between. My relationship with the other guy was pretty serious. Keep in mind that I was a good Catholic girl coming of age in the sixties, way before the sexual revolution reached the provincial environs of Natick, Massachusetts. Then Doug's mother became ill and he returned home on emergency leave. I was absolutely torn between these two boys and felt forced to make a choice. I chose Doug. Yet he was going back to Vietnam, perhaps never to return.

I was nineteen years old, a protected child of a Catholic up-bringing, sexually ignorant, immature and very naive. The only thing I had ever wanted up to that point in my limited life was to get married and have children. I never really considered that other avenues might be open to me. Doug and I became sexually active; me hoping we'd be married and Doug thinking about having to return to Vietnam. I got pregnant immediately. At first we planned to get married. We set a date, looked at rings and were counseled by a priest. But we never made it to the altar. Doug decided he could not marry me. I was devastated. My parents were mortified.

There was never any question that I could keep you; not in my parents' minds nor in mine, being the stupid little mouse that I was. I resigned myself to giving you up for adoption. I convinced myself that it was the selfless and unselfish thing to do and that I was going to make some childless couple very happy. Your birth was an un-speakable joy to me. It was the most wonderful day of my life—to see such a beautiful child and to know that you would be raised by two loving parents. It felt like it was the right thing for me to do, as painful as it was a few days later when I had to sign the final relin-quishment papers. That's why it seemed ludicrous to name you in the hospital, but it was required and I never was one to buck the system.

I could write reams about what it was like for me back then, but maybe I'll save it for another letter. I know you'd like to hear something about your biological father. I don't know how much was in the Catholic Charities files, and I'm probably violating some archaic and asinine stricture by divulging his name. A pox on them! Doug's full name is Douglas William Harrison. He was a bit over six feet tall, with light brown hair, fair skin and blue eyes. He lived on Jefferson Street in Natick. It seems to me his mother was Irish and his father was English-Irish. He had three brothers: Patrick, Michael and Andrew. He also had a sister, Linda. Before going to Vietnam, he attended Boston College and also worked for the telephone company.

I saw Doug only twice after he dumped me. He returned to Vietnam and was there throughout my pregnancy except for a short period of leave. While on leave, he came to see me at the home for unwed mothers (that's what they did with us back then, squirreled us away, out of sight) and we talked; about what, I can't recall. After our talk, I was overflowing with unreasoning hope that we would get together, yet we never spoke again.

The second time I saw him was years later, right after my breakup with Jim Merloni, my first husband. I was in a restaurant in Natick with my mother, and Doug came in with a woman and a little blond girl of about three. I assumed they were his wife and daughter. My emotions surged—shock, anger, resentment, shame. I stuffed them down along with my meal. I passed his table as I left and he said, "Hello." I stared daggers at him but could not speak. (This is another topic for an essay on resentment, perhaps better suited for my journal.) I don't know where he is now. If you want me to, I could try to get more current information, but I really have no wish to be in touch with him again. However, be assured that I have no problems with your getting in touch with him. I'm sure he is probably at least as well balanced as I am and that you won't find anything to dislike. He was a good person then, even if I do resent him sometimes, even now, for not loving me.

I have three brothers and three sisters. The oldest and my personal favorite, Ann, is married and has three kids, one grandchild. Her husband is senior vice president of an engineering firm in Boston. Next is brother Jed (Gerald), married, one daughter; he's vice president of a chemical firm headquartered in Philadelphia. He commutes there from Marlboro, Massachusetts. Next is Katy (short for Kathryn), married with two boys. After me is Barbara, divorced, two children and a boyfriend. After her comes Steve (we used to call him Biff), married and living in Framingham. Finally, brother John, born-again Christian conservative with five children and a lovely wife. He works in computers. I have included an old family portrait, sans John, the youngest, then unborn. My father used to line us all up on the couch at least once a year to take our picture. With seven kids, my parents were usually so busy that preserving our faces for posterity was always an afterthought.

I'm sorry that your parents had such a bad experience with Theresa's search for her birth connections and that they are soured on the whole thing. Perhaps if you assured them that I have no wish to usurp their place in your heart and that I seem perfectly normal. I'm sure you'll find the right time to tell them and that they will be relieved to know that my background is very similar to theirs. My father ran the Massachusetts office of a company that sold malpractice insurance to doctors and dentists. He grew up in Brookline, neighbor for a time to the Kennedys. My grandfather owned a manufacturing company and was also vice president of a leather-producing company. My mother moved to Brookline from Indiana, where her grandfather graduated from Notre Dame. Somewhere along the line, her family was famed for having the first indoor toilet in Fort Wayne. More family lore, on my grandmother's Protestant side, includes the dubious fact that we are descended from Oliver Cromwell, Lord Protector of England. Both my parents attended St. Aiden's School in Brookline as children and sent us to Catholic grammar school as well. So you see, we are fine, upstanding citizens, with only the standard minimum number of skeletons in our closet.

I would love to hear more about your youth. What is your mother like, and your dad? What kind of relationship did you have (do you have) with them? How did you and your family cope with Theresa? How did you feel about Catholic school? What was it like to discover your sexual identity? My prior experience with gayness is practically nil, but I will say that I think I harbor only positive preconceived notions. I am interested in anything and everything you want to tell me.

I hope you are settling comfortably into your new home and that it is everything you want it to be. I wish you great neighbors too. I look forward to your next letter.

As ever, affectionately (yet not effusively),
Ellen

March 1996
⌒∞⌒

Dear Ellen,

Thanks for your wonderful second letter and the essay you sent, which I think is fantastic. I just read your letter again, and I really appreciate how honest and direct you are. Thanks for starting to tell the story about Doug and how you came to give me up for adoption. It sounds like that was a painful time for you, and I appreciate that you're willing to dredge it up to tell me about it. I might at some point in the future try to contact Doug, so I appreciate the information, but I think that's a bit more than I can take on right now. I'm in no rush.

It's been really enjoyable getting to know you. I must confess that I've harbored a happily-adopted kid's paranoia about my roots. The night before I got your first letter, I had a nightmare about meeting my birthmother. We met in her dark, grimy bedroom, where she spent all her time. She was wearing the permanent-pleat polyester slacks my grandmother used to wear, had no social skills, and never left her room. Everything in the room seemed coated in a dank residue, and even the air was laced with it. I wanted to see if there was a family resemblance between us, but the whole thing was so weird that we barely looked at each other. I don't think we spoke at all.

Of course, this nightmare has nothing to do with you, my real-life birthmother; it was just a deep-seated, barely acknowledged fear of the unknown, a fear that I'd see the people I came from and they'd be nothing I would ever want to become. Which is why it's been especially great to replace those distorted visions with well-balanced and funny you. It's a massive relief to dispel those lurking anxieties.

When searching for a photo of me in 1989, you were right about my parents' having sent me to Catholic school. But even if you had been able to finagle a yearbook from Cardinal Spellman, I wouldn't have been in it. I went to Ursuline Academy, an all-girls school in Dedham, for grades seven through twelve. I'm enclosing here my senior photo. That hairdo was a daily miracle of teenage engineering—it took a handful of mousse, a high-powered blow dryer, at least fifteen minutes of painstaking curling-iron efforts and a long spray of superhold Aqua Net to create that pouf each morning. On my face were moisturizer, cream foundation, blemish concealer, blush, two colors of eyeliner, frosted green and pink eye shadow and my special blend of two lipsticks. I got up at 5:45 every morning to start getting ready, and during my intensive beauty regimen, no one was allowed in my room.

So there's a glimpse into my life in high school. Catholic school was an intense and life-shaping experience. On the positive side, I was groomed to excel. We were all being prepared for college— good colleges—and a lot was expected from us. My peer group was filled with hyperachievers. Two of my high school friends went to law school and are now clerks for Massachusetts supreme court judges. Another went on for a master's in nursing at Yale. Another is completing her Ph.D. in English. I started teaching at a university at age twenty-two.

They were all decent girls, and we had a lot of fun together. Being part of that group kept me motivated to succeed. It was a positive experience overall, even if it did get out of hand sometimes.

I remember once breaking down in tears senior year because the teacher had gone so fast in her lecture that I couldn't get all the information into my notes. I was sure I wouldn't be prepared for the upcoming test, which would affect my grades, which would keep me from getting into a good college, which would, of course, ruin my life.

I was a bit of a class comedian, priding myself on saying the sorts of things no one else would say, and saying them as bluntly as I possibly could. The nuns and lay teachers liked me, and I was a Good Girl for the most part, but every now and again I'd have to be taken aside for a private lecture on what was, and was not, appropriate to say. Once, when I was coeditor of the school newspaper, I was informed that jokes about elderly men in red string bikinis did not belong in the *Ursuline Blazer*. I was taken aside another time after the subject of birth control came up during a class. The teacher, who was a mother of seven, didn't appreciate my class-time speculation that she herself must not have been a birth-control user.

The worst thing about Catholic school was being rigorously molded into a line-toting arch-Catholic. We had daily religion class for the six years I attended Ursuline, two years of which were taught by a rabidly conservative woman from Iowa. And I bought it, all of it. I left Ursuline unforgivingly pro-life, homophobic and morally superior in my conviction that I would never have sex until I was married. Insufferable.

I was also trained to be an arch-heterosexual. The rabid Iowan expressed the Catholic party line on homosexuality without a trace of irony: "Love the sinner, hate the sin," she told us, nodding benevolently. We spent at least three months in our senior "morality" class planning our own hypothetical weddings. The stated aim was that we realize how expensive the whole thing was, and that we learn marriage was not something to rush into without serious thought. But what the assignment involved was planning what kind of flowers we'd have, what we wanted the invitations to look like, what the dinner menu would be, and where we'd go on our honeymoons. I actually spent an afternoon in a bridal shop looking at gowns. The unstated assumption behind all this planning was that each and every one of us would get married. To men, of course.

The amazing thing about it all is that I didn't question any of it. It seemed perfectly natural, and there were certainly no radical voices at Ursuline calling out, "Hey, this is fucked." I'm sure there were a few outcasts who felt that way, but they knew to keep their mouths shut. One girl in my class refused to regurgitate the pro-life dogma, circling "false" on a true-false test question that read "Life begins at conception." In return, she got a C in religion, bringing her GPA way down and knocking her off the honor roll.

The price of rebellion was high, but I didn't have to worry because, beyond my inappropriate humor, it had never even occurred to me to rebel. I was thoroughly indoctrinated in Catholic politics, and because I was happily dating a handsome boy, the heterosexual mandate didn't feel constrictive either. I didn't start realizing I might be queer until my senior year of college, and I didn't actually come out until the summer between my first and second years of graduate school.

This was after a long period of Catholic school detox. Thank god I went to NYU instead of Holy Cross, my second choice. After six years surrounded by friends who questioned Catholic teachings even less than I did, I was in Manhattan surrounded by people who found my perspectives odd, quaint even. I remember sitting in a dining hall my first year and discussing my righteous views on premarital sex: "I think it's far too special to squander outside a marriage." At the table was Shemetra, a no-nonsense Black woman. "Mmm, mmm, mmm," she said, shaking her head and scrutinizing me. "Girl, you really one of those?"

The story of my detoxification and political transformation is too big for this letter—next one perhaps. In short, I went from a pro-life, dogma-swallowing, homophobic prude to a radical queer activist who ate fire at a Christian Right prayer fundraiser last spring. The political group I was in, the Lesbian Avengers, is fond of dramatic media tactics; part of my training in the group was to learn to put out torches in my mouth, chanting, "The fires of hatred will not consume us, we take them and make them our own." I suspect your brother John and I would not get along.

I'm going to wrap up now. I fear if I keep going, I'll never get this off to you. This letter took a bit longer than I would have liked because my computer and printer were stolen from my apartment right before I moved, and I've had to rely on friends to do my computer work. (Too involved and ugly a story—perhaps the topic of my own journal entry on resentment.)

I'm enclosing here a piece I wrote about maxipads and an article I wrote for *Curve* magazine. I'm also sending along a copy of the Catholic Charities documents I received. I suspect they may contain some inaccuracies or distortions, so I'd love for you to go through them and fill me in. I'd also like to hear more about what it was like being squirreled away in the home for unwed mothers— such a hideous concept, so much shame surrounding the whole thing—and whatever other things you'd like to tell me.

Thanks for all your openness and affection. I'm looking forward to your next letter.

Fondly,

Katie

Dear Katie,

I thought I would die from the suspense of waiting to hear from you. It's terrible that your computer and printer have been stolen. I received your letter on Saturday and spent all weekend savoring the essence of you. God, that sounds obscene, doesn't it? Anyway, I thoroughly enjoyed your letter and your sense of humor, and got a great kick out of *Curve* magazine. Lesbianism sounds so damn powerful. Also your bio notes under "Contributors" made me laugh. Please describe a "speculum puppet show"—I can only imagine.

I have been much more attuned to gayness since getting to know you. Whereas previously I had little interest in it, other than idle curiosity, now I want to absorb as much information as possible as a way of getting to know you better. There was a young woman in my essay-writing class who told us all she was gay. Her name was Neon. She dressed in combat boots, shaved her hair except for some wild radish-colored sprigs on top and usually wore a rag tied around her head. She critiqued one of my essays, and I worked with her on her essay about San Francisco's public transportation system. I found her fascinating and regretted that she dropped out just before I got your first letter.

Because I am a forty-seven-year-old woman, I feel the power of women much more now than I ever did when I was younger. I'm glad that your gayness connects you to that power in such a big way and that you don't have to wait until you are middle-aged to feel it. I noticed that you say you *were* a Lesbian Avenger. Why not now? I hope you did not damage your mouth by eating fire.

It seems you have experienced both extremes of the sexual-political continuum. You went from the Catholic far right to the radical far left. I don't know if I'm expressing the terms correctly, but wouldn't you say that you went from one extreme to the other? You are right that my brother John would probably disapprove of your current orientation. He's less evangelical now than he was when he first had his divine revelation, but he's certainly no less fervid in his beliefs. He feels it is his duty to let his family in on the news that we can achieve salvation only through accepting Christ, and that not much time is left, according to scripture. He interprets the Bible very literally, believes in creationism and thinks that Revelations proves the world is going to end any day.

I take a more moderate view myself. I would say, if pressed to admit to anything, that I am an agnostic with Lutheran leanings. My husband John is Lutheran and we are raising the kids in the Lutheran church. We make sure they attend Sunday school and hope they feel the sense of community that church can provide. I long ago rejected Catholic dogma as totally unworkable in my life. It's my feeling that Roman Catholicism is pretty unworkable for human beings in general. You'd think that a religion that condemns premarital sex, birth control, homosexuality—any sexual interaction between people that is not intended for procreation—would be gung ho for masturbation. But no, Catholics must suppress and deny their sexuality almost entirely. Paraphrasing Chaucer's Wife of Bath, why would God give it to us if he didn't want us to use it?

Having read *Curve* magazine, I would like to know why some women shave their heads. To me, a woman's hair enhances her attractiveness. Is baldness a political statement, or are some women attracted to that look in a partner? I hope you don't mind my discussing this stuff with you. Be gentle with me if I come across as totally ignorant.

OK, let's get off sexuality and onto something completely different. Back to Catholics. I was really upset by the Catholic Charities report about your background. No wonder you had that nightmare about me before you got my letter. They made it sound as if you were spawned by a troglodyte.

The report is so cold and filled with distorted information, painting a picture of a highly dysfunctional family. Though Catholic Charities implies that I talked with their social worker on a regular basis, I met with a representative just twice. The first time was in December, as they report. The social worker, who was rather ancient and cronish, asked for facts and my parents and I provided them. My parents were with me at the meeting, as I recall.

Let me correct and clarify. My grandmother GaGa (my mother's mother), was not a diabetic. She lived to be ninety-four, was in good health and lucid to the end of her life. She was a small, stylish woman with a terrific sense of humor, and I loved her very much. Her husband, my grandfather Gus, was also a loving, wonderful man. As a child, I spent many memorable weekends staying with them at their home in Chestnut Hill. My grandfather would dance with me to Lawrence Welk on Saturday night TV. We went to the movies and out to dinner at elegant restaurants. But I have gotten off track here.

The report says I told the social worker that I was unable to take you home with me since I felt my home was "intolerable" because I was not close to my parents or my siblings and because my father had a drinking problem. Most of this is untrue. I have always loved my parents and siblings. At the time I was pregnant with you,

I was closer to my parents than I had been at any time since entering adolescence. My father was not drinking then and was as supportive as his religious convictions allowed him to be. He was very pissed at Doug for "getting me pregnant." When Doug refused to marry me, my father insisted I never see Doug again. This was my father's way of trying to protect me from further pain.

The report says that I "never wavered in my decision to put you up for adoption." That is true only in the sense that I never was able to voice my "wavering" because I felt I had no other options. And, as I said, keeping you was not an option; it was not even discussed. The shame for my parents was monumental. The only solution was to get me through the whole thing as quietly as possible, and then pretend it had never happened.

It is true that my father had a drinking problem. He was an intelligent, kind and devoted family man—until he had a few drinks. Then he became verbally abusive and a "nasty drunk." He was an alcoholic. His alcoholism had not caused difficulty for the family until I was in high school, and I was not even aware up to that point that he had a problem. My parents had a good relationship with each other and expressed love for us. As I told you in a previous letter, my father worked selling malpractice insurance, a business he took over from my grandfather Gus. When I was a senior in high school, my father went into detox and was sober for a while. But he started drinking again, had an accident with the company car (for the second time) and was fired. Forever after, my mother lamented the loss of the lucrative pension. He was never able to find another comparable job but was gainfully employed most of the time.

Even though the report states that my father was unemployed and my mother made only ninety-five dollars a week as a bookkeeper, my parents were pretty well off financially, even then. Though my father's family's fortune dwindled to nothing after the death of his father, my father had a military pension. He also dabbled in the stock market after taking some Harvard extension courses and did quite well. My mother's family was full of maiden aunts who left her portions of sizable estates. We did not suffer from a lack of resources.

I do not ever recall speaking at length in a counseling session with a Catholic Charities worker. I was counseled by a social worker at the Crittenton Hastings House (for unwed mothers). I admit I may have been uncommunicative in the beginning because I was dealing with so many emotions and was used to handling things on my own, as most teenagers try to do. But I eventually opened up and came to enjoy spilling my guts to a sympathetic ear. The Catholic Charities ears I encountered during my two meetings, however, were not in the least sympathetic, nor was the entire church establishment, in my opinion. From the beginning, when Doug and I met with a priest to discuss marriage, I was treated like a pariah. The priest discouraged the whole idea of us getting married and offered the possibility of adoption. The implication was that I was obviously not fit to raise a child.

The second and last time I met with the Catholic Charities representative was the day I had to sign the relinquishment papers. As my mother and I sat crying in the back seat of a car, the rep sat in the front and eyed us via the rear-view mirror. I think we drove to a notary and that was that. I felt cold, ill-used and sad as hell. I was still going through post-partum depression.

Katie, I have been writing for four hours here. I could probably write for four more, but my knees are killing me from sitting down all this time at the keyboard.

I also wanted to tell you that my best childhood friend went to Ursuline Academy. I wish my parents had not listened to me and instead had sent me to an all-girls school where I might have concentrated on my studies rather than on my social life. I was very definitely boy crazed. But that's another juicy topic for a later date.

I'd love to hear from you again ASAP. Our correspondence is a great source of joy for me. I must end because I am swamped with schoolwork. Need to write a "New Journalism" essay and a four-pager for English Literature, which I'm calling, "Humor as a Didactic Tool in *Everyman*" for my very persnickety, precise, prim professor. (Can you tell I love alliteration?)

With much affection,
Ellen

P.S. Send more pictures, *please!* Your high school picture looks more like me. Here is a picture of me taken a few months after your birth. (I wish my legs still looked like that.)

March 28, 1996

Dear Ellen,

My new computer has at last arrived, restoring my sense of balance and general well-being and allowing me to get a letter back to you more quickly. I was completely lost without a computer and printer. I had to put together a report for work, and printing it took four hours because I had to convert it to IBM and reformat the whole thing.

I sat down to write the same day I got your letter, so this one should get to you sooner than the last. I liked seeing that photo of you when you were twenty-one. I can definitely see myself in the shape of your face, and Cara said she could see similarities in our eyes. You look so young in the photo, it's hard to believe you'd recently had a baby. But I guess that's pretty much the crux of it, huh? You were so young.

I'd like to hear more about your parents, more about how they reacted to your pregnancy and whether or not they talked about it afterward. It was interesting to hear that the experience brought you closer together; I wouldn't have expected that. Did your brothers and sisters all know that you were pregnant, or was it hidden from some of them? Did you have friends to support you?

I'd also like to hear more about your decision to give me up. You said it was never an option to keep me—was that because of pressure from your parents, your own sense of things, a combination of the two? Was it hard to pretend that nothing had happened afterward? Did you ever regret the decision?

If you have any hesitations about how I'll react to your telling me about this, don't worry about protecting my feelings; I really do want to know about the whole experience. Before I got your name from Catholic Charities, I had no sense of anything that happened before I was adopted at six days old. Thinking about it now, it seems strange to say this, but I never really thought about it. Never thought about being born, never thought about being in the womb, never thought about the connections I had to a whole other family. It was like my existence before six days old was a thick blanket of fog, a blanket I never even tried to peer through. On the rare occasions when I did think about what led up to my adoption, there were only the vaguest of shapes in that fog.

Getting to know you has made me realize how little I've known about that part of my history. I can actually see the void, like when a can of paint spills onto the invisible man. Another eye opener for me was reading the book *The Other Mother* by Carol Schaefer, which describes Schaefer's experience of giving up a son for adoption. Seeing how much has been closed to me has made me all the more curious.

I appreciated your discussion of the Catholic Charities report in your last letter. After I got past my adopted-kid paranoia, I started suspecting that the report was unfairly biased. It seems like their goal in putting those reports together is not to provide thorough and accurate information, but to make the birthfamily look as bad as possible so that the adoptees think, "Whew! Glad I was adopted." Anyway, once I got your first letter, the report became irrelevant to me.

I'm thrilled that you're being so enthusiastic about discussing my life as a queer. I think that one of the worst things somebody can do after you've come out to them is pretend it doesn't exist. This has been one of the hardest things to deal with in my relationship with my mother. I wanted to come out to my parents for a full year before I finally did. I wasn't worried that they'd disown me or anything, but I dreaded the awkwardness it was going to introduce into our interactions. As time went on, though, it became more and more of a strain to hide it. So much of my life revolved around being queer—my intense involvement with the Avengers, the writing I was doing, my relationship with Cara—that when I talked to them, it was like wearing a gag. I valued my close relationship with them, and not being able to talk about my life was making me pull away.

My father called me right after they received my coming-out letter, and he was very supportive, but my mother didn't call for a month. When she did call, she acted like nothing had happened. I tried to get her to talk about her feelings, but it was like trying to get milk from a stone statue of a cow. Nothing.

My parents visited San Francisco that Christmas, the first time I'd seen them since I told them, and it was wonderful spending time together. They met Cara and were really warm to her, hugging her when they were introduced and inviting her along with us for a day trip we were planning. But since then my mother has never mentioned Cara's name, never asked how she is, or told me to pass along a "hello." Having my relationship, and my identity, so surrounded by silence is hard; it relegates some of the most important things in my life to the realm of the unspeakable.

Still, things are a lot better than they were before I told them. Now I can talk about gay stuff without being paranoid about whether they'd know I was gay, and I don't have to hide my relationship with Cara. Nothing could be more dehumanizing than having to do that at this point in my life. I'm also encouraged by the fact that they are coming along, my father more rapidly than my mother. It'll be a long process, and accepting that keeps me from being too frustrated.

I have, as you pointed out, moved from one end of the sexual-political spectrum to the other, and I guess I am radical far left as far as sexuality is concerned (and a lot of other things, come to think of it). Of course, I consider my beliefs to be just common sense, so I'd be more likely to categorize myself as moderate and everyone else as ridiculous. That pretty much sums up how I've always been. Though I've had drastic shifts in perspective, at each point in my life I've believed, with complete conviction, that my views were simply common sense. And when my opinions on an issue have evolved, I believe, with equal conviction, that I have been a fool for holding my previous views.

As far as your question about why dykes shave their heads, that's a tough one. I think it's partly political. Women who deviate so radically from society's rigid standards for female appearance often do it as a big "fuck you" to those standards. It's also an aesthetic choice. A lot of women do find a shaved head sexy—it's rebellious, it feels great when you run your fingers over it and, with the right bone structure, it can be exceptionally flattering. I think that among lesbian and bisexual women the range of what is considered attractive is much broader than the one you see in the mass media. Really butch women are sought after, for example, and there is much more acceptance of large, fleshy women.

Being part of a queer women's community has made me a lot more comfortable about being a big woman myself, something that used to be really painful for me. You mentioned the power of women that being a dyke connects me to, and I'd say that self-acceptance has been a really important part of that. As a straight woman, I never saw other women naked in real life. All I saw were the images in the mass media—images of borderline anorexic women who were carefully posed and had any "imperfections" airbrushed out—and I despised myself for not looking like that. Now I have a much more realistic sense of what women's bodies look like, and I don't need to have sex with the lights out anymore.

As for the speculum puppet show, that was a show I coproduced with a friend of mine last November. We got a bunch of other performers together for a two-night show at a local theater, and the first act was our puppet show. We turned a washing machine box into a puppet theater, painting it dark blue and adorning it with curtains and tin-foil stars. The show was a series of short skits with speculum puppets as the actors. Each speculum had a costume—there was Fabio speculum with a full head of flowing yellow yarn, a Lassie speculum who runs for help when her boy-master is run over by a Greyhound bus, and an archbishop speculum in a gown and tall, white hat, who interrupts his Latin chanting to make the moves on an altar boy speculum. We advertised it as "cerebral humor."

It's funny that you are asking about that. I had written a paragraph about the show in my second letter to you, and when Cara read it, she looked up at me, smiling and shaking her head. Maybe, she said, maybe I might just want to hold off on that one. It was like the time my teacher at Ursuline explained about the inappropriateness of the red-string-bikini joke.

In contacting you, I've been curious about whether there were, in the McGarry clan, some biological links to my being queer. For the most part it doesn't matter, and I actually resent the question "why are people gay?" because it implies that being gay is some abnormal thing that needs explanation. Nobody asks "why are people heterosexual?" because they consider it simply normal. Still, some part of me is curious about whether it can be traced genetically, and hearing that there were a bunch of maiden aunts on your mother's side raised my eyebrows. I wouldn't be surprised if some of them were, like me, funny that way. Has there ever been mention of that in the family?

And about why my participation in the Lesbian Avengers was phrased in the past tense, I was a really dedicated member of the group for more than a year and a half. I missed maybe five of the weekly meetings during the whole time I was involved, and I probably put in between six and twenty hours of work into the group each week.

And then, in the spring of 1995, I stopped. Couldn't be involved any more. I'm still figuring out why, but I'd say a lot of it was just plain burnout. I hadn't paced myself and had taken on too much responsibility. I was exhausted. Another big factor was that around that same time we had several frightening face-to-face confrontations with the Radical Right, including being targeted by a hate-radio talk show host who read our hotline number over the air and proclaimed that he and his posse were going to come after us. His posse left death threats on the hotline, made retching noises, told us we were disgusting. One male caller directed us to go "give head to Satan" and said, "I'm gonna cut your gonads out of your goddamned ovaries." By an unfortunate oversight, my home address was on the hotline's outgoing message. To top it off, the same day the talk show host targeted us, my father called to say they had received my coming-out letter.

With all this happening at the same time I just cracked, withdrawing from the Avengers and most of my friends and embarking on a frantic pursuit of serenity—going to the women's sauna at least twice a week and spending huge stretches of time reading in cafes. I think I averaged three books a week during that time. I'm not depressed anymore, but I have no desire to go back to the Avengers. Instead of running around doing activist stuff all the time, I've had more time to write and hang out with Cara. Plus, the group has really changed in the year that I've been gone. It's a lot smaller now and virtually none of the women who were in the group with me are still in it. I'm still an Avenger in spirit, though.

Anyway, I'm planning a trip back to Massachusetts in the first two weeks of July for a reunion with all of my cousins. If you're up for it, I'd love to meet you in person. I haven't set the exact dates yet because I wanted to make sure you weren't going to be in Thailand or Uruguay or something, so let me know in your next letter.

Enclosed are some photographs, and a bunch of color copies of pictures of me at different ages. The copies are not as sharp as the originals, but I opted for quantity over quality.

I look forward to your next letter.

Fondly,

Katie

April 1996

Dear Katie,

I would be really thrilled to see you in July. I'm thinking we could meet for dinner or lunch somewhere between Brockton and Chelmsford. I'm also thinking our first meeting would be most comfortable if we met alone. Please tell me what you think though, because I would be open to whatever would make you feel most at ease. I would love to meet Cara too, but my focus will be mostly on you.

I am thrilled at the prospect of meeting you in person, but I am also scared, as I imagine you are too, although you do seem like a much more daring and adventurous person than I am. I try to maintain a facade of bravura, but mostly I'm jelly inside. So, yes, I want to see you. I am happy that you want to meet me, yet I am a little bit scared that you'll think I am not worth knowing, or that maybe we won't hit it off, although I feel in my heart that we will because we have so many similarities and, of course, the biological connection.

I love the pictures you sent. I see so much of me in you. Pictures 11 and 12 especially could be me or my sister Barbara. In your younger pictures I see Doug's youngest brother, Andrew. The same blondish straight hair and round cheeks. Cara looks lovely and sounds lovely too, from the way you describe her.

It's very possible that there is a biological link within the family, on my mother's paternal side, to gayness. My grandfather Gus had maiden sisters or aunts (I'm not sure which): Aunt Mar, Aunt Ol (Olivia), maybe another. He also joked about a certain Uncle Dood who was "peculiar," whatever that meant. I also have a cousin who is gay.

You know, this is the fourth time I have started this letter to you. I feel a little overwhelmed with all the questions you asked in your last letter. I have been trying to formulate answers, but my feelings are a bubbling cauldron. I did read *The Other Mother* back in 1991, and I spent some time with the book again yesterday to refresh myself. My story is similar to Carol Schaefer's, yet I have not spent as much time as she has in examining the year of your birth and its aftereffects. As a way of excusing my apparent lack of introspection, I will tell you that I am a very practical person who does not spend time lamenting things I cannot change, or things over which I have no control. When things are bleak, I try to find something positive to focus on. It seems like a waste to me to get bogged down in negativity and depression, especially when you can't change the way things are. I was not always like this, but this is my attitude now and it has been working quite well for me. I am an optimist at heart, I guess. Back in 1969, however, I was an unformed, wimpy shadow of the self I have become. I allowed myself to be swept along on the tide of life like so much detritus. I felt no power in myself.

Once I became pregnant with you, I had no control. Doug had control in choosing to marry me or not. Then my parents took over, dictating what would happen next. For them, and therefore for me, there was no choice but to give you up for adoption. I would love to tell you that I fought my parents tooth and nail to keep you, but I did not. The major motivating factor in my life at that time was overwhelming shame, shame that fit me like a heavy winter overcoat soaked from a drenching rain, shame like a pea-soup miasma that I had to slog through.

I became pregnant with you in early October 1968, just before my twentieth birthday. The night I told my parents Doug would not marry me, I cried a river of tears. Tears that I was not loved by him, tears that we would not be married and tears that I would not be able to keep my baby. Those tears were not shed in the family home, though. My parents took me out in the car and we rode around for hours until I could "control myself." They couldn't have me making a spectacle in front of my little brothers, who were not to know of my situation. I still don't think Steve knows, and maybe not Jed either, because it is still not something I can discuss freely without having emotion choke off my air supply.

Right after Christmas, by arrangement through Crittenton, I was sent to live with a family in Newton. I felt as though I had been sold into slavery. They got me as a light housekeeper and au pair for their three children. I got a secret hideaway where no one would know me and where I could cultivate my shame like a virulent fungus. I had never been away from home before, and I was sent to live with people I did not know, just so other people—our neighbors, my siblings—would not see my growing belly. I was miserably homesick, absolutely friendless, isolated, alone and desolate. There was no one I could turn to.

You asked if I had friends to support me. I'd had many friends at that time and was a quite social person, but the shame was like a wall that imprisoned me and could not be penetrated. It was almost as though I fell right off the edge of the earth. I contacted no one and I ignored feelers from everyone. I was just too sick with shame and pride to allow anyone to see my ignominy.

I coped by immersing myself in books, just as you said you retreated into books after your unfortunate experience with the Radical Right. I had always read a lot, but when I was pregnant with you, I read maniacally. Not just three books a week, more like a book a day. Reading was my escape. I left my own miserable world and entered more pleasant places where I did not have to think about me. My social worker at Crittenton accused me of using books to avoid my problems, and she was right. Eventually, I learned to talk to her, but she struggled to elicit my feelings for a long, long time before I opened up to her. We started writing letters back and forth to each other and I was able to sort myself out.

During the time I was staying in Newton, I had Sundays off. I would get up as early as I could and ride to my parents' house in Natick, where I would sneak in the back door, hoping the neighbors would not see me. I retreated to my bedroom upstairs, usually. Before I got too big, I was allowed the run of the house. Later, I was relegated to my bedroom. If my grandparents visited, I could not go down to visit with them in the living room. As I write this, I am thinking how absolutely cruel this whole situation was. Yet at the time, it seemed the only thing to do and a sensible way of handling things.

I can get very angry about how I was treated, and believe me, I sometimes do. There were times when I was livid, blaming my mother for not telling me what it felt like to bond with a child. How could she have let me give you up? How could my parents have been willing parties to such a horror? Yet I could never give voice to this anger, never confront my parents with how I felt. I know they suffered too. I have to excuse them. I was the one who got myself into that situation. I was the creator of my own hell. I deserved to suffer, and I certainly was not worthy of keeping you.

In April, perhaps May of 1969, I moved into the Crittenton Hastings House off Oak Square in Brighton. My entire outlook changed when I got there. Far from being the "factory" Carol Schaefer describes, it was a beautiful old mansion with lovely furnishings and was staffed by wonderful, caring people. It was filled with lots of other girls just like me and I no longer felt alone. We had a little in-house newspaper, of which I was editor and publisher. We made friends with each other, bonding like socks with static cling. There were no pariahs, no outsiders. There was no rancor either, about who had boyfriends and who did not (as happened in Schaefer's book). We also revealed ourselves completely to each other and did not withhold our full identities. My closest friend there, Caroline, had worked at a brokerage house in Boston and still kept her apartment on Newbury Street. She was older and much wiser than I.

It was a wonderful time for me. We went on outings to Boston via the subway (with our phony wedding rings on our fingers). We would gather at the gate en masse when the ice-cream truck stopped by at early evening. We had long conversations all day long and into the night. Some of us also sat around the TV and knit baby things. I did not, however, because it seemed wrong that I could not knit them for you. I knit an afghan, which I never finished.

Only one of us at Crittenton at that time considered the possibility of keeping her baby. She and the baby's father continued to see each other. She said that as soon as they could, they would be married—he had promised her. I was suspicious and wondered why she had to be at Crittenton in the first place, and why they weren't married already, but I also admired her determination and courage at wanting to keep her baby. She thought that she would be able to put her baby in foster care until she was settled in her new life. I don't know how it all worked out for her.

We were aware that support services were not readily available for unwed mothers, and unless you planned to marry the baby's father, or were helped by your family, or had an independent source of income, it was impossible to keep your baby. There was also societal ostracism to deal with, a huge issue for me, the scared little mouse that I was. I was not strong enough, courageous enough, or even aware enough to fight the system. I also firmly believed that a child needed two parents. After having Jack and Gus, I am even more convinced of that now.

One by one, each of us at Crittenton went into labor and was whisked away to Boston Lying-In Hospital to deliver her baby. Caroline and I went within days of each other. She went first and I visited her in the hospital. She was sobbing inconsolably in her mother's arms and not up to visiting. I never saw her again, which is one of the sadder things about my experience because I was rudely awakened to the fact that the relationships I had formed with the girls at Crittenton were only temporary and could never be anything more than that. That old devil shame again. Why did we not rebel against it? I don't know—I guess we were thoroughly programmed to accept it, to embrace the shame instead of our babies.

The doctor who delivered you had the reputation among us girls as "The Butcher." All the other doctors we saw throughout our pregnancies were caring and nice to us. He, however, was a true creepazoid. My labor with you was swift—under three hours. I awoke at about 2:00 a.m. on one of the hottest days of the year. I immediately went in to take a shower, then called the housemother. She held my hand as we rode in a taxi to the hospital. I was drowsy at one point during your delivery and Dr. Butcher slapped me, yelling at me to watch. I think he wanted to make sure that I would never be so foolish as to get pregnant under those circumstances again, and that I would have no pleasant memories of your birth. I fooled him, though.

Your birth was joyous to me. I was so happy to see your wizened little body, all six pounds, thirteen ounces of you. You were beautiful with a lovely round head and perfect skin. I was elated and excited and called my mother almost immediately to tell her you were born. I was crestfallen at her reaction, though. She whispered into the phone at me, wanting to end the call as soon as possible. She said she would come in to see me as soon as she could.

The astronauts walked on the moon for the first time right after your birth. The other unwed mothers (in my six-person hospital room) and I watched them on the community TV as we cuddled our babies. Sometimes, the nurses would mix the babies up, giving us somebody else's baby. I always knew you, though. I also knew that I'd only have a few days with you before you were taken away.

I coped, as I had right from the beginning, by convincing myself that you were going to be raised by the two loving, lovely parents of my fantasy. That you would want for nothing. That you would have everything I could not give you. It made it bearable, just barely.

After you were taken from me, I returned to Crittenton. My parents could not take me home, they insisted, because I was in the throes of post-partum depression and awful pain from Dr. Butcher's botched (maybe on purpose) episiotomy. I spent days in a darkened room, isolated and desolate all over again. When I finally did return home, I had to pretend I had been away at school. Within the family, it was as if the previous nine months had never occurred. I never spoke about it again to my father, nor he to me. I'm sure he believed that if we did not talk about it that I would forget, making the loss of you easier to deal with. He died in 1975, a shell of a man. But that will have to be another one-inch frame.

I think my mother suffered with me, however silently. It was years before we could mention your birth to each other, and even then it was stiff and awkward for us, and I would always break down into choked tears. My relationship with my mother is another one-incher that will have to wait for another time.

For a while after your birth, when I was trying to create a circle of friends for myself again, I was quite open about my past. But I found that being so open turned people off rather than drew them closer. So I became silent and put 1969 in a drawer in the back of my closet. I opened that drawer up to my first husband, Jim. And I told John all about my past. I have two close friends who are also aware of your existence, as are my sisters Ann and Barbara.

Yet the shame will not leave me entirely, even now. I am ashamed that I did not fight to keep you; I feel that other people will ridicule me for that, because now it is so common for girls to keep their babies. I hate the very idea of having to explain myself and my motivations to people I care nothing for. I feel ashamed that I was so stupid back then as to not use some form of birth control—a real lack of brains there. And I feel ashamed that I even *feel* shame now and am still unable to open up that drawer for all the world to see. Shame is a permanent tattoo on my psyche.

I so want to share you with Jack and Gus and my mother-in-law, Ducky. I am so happy you and I have found each other at last that I want to proclaim it to the world. But then I worry that Gus will think that I might give him away too. Or that Jack will feel free to tell all his friends at school, and I'll end up having to explain myself to their mothers. So for now I remain silent. I wish I could be more like Carol Schaefer, who threw her shame away.

Perhaps I *can* be, with time. It's hard for me to admit, but the feelings are still raw. Maybe because they've been shut away. Perhaps shining some light on the shame will cause it to atrophy and die. Keeping secrets really sucks, as you pointed out so well in your letter when you talked about coming out to your parents.

Anyway, that's my story.

I love writing to you. You make me get down and dirty with my feelings and it feels so good to be open and honest with you.

Write back soon.

Much affection,
Ellen

April 18, 1996

Dear Ellen,

I'm always so happy to receive your letters. As soon as I mail one off to you, I start expecting yours and have to keep reminding myself that it will take at least a week or two. When I came home from work last Thursday, I was hungry and my back ached from falling down the stairs the weekend before—nothing serious, just a bruised ass and an out-of-whack back. Anyway, finding your letter on the kitchen table made my evening.

Thank you for answering my questions about being pregnant and giving me up for adoption. It feels good to have the fog lifted from that period of my life; I felt like I was reading a slice of history, especially the part about you and your roommates at the hospital watching the astronauts walk on the moon while holding your babies.

It was also a devastating story to read. I wandered around fragile and sad for several days after getting your letter. On Sunday I co-taught a workshop with a friend and was so out of it that I was more like a distracted member of the audience than one of the instructors. I'm so sorry that you had to go through all that; it's difficult to learn that my entry into the world involved so much anguish.

Getting to know you has been an intense experience for me, and it has opened up a lot of pain I didn't even know existed. I'd always thought of my being adopted as a completely positive fact of my life—and I still view it positively. But now I've become aware that, in addition to all the good, being adopted involves a tremendous loss. To lead the life I've led, I had to lose my connection to you, which now strikes me as incredibly sad. I wrote a letter to my friend Martin in Scotland this week and told him that it might have actually been easier if you'd been a complete freak. But then, of course, it wouldn't have been so joyous.

One of the things I found difficult about your last letter was seeing how much you blame yourself for getting pregnant and giving me up for adoption. From my end of things, it would be hard to muster even an ounce of blame toward you. If you hadn't given me up for adoption, I wouldn't have had the family I have, wouldn't have had the friends I have, might have become a very different person than the one I've become (though I'm realizing that my base personality would probably have been the same). Anyway, too much good resulted from it for me to feel any blame or regret toward you. I just wish it had been easier for you somehow, that you'd had more support and that there wasn't so much shame involved. And it might have been nice to not lose contact with you so completely.

One more thing. It might be selfish to say this, but I can't help feeling delighted that you had the "real lack of brains" not to use birth control. Cara's happy about that too.

I'm excited that you want to meet in person when I make my trip back East this summer, and I guess I'm a bit scared about it as well. I feel like we've already hit it off, so that doesn't scare me so much. Or maybe it does, come to think of it. I worry that something will go wrong, or that we'll have a polite lunch and then, after we've finished our coffee, head our separate ways: "Well, nice meeting you." It scares me too because it's such a big deal, and nothing in my life has prepared me for it: meeting somebody to whom I have such a powerful connection but who, until a couple of months ago, was a total stranger to me. And I guess I'm just afraid of all the emotions. I'm comfortable with concrete things, intellectual theories, humor, but emotions—they make me edgy.

I do know that you don't need to worry that I'll think you're not worth knowing. I already feel incredibly lucky to have you in my life. For that to change, your in-person self would have to be radically, tremendously, shockingly different from your written self. Like if you suddenly became some frothing-at-the-mouth Phyllis Schlafly character. Or Glenn Close in *Fatal Attraction,* smiling maniacally while I opened the gift-wrapped dead bunny you brought me.

The adventurousness you've perceived in me isn't as thorough as it might seem. Despite the fire-eating, I'm all jelly inside too. I wept in every movie I saw during the last year, and not just the obvious tearjerkers like *Il Postino* and *Antonia's Line,* but *Babe* and *Apollo 13* as well. I get teary at least once during every episode of *ER,* and emotional Coke commercials always move me. This, of course, is highly classified information.

Sometimes too I'm so riddled with anxiety, you'd think Woody Allen was my biological father. Every time I've sent off a letter to you I've busied myself with a new set of worries. With the first letter I was worried you'd end up being the birthmother of my nightmare. With the next, it took you a bit longer to reply, so I worried that you'd gotten freaked out and weren't going to want to get to know me. After my third letter, in which I talked about the more unconventional aspects of myself, I worried that you'd be shocked and repelled. And with my last letter, I worried that I was pushing you too hard to talk about painful things you might not want to talk about.

But each time I've gotten your reply, my anxieties have dissolved. As nervous as I am about meeting you, there's also a big part of me that feels confident that everything will be fine. With each of your letters—and with each set of my anxieties quelled—I've felt more and more certain that I can just be my complete, unedited self and you'll still be happy to know me. Such unconditional acceptance feels like a real gift.

I'm glad you think our first meeting should be just between you and me. Having a meal between Brockton and Chelmsford sounds good, although I worry that I'll end up blubbering and making a scene in public. This would do nothing for my butch image, which is already jeopardized by my embarrassing response to Coke commercials.

Since I don't get back East that frequently, I'd like to meet the people close to you, if possible, on this trip. Maybe on a separate day, or later that same day, I could meet John and Ann (and maybe Barbara?). And if Cara comes with me back East, I would like her to meet you too. If you want to introduce me as a friend or whatever, I'd also love to see Gus and Jack. That's completely up to you, though. I understand your reluctance to explain the situation to kids so young, and they might notice that we look a lot alike. Having said all that, it might be that meeting all the other people will be too much to take on. I guess we'll see how we both feel when it gets closer to the date.

Have you read any books about adopted people? If you have, or are planning to, I wanted to give you a warning: I usually don't see myself in those books. I read them because every so often a small bit or piece will apply to me. But for the most part they piss me off, especially Betty Jean Lifton's books, which have chapters like "The Adoptee as Mythic Hero" and "The Adoptee as Survivor." So melodramatic. I'd like to see a chapter called "The Adoptee as Average Schmo" or "The Adoptee Who Goes About Her Life." And actually, I'd rather not be called an "adoptee" at all. It sounds like something you need a prosthesis for. What pisses me off most about Betty Jean is that she writes as if her experience is the quintessential adoptive experience, as if she's speaking for all adopted people. I didn't appoint her to be my spokesmodel.

I also just saw the movie *Flirting with Disaster*, about an adopted man who can't name his baby until he finds his birth roots. Have you seen it? It got great reviews, and I'd have been thrilled to see a comedy about a topic so close to home. It was a total disappointment, though. Almost every character was just a hollow caricature, and the whole story was implausible. Most disappointing was that the main character's search for his roots was just a vehicle through which the movie could send him on a wacky adventure, encountering all sorts of kooky people, in which one thing after another goes wrong and then works out fine in the end. Basically, it sucked.

You may have noticed that I am a woman of strong opinions.

Anyway. You asked about my relationships with my parents in one of your earlier letters, and I've been stewing on that one for a while. It's hard to encapsulate something so complex, but I'll try to start anyway.

For the most part, I've always gotten on quite well with them. Of course, there were some rough spots. When I was a teenager I went through a surly period, especially with my mother, for no real reason. Puberty, maybe. Who knows. I was classically mortified by my parents during that time and wouldn't even go to the movies with them for fear that someone would see me. Then, when I was in college and graduate school, I became closer to my mom but had trouble with my dad, mostly because we can both be stubborn and opinionated. At that time I was discovering my politics and thought he was absolutely clueless about what was going on in the world. He, in turn, found me to be a humorless demagogue.

But the older I get, the more I appreciate my parents. I enjoy long phone conversations with my mother about the kids in her class and the neighbors, and I love her enthusiasm. Practically every sentence out of her mouth is an exclamation—"Isn't that wondahful!" or "Isn't that mahvelous!" or "Oh, isn't that amazing!" I no longer have ideological clashes with my father, and my coming out to him has brought us closer together. I appreciate his willingness to talk about my being gay, and this has been the first year in a long time that we've really listened to each other and respected where the other was coming from.

One of the main things I'd say about my parents is that they've always been unabashedly and completely proud of me. One whole wall in the den of the house in Brockton is covered with framed evidence of my accomplishments: my Phi Beta Kappa certificate, my National Honor Society pin, even minor honors like the Coach's Award I got when I was on the volleyball team in high school. They beamed at my graduation from NYU and traveled all the way to godforsaken Bowling Green, Ohio, when I completed my master's. (My favorite memory from that trip is picking them up from the airport in Toledo and passing through the part of the city filled with shopping malls, chain restaurants, and movie theaters. My mother, who had previously considered the Midwest to be merely part of the void between New York and California, looked out the window and exclaimed, "Oh, look! They have movies here!")

My father is especially proud of my achievements, even when they aren't achievements he would have envisioned for me. I didn't tell my father about the *Curve* article, but my brother did, and my father went right out to a gay bookstore and bought his own copy. Probably had to weed through a rack of gay male pornography to get it, too. A few months ago I told him about an experience at a cafe here in San Francisco. I walked in and noticed that the woman behind the counter was staring at me. As I tacked the flyer for Speculum Theater onto the cafe's bulletin board, she called out from across the room, "Aren't you Katie Hern, the famous lesbian humorist?" My father was just as delighted about it as I was, and since then, he's taken to using that phrase himself, leaving messages on my voicemail like, "Hello, this is David Hern, the well-known East Coast dentist, calling for Katie Hern, the well-known lesbian humorist." Just last week he sent me something in the mail and (discreetly) addressed the envelope to "Katie Hern, w.k.l.h."

My mother has a harder time feeling proud of things like that, and she can be pretty inflexible when she wants to be, but she's a good sport. She's had to be, with me as a daughter. When I was about seventeen, I perfected my impersonation of her, and not a family gathering has gone by since then without me doing it. When I picked my parents up from the airport this past Christmas, I was polite for about ten minutes before looking in the rear-view mirror and commenting on the blonde highlights she had put in to cover the gray in her hair.

"How you doing back there, Blondie?"

"Oh!" she scolded, "You're a brat!"

My mother refuses to play Pictionary with me anymore because I've teased her too much: "No, I'm not playing! You're horrible!" I really couldn't help it, though. Her style of playing is to draw an unintelligible shape and then, wide-eyed and holding her breath, point at it frantically until the timer runs out. Her partners stammer, "Uh, dog? Person? Africa? Could you draw something else? Mosquito?"

My father's a good sport about my teasing too. About eight years ago I made a card for his birthday with cartoon depictions of all the things I found embarrassing about him, like a sweater of his that I hated and the pair of canvas shoes I called his "Don Johnson wannabe slipper shoes." There was also a cartoon labeled "revealing yard-work attire," which depicted him holding a rake and wearing pants that hung just below his butt crack. He still has the card taped to the wall of his office.

So that's at least a glimpse into my relationship with my parents.

I'm glad that you're enjoying our letters, because I am too. Even though getting to know you has been painful and scary at times, it has also made me feel a lot more grounded. Seeing so many of my own traits reflected in you, I feel like I know myself better. And the things I like about myself, like my humor and irreverence, feel a lot more permanent and rooted. I'm looking forward to July.

Write back soon, and send more photos and writing.

Fondly,

Katie

April 25, 1996

My dear Katie,

I got your letter today and I am overwhelmingly grateful to you for expressing such sympathy and kindness. I did not mean for you to feel saddened by my experience; I just wanted to answer you honestly and have you understand. But empathy just poured from your letter and brought tears to my eyes. Undoubtedly, you *are* the world's best person.

I also want to assure you that I too am delighted that I did not use birth control at nineteen. I love the fact that you are a wonderful presence in the world. I have never regretted your birth. I only regret that I was so willing to swallow the Catholic bullshit that somehow made me think that having sex with Doug was OK as long as I loved him, but that birth control was not OK.

I also believe that there is no need to feel a sense of loss anymore, for either of us.

I find it astonishing how much alike we are. Perhaps it's because we are throwing everything we have in us into these letters to each other, and I am able to see all the way into your core. I did not feel this same sense of identification with my own mother that I feel with you. I feel like you are a more evolved version of myself: better educated, funnier, more in touch with your feelings, more self-assured and a far superior writer. Don't get me wrong, I'm not saying I don't like the me I am. I'm just saying that you are a really terrific woman. I too feel lucky to know you—incredibly lucky.

I also cry at the least provocation (and subsequently become totally unable to squeeze any syllables from my constricted larynx). And I too experience high anxiety while awaiting your letters. I was freaking yesterday when no letter came from you. Perhaps we should think about e-mail. (Not that I know how to use it, but I'm sure John would be happy to teach me. It'll give him a sense of purpose other than studmuffin.) I guess as we write more and more to each other, we'll feel more confident in not losing each other to shock or disgruntlement or hurt feelings or whatever else we may think we inspire. Please do not worry any longer that I might try to push you out of my life. I want you in my life for as long as you want to be here.

I have been trying to imagine Woody Allen as your father. I read somewhere that "sex is the most fun you can have without laughing," which seems kind of skewed. I always laugh during sex, don't you? Imagining myself with Woody is good for a laugh but, nope, can't *really* see myself in bed with him. I like tall men—they make me feel smaller, more delicate.

You may note that I am using my full name, Ellen McGarry Carlson. This is a conscious move toward integrating my unwed mother self out of the closet and into my current self. I started to use McGarry again soon after you reentered my life. (I had not used my maiden name since marrying in 1972.)

I can't wait to see you. Even if we embarrass ourselves by displaying copious amounts of emotion, we can do it together and present a united front against those at neighboring tables who might gape at us open-mouthed. I look forward to your letting it all hang out and I shall try to do the same. My sister Ann was very disappointed that I was keeping you all to myself, and she will be delighted to know that you want to meet her. How about for our second meeting you come here to my house with Cara so you both can meet John, Jack and Gus. Then you and I and Ann and Cara can go out somewhere. Having the two kids and no baby sitter, I don't get enough chances to go out. You talk about all the movies you've seen. The only ones I've seen lately are *Babe* and *Muppet Treasure Island*. Not that I want to see movies while you are here. I want to talk and maybe show you family albums if you want to see your genetic ancestors—stuff like that.

I haven't read any books about adoptees because I did not want to give myself anything more to worry and feel guilty about. As I mentioned before, when I began my search for you, I went to some meetings where mostly unrelated adoptees and birthparents mingled. Everyone talked about their experiences and some were mind-blowingly sad. One birthmother had found her son, who was pro-foundly retarded. Another had tried to get in touch with her daugh-ter and was being sued by the adoptive parents. An adoptee said she hated her adoptive parents, who were abusive, and she recounted a very traumatic life. But by and large, most of the adoptees seemed happy to have been adopted. They were searching for "roots" or some kind of genetic identity while not wanting to hurt their rela-tionships with their adoptive parents.

On rare occasions, I've watched TV talk shows and have seen adoptees struggling with issues of abandonment. I don't get the sense that you feel abandonment, though. If you would like to recom-mend a book to me, I will read it, but mostly I have been relying on your own account. You are so good at expressing yourself, I haven't felt a need to delve into a book to understand your position.

How about I tell you a little bit about my mother, who died of colon cancer in March 1993. Her name was Suzanne and she died at the age of seventy-eight after battling cancer for three years. For a good portion of those three years, she allowed her more negative qualities to dominate and she was difficult to deal with. The women in my family all seem to have the "critic gene," which causes us to be overly hard on members of our family—flaming bitches, essen-tially. Some of us have been able to turn the gene into a recessive one. For instance, Ann is never critical and I try hard to squelch the tendency, because I know so well what it feels like to be subjected to it.

My mother was always very concerned with appearances. She wanted us all to look perfect, or to fit her ideal of perfection anyway.

For me, that translated into being thin and perfectly dressed. There was a lot of stuff like, "You're not wearing *that*, are you?" and "*What* have you done to your hair?" and "Are you putting on weight?" Once I was sitting across from her in a restaurant and she said, "Your face is pretty except for the fact that your eyebrows are too far apart." (Like I had some control over how they grow, for God's sake!)

Toward the end of her life, rather than try to have real dialogue with my mother, I mouthed pleasantries, ignored what had degenerated into downright nastiness and just chalked it up to her illness.

Before she became ill, my mother was wonderful. I was never closer to her than during the time I was between marriages. She was extremely supportive, concerned and loving. My mother and I spent lots of time together just because we enjoyed each other's company. We would go out to fine restaurants, go on shopping sprees, go to plays in Boston, and we traveled. Not too long after Jim left me, my mother and I went to England, then sailed back on the *Queen Elizabeth 2*. It was a great consolation prize for me and we had a terrific time. In 1984 we went to Florida together for three weeks and were joined by my Aunt Joey for one of the weeks. One of the best trips of my life.

My mother was a very stylish, perfectly coifed woman who never left the house without her clothes pressed, her heels on and her nails lacquered (a trait passed down through generations of the women in my family since the invention of nail polish). She expected everyone else to be the same way. It was traumatic for her when she lost her hair and her legs swelled from chemotherapy. She could no longer look the way she wanted to. She had always prided herself on looking and feeling young. Cancer made her an old woman and she railed against it. She became negative and unhappy because so much of her sense of self-worth was tied up in her appearance, which was really too bad because she had a lot to feel proud of.

As we age, my sisters and I get heavier. We are less able to look as lovely as our mother would have liked us to look. As for me, comfort takes precedence over style; I barely give a shit about clothes anymore. I can't find *anything* I look good in. I'm especially pissed today after searching the women's racks at Macy's and finding nothing even remotely attractive to wear to my nephew's wedding in May. Anyway, mostly I just wear my school uniform: jeans and one of John's shirts. Kind of sounds like butch attire, but I accessorize with nail polish, lipstick and earrings, and I never wear combat boots.

On to another subject. Tell me more about Cara. What does she do for a living? How did you meet? I hope she can come to Massachusetts with you.

And how about your brother, Matt? I'd like to know more about him.

We are sending the kids to camp for the first time this year: Camp Calumet, a Lutheran camp at Ossipee Lake in New Hampshire. John and his brother went there as children. I am a little worried about Gus being homesick. He will be eight on August 1 but he is a young eight and still loves shows of affection from his mom, unlike Jack, who I have to tie down to give a hug. John and I are looking forward to having some real quality alone-time together. In our eleven years of married life, we have only been away from the kids once: for one glorious weekend on Martha's Vineyard.

I send along some photos, including one of me in a bikini with Jim, from my Charlie's Angel–wannabe phase. When this picture was taken, I weighed about 117 pounds. I look *absolutely nothing* like the picture now. I am also sending an almost-three-year-old photo of us taken at our summer home in Maine.

So write back soon. Maybe send an e-mail address. John tells me I have one, too, but he is at Cub Scouts with the boys right now so I can't ask him what it is.

Much affection,

Ellen

May 1996

May 3, 1996

Dear Ellen,

Thanks for all those photos. I was struck by the similarities again, especially in that one from your confirmation. There's a photo of me taken this past Christmas in which I look just like that—older and butcher, of course, but with the same head tilt and half smile. (I'll try to copy it and send it if it won't delay this letter too extraordinarily.) Do you want the photos back? You said earlier that your parents didn't take too many photos when you all were kids. If they're scarce and you don't want to part with them, I could send them back.

I think you look worlds better now than you did in that bikini photo you sent. Worlds better. I'm glad you're past your six-Cheerios days. I hate to see women fighting their bodies. It involves so much self-hatred and is such a hideous waste of time and energy. I did it myself when I was in high school. Around my sophomore year I started taking only half a sandwich for lunch. For dinner I'd eat a Lender's bagel with nothing on it, or a cup of fruit yogurt. I dropped thirty pounds and people showered me with praise. I just shrugged it off, acting like I'd barely noticed the change in myself: "Oh, I've not even been trying to lose weight." But I never felt like it was enough, never felt at home in my body. I wore superbaggy clothes and fixated on the little pouch my stomach made when I sat down. I would stand in front of the mirror naked, barely able to look at myself, and fantasize that I had a tool to slice off portions of my body, like a sculptor's wire slices into a block of clay. I'd trim off my hips and then move on to my inner thighs, sculpting and shaping until they no longer touched together. I also fantasized about breast reconstruction and jaw surgery that would keep my gums from showing when I smiled.

Even at my thinnest moments, I was always on edge, silently frantic that I'd balloon out of control. There's a part of me that looks back at photos from my junior and senior years of high school with longing. But the more sensible part of me knows that what I was doing was totally unhealthy and that my body just wasn't meant to look like that. I'm built to be big, and I'm starting to like that about myself. I like my strength and the fact that my size makes me a more formidable presence—less easy to take advantage of, less of an appealing target on the street. And I like the roundness of my body too. I'm still not a poster child for self-acceptance, but I don't fantasize about that sculptor's wire anymore.

I go to a women's bathhouse in San Francisco, and there's every type of body you could imagine there—from massive women taking up two spaces in the sauna, to birdlike women who look like they'll snap if there's too much sloshing in the hot tub. Going there has really changed the way I think about women's bodies in general, and mine in particular. When I moved to San Francisco, my friends used to encourage me to go and I'd snort, "Walk around naked in public? To relax? I don't think so." But once I got past my shame, I found it really liberating to go there. And I do relax. Naked, in public. What amazed me most was seeing that even thin women have cellulite and rolls of flesh. This was terrific news after a lifetime of comparing myself to the media's distorted images of women.

Thanks for all the wonderful things you said about me in your last letter. I think they're not entirely true, but they were good to hear anyway. I smiled when you commented on my being in touch with my feelings; I'd say I'm much more likely to shut them out entirely or have delayed responses to them. After I received your last letter, I barely felt anything for two days. Then, Saturday afternoon, I noticed that I felt uneasy and it took the whole day to figure out why. Had I been condescending to my neighbor? Was something wrong between me and Cara? At midnight, lying awake in bed, it occurred to me: "Gee, maybe it has something to do with reading the story of my birth." When I do have feelings I don't like (pretty much anything that isn't carefree and gay), I try to eliminate them as quickly as possible. Solve the problem and get over it, by any means necessary. Right away.

I probably just come off as more in touch with my feelings because of the letter format. I'm much more comfortable writing about personal things than speaking about them. When we meet this summer, you'll probably find me a lot more contained. Maybe not, since I've already been so open, but it's likely.

Anyway. I'm excited about seeing your house and meeting Gus, Jack, John and Ann. Cara is almost definitely coming back with me, so you should get to meet each other. You said Ann was disappointed you were keeping me all to yourself. Have you not let her see the letters? I don't mind if you show them to the people close to you—John, Ann, pretty much whoever you like. I had actually been assuming that you'd show people. I hope you don't mind that I've shown our letters to Cara and a couple of other close friends. To me, it feels like too major of a thing to keep to myself. But I'll stop sharing them if that makes you uncomfortable.

I enjoyed reading about your mother in your last letter. That genetic predisposition toward nail polish seems to have skipped a generation with me, but I do have the critic gene you mentioned. John Francis, a friend from college, named my judgmental, stern side Sister Huberjean. I try to keep her in check, but she does like to take over. She's harder on me than on anyone else, especially when I'm starting a new piece of writing—"Oh, aren't you so clever" and "You're writing about this again?" and "You're so selfish, exploiting your family like that." Sister Huberjean has a sharpshooter's accuracy for my vulnerable spots.

Reading about your mother, I realized that I still don't quite have a grip on the fact that your relatives are also my relatives. I've pretty much integrated the fact that you and I are related, but I still catch myself reading about your family as if I'm just an unconnected observer. With the last letter I had to keep reminding myself, "She's talking about my genetic grandmother." The same thing happened when I read the Catholic Charities report for the first time. Eating a burrito in the taqueria near my house, I read through it with calm detachment, as if they were talking about somebody else. Only when I reached the line "Your mother named you Sarah Elizabeth" did it hit me: Shit, it's me they're talking about.

You asked about Cara. She works as a paralegal at one of the country's top immigration law firms. She helps get the cases ready for people seeking political asylum, including gay people seeking asylum from homophobic persecution, and she gets to use her fluency in Spanish with some of her clients. She had trained to be an emergency medical technician (one rung lower than a paramedic) and even got her certification, but then this paralegal job fell in her lap. She's overworked, but she enjoys her job and feels like she's always learning new things.

We met through a mutual friend of ours, someone I knew through the Lesbian Avengers and Cara knew from college. We had our first kiss at the Castro Street Fair, one of the big gay fairs of the year, where I was working as a kisser at the Avengers' kissing booth. Cara paid, I believe it was, a dollar for an ear nibble and kiss on the lips. This was before I knew her very well. We'd only briefly met once before, and we didn't start going out until a couple of months later, so to be honest, I didn't quite remember the kiss. On our second or third date, the Castro Street Fair came up in conversation.

"Hey, you should have gotten a kiss from me at the kissing booth," I made the mistake of saying.

"I did," she replied, smiling calmly while I squirmed.

Given the way things went in the beginning, it's actually a miracle that we made it this far. When we started dating, I was a prickly bundle of commitment phobia. I'd debated asking her out for more than a month but didn't because I didn't want it to get too serious. When I finally did, it was because I'd gone out with someone else two nights before and felt like, with two women in my life, neither relationship could get too out of hand.

I'm self-protective by nature, but I was especially wary of romantic involvements because my first relationship with a woman was a disaster. That was in Bowling Green, only months after determining that I wasn't quite the heterosexual I'd thought I was. She was a Ph.D. student and ten years older. We stayed together for six months, and I felt more trapped and miserable every day. It was hard enough coming out, but being with her made my first year as a queer one of the worst times of my life.

Anyway, after that experience I was fiercely antirelationship, dating either two or three people at once or no one at all. Things were stop-and-go with Cara at the start. We saw each other once a week, at the most, and she refrained from calling me too often so that I wouldn't feel boxed in, a very wise move on her part. Gradually, over the next couple of months, we started seeing each other twice a week and talking on the phone a little more. I started to feel less skittish, and having a girlfriend no longer seemed like being dropped into a pit of vipers. Then we progressed to three or four times a week, and eventually, after a little more than a year, we started living together in a house with our friend Jo. Now I couldn't imagine not having Cara in my life. My friends like to tease me about my transformation: "I don't want a girlfriend," they quote me as declaring, "I am nonmonogamous."

What else can I tell you about Cara? She's a bit shy around people she doesn't know but not the blushing, stare-at-the-floor kind of shy. Just quiet and watchful. The first time we were introduced, I was most struck by how steady her gaze was, how confidently she met my eyes and how firmly she shook my hand. Like nothing could faze her. That's pretty much the way she is—calm and grounded, with an offbeat sense of humor that sneaks up on you.

You also asked about my brother. Matt's an industrial designer for a firm in Palo Alto. Right now he's designing an office chair for a Japanese company, and before that he designed a new model for cellular phones. When he worked in Boston, he designed a camera for Polaroid. He loves objects, especially clothes, which fill up almost every centimeter of closet space in the apartment he shares with his partner Jane. He moved out to San Francisco before she did, and when she came out a few months later, she had to go buy a new wardrobe for her things because there simply wasn't enough room for them.

Matt just bought two new pairs of shoes, and every time I've gone to his house since then he has brought them out. "Dude!" he says, hurrying from his bedroom, balancing one of the pairs gently in his palm, like a waiter displaying a fine bottle of wine. "What d'ya think?!" He trails his fingers along them and points out their advantages. "Styling square toe, Italian leather, and . . ." he sucks in his breath, "check out these soles."

Jane is an English woman and also a designer, and she and Matt have been together for about eight years. She's like a member of the family now and they're very good for each other. She's much more Spartan about possessions and without her influence Matt would probably never get rid of anything. She's sort of a grounding influence for all Matt's nervous energy.

Matt has been watching my experience with you out of the corner of his eye, but so far he's deflected any discussion about pursuing his own birth roots. Today, though, he called and asked me to print him a copy of the letter to Catholic Charities requesting birth records. He says that my finding you has made him realize that there are actually people out there. Like me, he'd never really imagined it so concretely before. I think one of the things that's been holding him back has been the fear that his birthmother might be dead, or that he might not be able to get her name and address, or that his experience wouldn't go as well as mine. It's going to be a drag if his birthmother hasn't opened the records to him. That makes everything so much more difficult and complicated.

I'm going to wrap up now. I do have an e-mail address, but I'd prefer we didn't do e-mail, at least not until I become more of a computer geek. I just got on-line and, as a certified technophobe, I'm not at all comfortable there yet. Plus, even though it takes longer, I really like getting a big envelope in the mail, something I can hold in my hands. And I hate the way things look on e-mail. The font is so impersonal, and there's all that code jibberish. I'd rather wait an extra two or three days for the treat of a letter.

Anyway, Cara just got home from work, and I need to cook us

some dinner. (I cook, she does the dishes.) I look forward to your next letter.

With love,
Katie

Dear Katie,

An emotional thank you for the Mother's Day card. I was moved that you signed it "with love." But I don't want to go all stickily effusive, making both you and me uptight, so I'll just leave it at *Thank You.*

I received your letter Saturday and this is the first chance I've had to sit down and write. John, his brother Paul, Paul's wife Diane and I spent Saturday moving John's childhood bedroom furniture up from Ducky's house in Needham to Jack's bedroom here. Jack and Gus have been sharing bunk beds since we bought this house three years ago, and we intended to move the stuff ages ago but other jobs always got in the way. Anyway, now the boys are happily ensconced in their separate bedrooms, and John and I can have some peace and quiet at bedtime instead of listening to a full hour of chitchat and giggling broken up by our steadily escalating voices and threats.

Yesterday we had Ducky, Paul and Diane here for Mother's Day. John made spaghetti and meatballs, garlic bread, a salad and ice-cream cake for dessert. He grocery shopped, cooked *and* cleaned up after himself, which was a wonderful gift for me. He even prepared shrimp and crackers and cheese as hors d'oeuvres. Such thoughtfulness and culinary imagination in one 250-pound package—and he's all mine!

I identified with you very much when I read about you and Cara and how your relationship got off to a rather shaky start. It sounds almost eerily familiar: "skittish," "boxed in," "dating two or three people at once." You could almost substitute John's name in place of Cara's and you'd have my story. The feelings are the same.

As I told you before, John was one of my programming students at the computer school where I worked. My job as director of placement was to secure twelve-week internships for the students and help them find permanent jobs. It was necessary for me to spend lots of time with each student to encourage, motivate and review progress in the job-search process. When I first met John, he seemed exceedingly nervous and blathery. I thought he was uncharmingly goofy and very possibly unemployable. How could this guy who couldn't form a complete and coherent sentence ever go on an interview? I didn't think I had much raw material to work with in his case, but I was driven to maintain my 100 percent placement record, so I did the best I could. He told me that if and when he did secure a job, he was going to take me to dinner to thank me and celebrate. I thought to myself, "A job? Humph . . . that will be a long time coming." Much to my surprise, he interviewed quite well and got a job right away.

John called immediately to let me know and to set a date for dinner. I knew that he was attracted to me, but I did not consider him datable at all, and I did not consider it kosher to date my students anyway. However, I was thrilled that he had gotten a job and I felt such an event deserved a celebration of some sort, so I consented to dinner, with the stipulation that he not consider our having dinner a date. He agreed.

During dinner John confessed that he had a big crush on me and wanted to pursue the possibility of seeing more of me. I informed him that at thirty-four, I was divorced, ten years older than he, and had been dating another man for nearly five years. He told me he had always liked older women and wanted to know why I had not yet married the five-year guy. I told him I had absolutely no interest in marrying again. He took it as a hopeful sign that there was room for a big, nurturing guy to change my mind about marriage. (He told me months later that his experience with "older women" had been a crush on an eighteen-year-old camp counselor when he was only eight.)

John slowly insinuated himself into my life. I saw him once a week to begin with and subjected him to all manner of torture. I dated others even though I knew it hurt him, I continued to see Tom, my five-year guy, and I balked at any kind of commitment. As John and I became more serious, there were a few times when he took me to shop for an engagement ring and we'd pick one out together. But then I would freak and break up with him saying we were "incompatible" and marriage would never work. At one point I even told him he had the wrong pheromones and not to take it too personally.

Yet John persisted. He ignored my no's and kept coming back. Though I was very dense and it took some time, I eventually saw that there was no man in the universe who was more right for me than John. He is kind and sweet, with a goofy sense of humor. He's wonderful with kids because he gets right down to kid level and really relates to them. He is devoted to his mother, which supposedly indicates that he will also be devoted to his wife. And he certainly is. I have never been with anyone who has cared so much about me and who has been so selfless and unselfish with his love. He is also unfailingly honest, a hard worker, highly determined and motivated, very generous and not the least bit remote or reserved emotionally.

John has a big loud personality. It is impossible for him to whisper. He takes up a lot of space when he enters a room, and not just because he's big physically. He's a great schmoozer and likes to talk. He is naturally gregarious and most people really like him. Not to say that he doesn't have some faults, of course. He eats like a barbarian, chewing with his mouth open, and when we have chicken, creating bone piles off to the side of his plate. I fear I will never be able to teach the kids good table manners with him as an example. He is also free with the four-letter words and considers them to be an integral part of everyday language. Jack and Gus have picked up quite the vocabulary. Mostly he is just very comfortable with himself and not inhibited in any way whatsoever, which makes him the best kind of partner for me. I love him more than words can express.

You say you are not so in touch with your feelings as I may have perceived from your letters, and that you tend to shut out your feelings or have delayed responses. I am the same way, and I had always thought it was because of my inhibited and repressed Irish Catholic background, coupled with the fact that I had to shut myself down to such a great degree during my pregnancy with you. I find it enlightening that this trait actually seems to be genetically inherent.

I recognize the need in me to be in control. This need manifests itself in lots of different ways. Like I feel really discombobulated if my house is a mess and things are out of place; perhaps I'm a bit anal-retentive in that regard. And I hate to cry in the presence of other people. And it bugs the hell out of me when someone is overly effusive, greeting me like some long-lost relative when we just saw each other last week. I usually don't mind meeting new people and am not a wallflower or shy in that way. I really like to get to know people and am very interested in what they have to say. It's when they start asking me questions about myself or try to take the relationship to the next step that I tend to get uncomfortable. I can come off as quite aloof. God, I hope I will not come across as aloof to you when we meet. I don't want us to have any walls between us or have us feel like prickly little porcupines emotionally.

Regarding the photos I sent you, you may keep them all. I don't have a copy of the bikini photo with my first husband Jim, but I don't really care because that person bears so little resemblance to me now. Again, not just physically. I didn't even feel like her back then. Weird, isn't it?

After Jim left me, I came into my own. I blossomed, to use the old cliché. I quit my job in the stifling, patriarchal atmosphere of insurance, where I always had to be negative and tell people what they could *not* have (in claims adjusting), and took the job at the newly hatched computer school, where I tried to help people see what they *could* have. When the school first started, we trained the handicapped and economically disadvantaged under the auspices of a government-subsidized program. Later we became a private school open to all. I felt like I was doing something really worthwhile, and there was nothing more gratifying than seeing the students have success in good-paying jobs and go on to satisfying careers. I developed healthy self-esteem and a strong sense of independence. I dated a lot and it was always me who was in control. I called all the shots in the relationships and I figured if a man didn't like it, there were always more fish in the sea. And the really funny thing was, they loved it. The more I pushed them away, the more they wanted me. I was still inhibited and repressed inside, though. John came along and recognized the true me and cultivated me "like a little rose bush," as he used to say.

I am not inhibited with John (maybe still just a little bit, he'd probably say), but I could never ever see myself comfortably parading this body around a women's bathhouse. I have gone skinny-dipping in Maine in the dim light of dusk, but that's about the extent of any public nakedness I would consent to engage in, I'm sure.

Why did you want breast reconstruction when you were younger? I can't say I ever wanted to have myself operated on, but I was envious of other women who had small, delicate looking nipples. The thing I hate most about my body is that it's hairy. I am very high maintenance and have to shave my legs every day. It's like I got some gorilla blood but the rest of the family did not. Isn't it awful what we women put ourselves through? A man can have the biggest paunch in town and still feel like he's God's gift. Although I guess they suffer the same kind of anxiety if they think their penises do not measure up.

Speaking of men, tell me why you refer to yourself in the *Curve* article as bisexual rather than strictly lesbian. Is it because you have had relationships with men in the past and were attracted to them sexually? Just tell me if I am overstepping any boundaries in asking you these kinds of questions.

I am having such a good time writing to you. But I must end because I have a final this afternoon. I have also been writing this letter in snatches over the past two days, and I want to get it off to you because I know you look forward to receiving my letters as much as I look forward to getting yours.

Write soon.

Love, with some noneffusive shows of affection so as not to scare you off,

Ellen

P.S. Yes, I have shared your letters with John and Ann and, no, I am not uncomfortable that you share mine with your friends. In fact, I like it.

Dear Ellen,

I'm glad you liked your Mother's Day card and that John made such a feast for you that day. I loved reading about how you two got together, especially when you described him as "uncharmingly goofy" and "blathery." And I laughed out loud at the image of him swearing and leaving piles of chicken bones by his dinner plate.

The stories of our relationships are strikingly similar, and it does make me think there's a genetic link. But I suspect you were also right about the things in your life that triggered your closing off: your pregnancy with me, growing up Irish Catholic. In my case, I think it was triggered by the Catholic thing and the emotional chaos that surrounded my sister when I was growing up. It's probably also related to being adopted.

I just reread some of our letters and noticed that in my first letter I assured you, with unwavering conviction, "Some kids feel abandoned and hurt by having been given up for adoption, but I've never been one of them." That's true; I've never consciously felt either of those things. But over the past few months, I've been realizing that there's a lot going on beneath that confident "I'm adopted and I'm fine" exterior.

When I was around nine or ten, I was consumed with the fear that my parents would die. I needed to know where they were at all times and started calling all of their friends if they weren't home when I expected them to be. One afternoon, while walking back from school, I became so convinced that they'd been killed that I ran the whole way home. When I threw open the back door, gasping and frantic, I found my mother doodling absentmindedly on a newspaper and talking on the phone.

Even now, at age twenty-six, when I imagine the worst thing that could happen to me, it's always losing somebody I'm close to. I'm prone to big waves of panic about my relationship with Cara, and I keep almost everyone I know at arm's length, the way you described in your letter. It's not intentional, and I've only realized this in the past few months, but it's definitely my pattern. In graduate school I was involved with an English man named Martin, who planned to move back to London when our master's program was over. This gave me the perfect opportunity to keep him at a safe distance. Even though we spent five or six nights a week together for a whole year, I had it all planned out: We would stay together until we graduated. And then we would break up. I actually broke up with him sooner than that to get involved with my first girlfriend, and when he tried to get me to reconsider, I was genuinely surprised that he could be so upset: "But Martin," I told him, "we were just going to break up at the end of the year anyway."

When I think about how shut down I've been, I get the vision of myself as a pale, attic-dwelling agoraphobe who hides under the bed when the doorbell rings and has curling, six-inch nails. I'm not exactly shy or reclusive, but when someone tries to get beyond my brash outer layer, I suck in my breath and duck out of reach. Or at least that's how I've been for a long time. It does seem to be slowly changing, thank god.

I guess the point is that, like the adopted people you met in that support group, I do apparently have what therapists call "abandonment issues." I've always resisted attributing any problems to my being adopted, resisted the idea that being adopted had any impact on me at all. When I'd hear an adopted person even mention words like "loss" or "abandonment," I'd practically snort,

"Christ, get over it!" I still don't think that having been given up for adoption was solely responsible for the fears I have; a lot of different things have probably contributed to those fears. But I do think that being adopted is part of it.

I hope that reading about this doesn't set off a Pavlovian surge of Catholic guilt in you; I meant it when I said I don't feel any blame toward you. I think that a sense of loss and abandonment may just be an unavoidable part of being adopted, even in situations that worked out as wonderfully as mine did.

Whew. That was a bit heavy. If I were a lounge singer, I'd lean suavely onto the piano and say, "OK, folks, I'm going to change the mood a little now." How about an Ursuline story to lighten things up?

In ninth grade I sat in the second row of Sister Agatha's Latin class. She was a tall, dignified woman who wore cranberry-colored wool skirts and frilly blouses rather that the standard nun-wear of veils and no-nonsense polyester suits. She liked being able to pass.

Looking back from my reasonable, adult vantage point, I'm sure she was a good woman. She liked her students and organized student trips to the theater in Boston. But when I was in ninth grade, I couldn't stand her. I hated her classes, I hated the way she'd force a hug on you and suffocate you in her shelflike bosom, and I hated the way she pronounced "water" in an affected English accent: *woh-tah.*

In her classroom we were prohibited from uttering the sentence, "Can I go to the bathroom?"

"It's crass and unladylike," she told us, her strong Roman nose lifted disdainfully. "Instead, you may say, 'Sister, may I please go where the Queen goes alone?'"

I could barely keep myself from groaning when she spoke, and I didn't keep myself from making faces. She knew I didn't like her, and occasionally, if I was talking in class, she'd pelt me with an eraser from across the room.

But on this particular day, I wasn't looking for trouble. I wasn't rebelling or trying to shock anyone. I was, very simply, uncomfortable in my pantyhose.

It was the fall, and when I got up that morning, there had been frost on the windows. I'd decided, with a fourteen-year-old's fashion logic, that wearing suntan-toned pantyhose under my knee socks would be not only warm but also an attractive complement to my green-plaid uniform. It struck me as a very mature wardrobe choice.

Later that morning, though, with the heater going full blast in Sister Agatha's classroom and the sun beating through the windows, the choice didn't seem so wise. My whole lower body was compressed and sweating, the crotch had inched down to mid-thigh and the elasticized control-top was slicing me in half.

So, while Sister Agatha proudly conjugated verbs at the blackboard, I started taking off my pantyhose. I peeled off one knee sock, then the other, and then lifted myself slightly out of my seat and slid the pantyhose down beneath my plaid skirt. But pulling my right foot out of the hose, I was stopped in my tracks.

"*What* are you doing, Miss Hern?!"

Up until that moment I hadn't expected any controversy. Hadn't expected anything, really, except the relief of being out of those pantyhose. Still bent over, with one leg in and one leg out, I lifted my head. Sister Agatha's nose was thrust toward the ceiling, and she was staring at me so intently I thought I might burst into flames.

"I *said*, What are you *doing?*"

I couldn't move. I couldn't speak. The classroom was completely silent, and I was aware of every muscle in my body.

"Do you think it is appropriate for a lady to take off her hose in public?"

Sister Agatha's nostrils had expanded to enormous proportions, and she was breathing so fiercely, trying to maintain her composure, that they were quivering.

"Tell me, Miss Hern, is that appropriate behavior?"

"Uh, no, Sister."

"'No, Sister, *what?*'"

"No, Sister, it isn't appropriate."

"Then *why,* please tell me, are you taking off your hose in the middle of my classroom?"

I thought about the question for a few seconds, trying to determine what the right answer might be. This was Catholic school, and I'd developed a genius for figuring out what teachers wanted to hear and feeding it back to them. But there didn't seem to be a right answer this time.

"Miss Hern?"

"Because they're uncomfortable, Sister."

I heard a few titters escape around me, but Sister Agatha never took her eyes off mine. She was still holding the chalk midair at the blackboard. My skin was burning, and I wondered if I'd ever again be able to face my fellow Ursuline girls.

"Well?" Sister Agatha asked.

"Well, Sister?"

"Do you wish to be excused? To visit the restroom?"

She used the word "restroom." To Sister Agatha, "restroom" was almost as crass as "bathroom." I nodded but couldn't move. The situation was even more grave than I'd thought.

When she finally turned back to her verbs, I gathered up my socks and rose from my chair. And with every eye in the classroom on me, I went where the Queen goes alone. Dignity is hard to come by when you're walking with one half of your pantyhose still on and the other half loose and baggy in your hand.

Finishing up that story made me realize how much I love writing to you. In *Bird by Bird,* Anne Lamott suggests that for inspiration writers should imagine that they are writing for someone in their life. I think she calls it "writing a present." This is one of the many unexpected pleasures of our letters. I'm a notoriously lazy writer; I'll usually find anything to do rather than write. Ironing even. But because I want to tell you about my life, I sit down and do it. I don't think that the Sister Agatha story would have ever been written if it weren't for these letters.

I love the questions you ask, especially the ones about queer stuff. I've repeated the "why do women shave their heads?" question to almost all my friends, who have laughed and simply said, "God, how'd you explain that one?"

In regard to my teenage dream of breast reconstruction, I didn't seriously want it, never researched plastic surgeons or anything. It was just part of my self-hatred. I thought that everybody had *Play-boy* tits but me. Now I look at *Playboy* and cringe; the women all look so unnatural: hairless except for a blonde racing stripe at their crotch, with airbrushed skin that looks like the rubber Barbie's legs are made of, and breasts that look like they were designed by a horny teenage boy with access to a plastics lab.

And about why I call myself bisexual rather than lesbian, that's even more complicated than the shaved-head issue. I've been involved only with women for almost three years now, and I'm in a long-term, monogamous relationship with a woman. But I call myself bisexual. I guess for me it boils down to potential: I have the potential to be attracted to and involved with both men and women. I've had good relationships with men, and I do find some men attractive, so it would feel dishonest to erase that by saying "I'm a lesbian."

I'll wrap up now because the length of this letter is getting excessive. I'd like to hear more about your decision to search for me in 1989. What led up to it? What did you hope would happen? How did you feel when you got my name and address? How did John react to your decision to search? And what happened on those trips you took down to Brockton? Did anyone go with you? Did you stop outside our house? Did you see anyone? When was it exactly? Would I have been away at school in New York? What was going through your mind when you were there? Details, I want details.

One more thing. What time was I born? From one of your earlier letters it looks like it was around 5:30 a.m., but I couldn't figure it out exactly.

I framed that photo of you that you sent with your first letter, and it's on my bureau, alongside three other pictures: one of me with my parents, one of Matt and Jane, and one of Cara and me. Having it there makes me very happy.

I can't wait for your next letter.

With love,

Katie

June 1996

❧

June 3, 1996

Dear Katie,

As your impending visit gets closer, I find myself wishing I could diet down to more reasonable tonnage, have a quick face-lift and repaint my house. I so want to make a favorable first impression on you. I hate to admit to such squishy, quivery insecurity, so I will pretend I didn't write the preceding. I will just say that I am really looking forward to seeing you, and I hope it won't be a humid day so my hair will behave.

My heart cockles were warmed when you wrote that you have my picture displayed alongside your family's. I have your picture—the big toothy grin one (my favorite)—on my bureau next to pictures of Jack and Gus. They have not yet asked who you are (kids are so self-focused at their ages, I don't think they have even noticed yet). I am still debating daily with myself whether I should tell them that they have a sister. John says if we tell them, we must also tell his whole side of the family (a network of innumerable aunts, uncles, cousins, second cousins, thirds and so on), so that the kids will not be burdened with keeping a secret. John thinks the fact that I was an unwed mother who had to give her child up for adoption is nothing to be ashamed of and people will understand.

My bold independent side says, "The hell with what anybody thinks." My gelatinous, milquetoast side says, "Ohmygodin-heavenellen, how can you even think that they won't belittle you behind your back, and think of all the explaining you will have to do!" My emotionally evasive, Scarlet O'Hara side says, "Fiddledeedee, I'll think about it tomorrow." It just seems easier at this point to stay quiet. But maybe I will float a trial balloon with John's mother Ducky, truly a most loving and sensitive person, and see how she thinks I should handle it.

I have been thinking a lot about your admission of some "abandonment issues" in your most recent letter. However, the instances you cite as being possibly adoption-related are so similar to mine that I have a hard time making the connection to adoption causation. Let me explain.

My earliest dream-memory is a nightmare I had when I was about three or four. In this nightmare I was hiding, terrified, behind a hedge in the backyard, watching as my parents were cooked in a huge black pot by cannibals. I woke up screaming. Also at four, when I attended kindergarten, I hated to leave my mother to go to school and would try any excuse to stay home. This behavior went on for years. My chronic malingering got so bad that at the age of nine, when I suffered a hemorrhage a week after my tonsillectomy, my mother tried to send me to school, not believing me when I told her I had been vomiting blood. It was only when I fainted and fell down the stairs that she took me seriously.

I also remember an incident when I was about eight or nine, when I was next door with a neighbor family, watching a movie on a Sunday afternoon. I started to have unreasonable fears that something had happened to my parents and family, and I began to cry. I tried to stifle the crying but soon was sobbing uncontrollably. The neighbors assumed I was crying because of the movie. I just wanted to get out of there to run home.

When my first husband Jim left me, I feared that I was unlovable and doomed to live my life unconnected. My mother was my life-line then, and I again was plagued with fears that she would die and I would have no one in the whole world who loved me. My self-protective cloaking devices became fully activated and I pushed people away so I would not be hurt again.

So are these kinds of fears caused by external events in our lives, or are they somehow part of the personality? I asked John if he'd had childhood fears like imagining his parents had disappeared or died, and he said no. Jack also said no. But Gus said yes. He is more like me and less like John. So I guess the answer is both.

Perhaps because there were so many children in my family, I did not get the attention I needed. I was a painfully shy, self-conscious child, not so much an "attic-dwelling agoraphobe," but one who hid behind my mother's skirt, afraid to talk to people, and with nails chewed down to the quick. Or perhaps, as researchers are apparently now discovering, there is a shyness gene that shapes my personality, so I am occasionally plagued by insecurity, stage fright, telephonophobia and generalized feelings of unworthiness.

Mostly when I am feeling insecure, I take a big injection of unconditional love from John and the kids and I feel better. For me, love is the answer. To everything. Give me a couple of hugs and I will feel good in the morning.

I will believe you when you say that you don't feel any blame toward me. In reading your letter, I did not feel, as you so creatively put it, "a Pavlovian surge of Catholic guilt." What I felt was a surge of identification and familiarity. Maybe I am obtuse, though. From your first letter, John said that he could feel your hurt, whereas I took what you wrote more at face value. Whatever the case, I want to assure you that I want to know you and have you in my life. We can live in the present and "heal the past." I hope you will want to know me too, after we meet in person.

I loved your Sister Agatha story. I laughed and laughed at your line, "She liked being able to pass." I'm sorry you had to suffer with her, but it is such a classic Catholic-school story: full of abject humiliation, pettiness and punishment. I have a few stories like it too. For some other time.

You asked about my search for you in 1989. After I had Jack in 1986, I was filled with a vast sense of loss that I did not have you in my life anymore. Giving birth to Jack brought back a thousandfold the memory of your being born and holding you in the hospital. I also felt intense anger that I'd had to suffer so much simply for exercising my human sexual nature. I felt that the punishment definitely did not fit the crime. But even though I had lots of time to think, I had to pour all my physical energy into taking care of Jack. We bought our first home, a condo, when Jack was seven months old, and I became pregnant again when he was nine months. I was extremely busy so I never got beyond the thinking stage.

I miscarried that pregnancy but soon was pregnant again with Gus, who was born in August 1988, twenty-six months after Jack. Having two children in diapers leaves very little time; some days I didn't even get a shower until John got home from work.

All the while, I thought of having lost you. After about five months I was able to grab more snatches of time for myself, and I decided that I would find out what had happened to you. I had seen some reunions on TV and garnered the name of ALMA (Adoptee Liberty Movement Association), an organization founded by an adopted woman who wholeheartedly believed that adoptees should have open and unrestricted access to their birth information. ALMA group meetings were held all over the place. I attended one in North Andover and met an adopted woman who had her birthmother living with her; they had found each other after thirty-seven years. I also met another birthmother about my age who was a member of the more militant group, CUB (Concerned United Birthparents). She had secured information about her daughter, who was in her first year of college at the time. She wrote to the girl's parents and expressed a desire to be in touch. The daughter's adoptive family was southern and military, and adamantly opposed to any contact whatsoever between their daughter and her birthmother. They hired a lawyer who wrote back to the birthmother threatening a lawsuit should any further attempts to contact their daughter be made.

I came away from that meeting having seen polar opposite outcomes of the search process. One was very happy, one was really sad. But all parties strongly believed that seeking and finding was justified, nay, even necessary, for both the adoptee and the birth-parent. I took folders of information about searching and a how-to guide to start me on my way.

The first step was to contact the maternity home and the adop-tion agency. I wrote to Crittenton and received a sympathetic letter telling me they had not heard from you. Not being the adoption agency, they had no pertinent information about your adoption, but if I wanted to, I could authorize their providing what informa-tion they had to you, should you ever ask.

Then I wrote Catholic Charities. A woman named Christine O'Shea sent me what they referred to as "nonidentifying informa-tion" (called a "Profile—Adoptive Couple," a copy of which I send here), along with a copy of my agreement for adoption (I assume to remind me of the rights I had signed away). They said that I could make an appointment if I had any questions about the material. Notice the profile refers to your parents as "warm, friendly, and attractive," very unlike how they pictured me. Did you have a copy of this before? Anyway, her letter also sounded semi-sympathetic to me, and I had heard stories of some social workers being very forthcoming with information, so I called to make an appointment to see her in January 1989.

I made arrangements with my mother to watch the children so I could go meet O'Shea. My mother was nearly as interested in meeting you as I was and was willing to do whatever was necessary to see that I found you. I bought a new black sweater, which I thought made me look thinner so I would create a good impression, and off I went to my appointment in Malden.

When I got to the office (a rather rundown place it was), I sat in the waiting area for a good long time feeling alone and under scrutiny. O'Shea finally arrived and ushered me into her office and closed the door, hush-hush-like. I told her my reason for being there. I said, "There's no longer any need for unwed mothers to feel stigmatized, since so many girls keep their babies nowadays." She said, "Oh, no. I don't think that's true at all. As a matter of fact, I know a girl right now who is so ashamed she won't come out of her room. She is anxious to have her baby born so it can be adopted." I thought to myself, "Gee, as a social worker, shouldn't you be helping her to get over that?"

Then she went on to say that she could not provide me with any information about you that might lead me to you. I think she truly believed that it would not be right for me, a birthmother, to interfere in their process. She admonished me to stop my search. She told me I could leave my permission in the file to open my records to you, should you request them. She did say that more adoptees contacted her office than birthparents and also that she had set up meetings between adoptees and birthparents, with "90 percent resulting in happy contacts."

I came away from the meeting feeling summarily dismissed. I felt I had been treated, once again, as the merest peripheral and insignificant party in the adoption process. My feelings were of no concern to Catholic Charities. But maybe I was overreacting and projecting my own sense of shame onto O'Shea's dealings with me. I have been looking over my files from that time and find my notations from our meeting where O'Shea told me that there was a good chance your family was still in Massachusetts, that you were probably the last child adopted by your parents, and that your father was "good friends with the Monsignor." So she did not entirely shut me out.

In any case, I came away feeling angry that they would not give me your name and address, perhaps implying that I (as a birthmother) was too unstable to handle the information properly. I rode home mumbling to myself and fueling my retrorockets of rage. I vowed I would find you despite Catholic Charities.

In February I contacted the Adoption Connection, headed by another adoptee. This is a support group like ALMA, and very active in Massachusetts. I enrolled as a member, put my name into their registry, and attended a couple of meetings. These meetings were huge, attended by adoptees, birthmothers and adoptive parents. (There may have been birthfathers there, I can't remember.) Experiences varied widely—good, bad and ugly. But the meetings took place in far-flung towns that were very difficult for me, a mother of two little kids with a husband in grad school and working full-time, to get to. I had to stop going to them. I did find out, however, that for a small fee, I could have someone do my detective work for me to find your name and address.

In January 1990 I had your name, address and phone number. I was thrilled. John was thrilled. My mother was thrilled. I told my friends. I even told Jack and Gus, who were, of course, too young to understand. The very next day I called the Brockton police for directions, strapped the kids in their car seats, and off I went to scope out your house. I drove up and down and around the street a few times, seeing no one, thinking how stupid I was to think that I might see you, especially in the middle of the morning. I also knew I couldn't just sit there all day because someone in the neighborhood might think I was casing the joint for a robbery. I took the kids to McDonald's near the Westgate Mall and wondered if every young female face I saw was perhaps yours. I decided I needed to get more focused in my quest to see you.

I sat down and composed a letter to your parents that started, "This letter may come as a bit of a shock to you, but please be assured that I do not wish to cause you any problems or heartache. I have waited nearly twenty-one years to seek my daughter—the passage of time has not softened the pain nor filled the empty space in me." Katie, you can see my draft of this letter when you come, if you like.

I never sent the letter, of course. What I did do was try to get more information about you. John drove me and the kids down to Brockton one Saturday. We went to two different libraries to look at high school yearbooks just so I could see your face. Not finding you in Brockton's yearbooks, we drove over to Cardinal Spellman and sat disappointed in the parking lot because the school was closed. For weeks afterward I tried to think of a way to get yearbooks from that school.

I tried to find out if you had a driver's license and was told there was no license issued to a Kathleen Hern. (I did not have your middle initial then.) I also tried to find out if your dad had a practice in the Brockton area and couldn't find one. It was then that I began having all kinds of scary imaginings. What if the reason you were not in a yearbook and had no license was because you were handicapped or retarded? Or what if your parents took out a restraining order on me? Or what if your father was a drunk who had lost his practice? These kinds of scenarios had occurred in other searches I knew.

Then I called your house a couple of times and hung up without talking. Your mother's hello-voice sounded lilting and happy to me. Once, I even screwed up my courage and called with the flimsily formed idea that I would pretend to be conducting a survey. But like I told you before, I am a lousy liar and an inept and uninspired detective. Your father answered, I asked for you. He said you were no longer living there, asked if he could take a message and who I was. He sounded very nice. I fumblingly replied that I was just an old friend and hung up quickly.

So there were many reasons why I finally gave up the quest to see you. First, I figured you were nearly twenty-one and able to make up your own mind if you wanted to find me, and I would rather be in touch with you directly than going through your parents (nice as they sounded). Second, your parents sounded pleasant and all appearances indicated you lived in a well-kept home. Third, the shame thing—I felt I had no right to enter and disrupt your life. Fourth, I was scared I'd open a can of worms when my own life was so good. I had two happy and healthy children and a terrific husband. I could not risk their happiness by exposing them to anything like a lawsuit or negativity from your parents. And what if you hated me? That was too hard for me to face. Finally, there was always the scenario I had kept in my head from the time you were born: that you would contact me someday.

So here we are. I am so happy you found me and I am thrilled with our flowering relationship. I feel so at peace when I write a long letter and send it off to you. And so much happiness when I get a letter back from you in return. You have filled my heart's empty space.

Now I want you to tell me what prompted you to begin searching for me. How did it feel when you were able to get my information so quickly? What did you think about during the month of January before sending the letter? Did you try to get additional information on me before sending the letter? Have you thought any more about contacting your biological father?

To answer your other question, you were born at 5:10 a.m. Is this just for your general data store or do you want to get your horoscope done?

Back to your last letter. I was surprised and amused to read that you call yourself a "notoriously lazy writer." I too will avoid sitting down to write unless I'm under some class deadline. I had thought it was just my slothful, unmotivated self. I recently got my portfolio of work back from my professor. She gave me lots of suggestions on where to send my essays to get them published, and I have been avoiding composing my enticement letters to the different magazines. There are lots of reasons in my head not to send my stuff out—some reality-based, some insecurity-based. Whatever. I know I have to do it because I've signed up with her again next semester and she will ask me about my progress.

Next time I will send you my last available essay (I haven't yet written anything else), which details my efforts to find out more about the writer's market. I'd send it this time, but this letter is so long you'll have enough to read.

Write soon.

Love,

Ellen

P.S. You've mentioned Sister Huberjean, your alter ego, a couple of times. Is there some allusion of a literary or cinematic nature I am missing? I tried to find some reference to Huberjean on the Internet and came up with zero. Educate me.

June 7, 1996

Dear Ellen,

I got your letter yesterday and was really touched by the story of your search for me. And hearing that you'd called the house and asked for me was mind-blowing. It's hard for me to grasp that you were so intent on finding me while I just went about my life of paper-writing and residence-hall government, entirely oblivious to it.

I remember the time you called quite clearly. I was at NYU then, and my father mentioned it to me during one of our weekly phone conversations.

"Somebody called here looking for you," he told me.

"Who was it?"

"She didn't leave a name, but she asked for Kathleen and said she was an old friend."

"Did you give her my number here?"

"No, I didn't know if I should. I told her that you were no longer living here and that I'd take a message if she wanted, but she didn't leave one."

"Huh. That's strange."

I couldn't figure out what old friend would be calling me Kathleen and wouldn't know that I was living in New York. I wished that my father had given the person my number so that I could find out who it was.

I don't know what kind of reaction you would have gotten from me if he had given you my number. My first instinct is usually politeness, but you might have also found me detached and distant, not out of maliciousness or spite, but because it would have been such a shock. Like I told you before, I'd never thought much about my birth roots. I think I actually kept myself from thinking about them, out of a sense of loyalty to my parents and maybe out of self-protection. So if there was suddenly a human being on the other end of the phone who said she was my mother—and it wasn't the mother I'd always known—I wouldn't have been able to comprehend it. It's hard for me to comprehend it even now.

You asked for the story of how I came to search for you, and I'm afraid it's not as heartwarming as your story. Once or twice a year for the past five or six years, I'd thought about contacting Catholic Charities for my medical history. That was the only curiosity I would allow myself. I've always adamantly denied any interest in finding my birthparents. "I have parents," I'd tell people who asked if I wanted to search.

Then last spring and summer I worked with a student at JFKU who was doing her master's thesis on therapy for adoptees. She herself was adopted and had recently reunited with both her birthmother and birthfather, and she was writing about her search and the difficulties involved with being adopted.

"Not all adoptees feel like you do," I warned her frequently. "Your paper needs to acknowledge that there are a wide range of experiences adopted people have."

It was a good piece of advice, but even as I said it, I could hear that there was a defensiveness behind it. And when I gave her my standard spiel—"I have no interest in searching for my birthparents"—I knew the explanation was a little too quick, a little too pat.

As her teacher, I had to stop being so scornful of adoptees who said they felt hurt and abandoned because, if I'm remembering it right, she herself had felt that way. My "get over it, crybaby" attitude just wasn't going to work when I was trying to help her articulate and organize her thoughts. And reading the sections of her paper that described her own experiences, I could see how incredibly disrespectful my perspective had been.

Since this was her master's thesis (it ended up being more than one hundred pages long), I saw her almost every week for a couple of months. I couldn't avoid the subject of adoption, and I couldn't get away with the dismissive, superficial way I'd talked about it in the past. I started thinking about being adopted in ways I never had before and started looking at my own defensiveness.

Around this time I happened upon the book I mentioned in my first letter to you, *Within Me, Without Me*, which told several birthmothers' stories. I was moved by how painful their experiences had been, and I was furious about how they'd been treated. One day, about halfway through the book, I decided to send off to Catholic Charities for my records. A small part of me hoped that you had opened the records to me and that we'd get in touch, but mostly I didn't think about it. As with most emotionally intense things, I just held my breath and did it. I didn't let myself imagine what might come of it, and I didn't acknowledge to myself what a major thing I'd initiated. I told myself I mailed that letter because I was curious and that I would just wait and see what happened.

So, not having prepared myself at all, it was shocking when Karen Hawthorne from Catholic Charities called me, out of the blue, and read off your name, address and phone number. I hadn't even gotten anything in the mail about it, and suddenly, there it was in front of me. This woman is my birthmother. As Hawthorne talked, I doodled cartoon people on the scrap paper in front of me; their faces all ended up looking stunned and bewildered.

For at least a week I had to struggle to remember your name. It just wouldn't register, I couldn't absorb it. I ended up having to devise memory tricks for myself. For your first name I thought of another woman named Ellen that I know, for your maiden name I thought of a San Francisco street called Geary Boulevard, and for your married name I thought of Johnny Carson with an L thrown in.

It's such a different story from yours that at first I was reluctant to tell it. But I've kept myself from feeling bad about it by telling myself that the experiences of birthmothers and adopted kids are, by nature, very different. You were twenty when you had me. You remember the nine months of pregnancy, the labor, the moment of birth. You remember holding me while the astronauts walked on the moon, and you remember signing the papers in the back seat of that car while the social worker in front peered at you through the rear-view mirror. And from then on, you were conscious of the fact that you didn't have me in your life.

I remember nothing of that, and growing up in a loving family, I didn't feel the loss. The goal in Catholic Charities's closed-adoption system was to replace one set of parents with another and erase all traces of the first set. And for me, it worked. Complete erasure. I don't think I really understood that I had another set of parents. There was no way to conceptualize two sets—two mothers, two fathers. It was an either/or thing.

This is one of the things I struggled with during that month between getting your name and sending off my first letter. The very language of it all felt like a betrayal of my family. I worked out a lot of my confusion in a plain spiral notebook. The day after my call from Hawthorne, I wrote,

I don't want to use words like "mother," "grandmother," "brothers." They feel wrong—far too intimate to be attaching to strangers. . . . I have a family. I have a mother. I have a father. A sister I prefer not to interact with. And a brother I'm becoming good friends with. Two grandmothers, both dead, and never very much fun to be around when they weren't. But there's a whole what-if family out there. . . . I feel numb—need to keep reminding myself that there are people out there who are, in some way I can't get a grip on, my family. A different kind of family, so different the word seems wrong.

A month later, having received your first letter, I tried to understand the way I reacted when I first read the Catholic Charities report. In my notebook I wrote:

Sitting there with a drippy burrito in El Farolito, it hit me like a cartoon piano falling from the sky, or an anvil dropping on me, leaving me flattened with dizzy stars spinning around my head. "Your mother named you Sarah Elizabeth."

No, my *mother* named me Kathleen Mary. My *mother* is swimming at Massasoit Community College right now for the arthritis in her left knee. My mother's name is Mary, Mary. It's Mary. Not Ellen.

I just couldn't understand it, didn't have any place in my mind to fit "birthmother," and it felt like this new information was squeezing the only mother I'd known out of her place. I'm still in the process of creating that space, trying to understand where you fit, and still trying to comprehend that acknowledging you is not a betrayal of my other mother.

I've always been superprotective of my parents. I remember one evening when I was about ten and my mother had organized a craft-making class in our basement. She and about six other women were sitting around a long table and making lampshades. I was on the cellar stairs watching them and listening to them talk. They chatted easily with each other as they worked, and the conversation moved to the subject of pregnancy.

"My labor with Chrissy was eighteen hours long."

"God help you. Mine was only six, but it was a terrible six."

"I could barely walk for the last month I carried Michael."

My mother concentrated on her work and said nothing, her back rigid. From my perch on the stairs I held my breath and willed, with all my might, that they not try to involve her in the discussion, that they not make her say, "I couldn't have children of my own." I didn't want her to have to feel bad.

Along with the feeling that I was being disloyal to my parents by contacting you was the feeling that Katie Hern, the person I'd spent twenty-six years becoming, was suddenly in jeopardy. I put it this way in my notebook: "If things had gone differently at just one moment in the past, the moment Ellen was told she had a healthy baby girl, a whole universe would have collapsed and sprung into a different form."

That feeling was most triggered by learning my original name. The name represented for me a whole other life I almost led, and a whole other person I might have become, a possibility that terrified me. Unable to sleep one night, I ranted for two and a half pages in my notebook about "Sarah":

Sarah to me is a thin, pale-skinned, delicate woman, a woman with long, straight hair pulled back into a tasteful ponytail at the nape of her neck. She wears floral, full-skirted dresses and low-heeled delicate shoes. A woman who laughs quietly into her gentle, polite palm, who blushes and apologizes easily. Sarah is by no means hearty. Or aggressive. Or loud. Sarah wouldn't dance and sing in the supermarket produce section. She'd never take up that much space, not want to impose on anyone else's shopping experience. . . . Sarah moves unobtrusively through life, hoping nobody will notice. She doesn't want to make a fuss. I am not Sarah.

No offense, Ellen. Sarah is a perfectly nice name and all, but before I got to know you, it was threatening and unsettling to learn that it had been *my* name. What was most reassuring for me during all of this were your letters. Seeing myself reflected in you helped me to understand that even if my life had gone differently and I had remained Sarah Elizabeth, I wouldn't have become the kind of Sarah who blushes, apologizes and covers her mouth when she laughs. I might have still danced and sung in the produce section. My identity stopped feeling so tenuous.

You asked if I tried to get additional information about you between January and the beginning of February, when I sent my first letter. No, it didn't even occur to me. I guess I just needed that month to get my head together. In the entry I wrote the day after I got your name, I closed by saying:

> I feel like I haven't caught up with the information yet.
> Don't know
> how I feel
> what I think
> what I'll do or say

or what I want.

What do I want?

So that's the gist of my "search" for you, which wasn't really a search at all, more like a stumbled-on find. Reading the story of your search made me feel loved and appreciated. Mine's not going to do the same for you, I'm afraid, but it's honest. And I've never regretted that spur-of-the-moment letter to Catholic Charities. When Matt was considering starting his search, I warned him that it was going to bring up all sorts of issues he didn't expect and affect him in ways he couldn't predict, but that I thought he should do it. Even at the most difficult times, I've always felt very glad to be able to get to know you. And I'm no longer rocked by the tumult I experienced when I first got your name. In fact, over the past few months I've felt more and more grounded, more firmly rooted in the identity that felt so threatened by the name Sarah. I could even send you a Mother's Day card without feeling like a complete traitor.

I have one more question about your search. You said that you told Gus and Jack when you first got my name. What did you tell them? And how old were they exactly? Do you think that Jack might remember that?

I sympathize with your dilemma about telling the kids (and therefore the entire extended family). I've been thinking about it and remembering what I was like as a kid, and it occurs to me that Jack and Gus might know more than you think they do. I always knew more about what was going on in the family than my folks suspected. If there was an argument or an emotional issue being discussed, I'd sit at the top of the stairs and strain my ears. And there wasn't a single corner of the house that I hadn't investigated.

I knew what was in my mother's desk and where my teenage brother hid his porno magazines. Matt was the same way. Unless Gus
and Jack have far more advanced ethical systems than Matt and
I did at their ages, I think they're probably going to find out on
their own if you don't tell them. But I don't mean to freak you out.
I might not have become such a snoop until I was a little older,
and maybe you've been really careful about what they might see or
overhear.

I could totally relate to your writer's market essay. I too had
grand visions of a career in writing. When I finished my master's
and moved out here, I planned to support myself as a freelance
journalist. But I eventually had to admit that I wasn't cut out
for that kind of insecure, will-I-be-able-to-pay-my-rent life. At
every gathering of writers I go to, I hear the same thing: It's next
to impossible to completely support yourself with your writing.
So the answer for me is a twenty-eight-hour-a-week job that I
love (with clear boundaries about not taking work home with
me), and then Fridays and weekends for my life and my writing.
It's worked out pretty well so far. When I didn't have a steady,
secure job I couldn't write at all because I was so anxious about
becoming destitute and having to move back in with my parents,
tail between my legs.

OK. I need to wrap up now. My ass really hurts from sitting so
long, and Cara rented *Absolutely Fabulous*.

As always, I look forward to your next letter.

With love,

Katie

DATE: June 13, 1996
SUBJECT: An e-mail hello

Dear Ellen,

I'm getting the hang of this Internet thing and thought I'd send you a trial e-mail to pass along some news: I've composed the letter to my parents about reuniting with you, and now I'm sitting with it for a day or two to see if there's anything I want to change. Once I had written the letter, I felt a lot better about the whole thing, and I'm now certain that it's going to be fine. I just had to reach a certain point of comfort myself to be able to discuss it with them in a loving and nonthreatening way. I'll send it off in the next few days so that they have some time to get used to it before I arrive.

Oh, by the way, when are the kids' birthdays, and when is yours? Mine, as you know, is in just over a month.

I'll wrap up now and try to be patient for your response.

Love,

Katie

DATE: June 14, 1996
SUBJECT: Ellen spelled backwards is Nervous Nellie

Dear Katie,

I got your letter in the mail yesterday and I will compose my reply letter today and over the weekend. Meanwhile, I love that we can send notes back and forth over the Internet.

Gus will be eight on August 1. Jack just turned ten on May 26. John will be thirty-eight on July 7. (Nearly all of my really significant relationships have been with Cancers.) My birthday is October

27. Did you know that Scorpios are the most detested sign? I read that somewhere.

Regarding your feeling much better after having composed the letter to your parents, have you read Joan Didion's essay, "Why I Write?" I got chills when I first read it because I identified so much with it. She says essentially that she writes in order to think: "Had I been blessed with even limited access to my own mind there would have been no reason to write. I write entirely to find out what I'm thinking, what I'm looking at, what I see and what it means. What I want and what I fear."

I have always written as a means of sorting myself out. Writing makes things clear for me and organizes my jumbled thoughts. I feel I'm not very quick on the uptake a lot of the time in conversation. I'm not one for snappy retorts or immediate insights. I need time to chew on things. Given enough time, I can be *brilliant*. Yeah.

Anyway, is this how you feel too?

I really would like a recommendation from you for a book by an adoptee that expresses feelings you identify with. And do you have a copy of that one-hundred-page thesis you mentioned in your last letter?

After reading that letter, I feel like I need a support-group meeting. I very much appreciate your honesty but I have to tell you, it made me feel vulnerable and emotional. It was painful to read that you hated the name Sarah Elizabeth, my all-time favorite name. Also that you are still trying to understand where I might fit into your life.

I want to reassure you that I do not want to take your mother's place in your heart (and I know that you would never want that either). I just want to be your friend. I want an open and honest relationship with you. I will spend some time writing about this stuff in my letter to you. I just need to digest and process it a little more so I can be clear.

Geez, this e-mail is getting way long. I'll end for now and get started on my reply to your letter.

Love and a hug,

El

⸎

DATE: June 14, 1996
SUBJECT: Re: Ellen spelled backwards is Nervous Nellie

Dear Ellen,

I'm really sorry if what I said in my last letter hurt you.

As I was mailing the letter, I wondered if it was a bit too raw to be sending you. I should have sat with it a few days longer rather than mailing it straight out. It was an example of me figuring out something by writing about it, figuring out the things I struggled with after getting your name from Catholic Charities, and I don't think I gave myself enough time to translate those raw emotions into a form that would be easier for you to take.

I think attending a support group might be a really good thing for you to do. This experience would have been a lot more difficult for me if I hadn't had therapy once a week.

And I'll look again for books that might give you a context for understanding the difficult things I'm telling you. I pulled something off the Internet that I'll send along with this e-mail (or I'll try to send along—let me know if it works). It's an overview of the issues involved with adoption, and it's a decent place to start.

The one thing I want you to know is that, even though I had a lot of resistance and defensiveness to overcome in order to develop a relationship with you, getting to know you has been one of the most wonderful experiences I've ever had. I feel blessed to have you in my life, and you don't need to worry anymore about driving me away. Or that I won't like you when we meet. Or that your hair will be too frizzy or your hips too wide.

I love you.

Katie

DATE: June 14, 1996
SUBJECT: Thanks

Dear Katie,

You are so sweet and kind and sympathetic. But I don't want you to protect me from feeling the emotions that you want to convey in your letters to me. I want you to be as open and honest as possible, even if your feelings are raw. It's OK for me to feel that rawness too, as painful as it may be.

It really helps me to be reassured by you. Thank you. Sometimes I am overwhelmed with the connection to you and the emotion I feel and I worry that I might lose you again.

John and I spent some good alone-time last night just talking about our e-mail (yours and mine) and your last letter. He knows I can sometimes get carried away with my imagination, and he does a great job of keeping me grounded in reality.

I am going to look into the Adoption Connection group again to hook up with some meetings. They'll be able to give me some input about telling Jack and Gus too.

Just talked to Ann. She thinks I should tell the kids because, like you, she thinks they are getting near to the snooping age and will find out through their own devices. She thinks I have nothing to hide, shamewise. She feels Jack can intellectualize it, and she pooh-poohs my concern with Gus's sensitivity and says that as long as I reassure him (on a frequent basis) how much he is loved (and Jack too), they will be fine with it.

I'm afraid I shocked Gus terribly yesterday when I answered in the affirmative that I had once been a smoker. We have them programmed to be disgusted with smoking and he just could not believe that his own mother at one time did such a nasty thing. He's at the age still where his parents have tremendous powers; we are somewhat godlike to him. I don't really want to be godlike, but I don't want to take away his innocence either. It's such a pure and beautiful thing.

You still have not told me where Huberjean comes from. I know she is like my Sister Mary Misconception, only French. What or where does the name come from?

I love you too, Katie.

Ellen

DATE: June 14, 1996
SUBJECT: Re: Thanks

Dear Ellen,

I'm glad my e-mail today was reassuring for you. It knots my stomach to know that my letter upset you. I think there may be no way to avoid some of the painful issues we've encountered, and I'm glad that the relationship we're building is so honest. I am going to try to be more gentle, though. And you really don't need to fear losing me again. That would devastate me as much as it would you.

You might take a look at a book called *Being Adopted: The Lifelong Search for Self,* by David M. Brodzinsky, Marshall D. Schechter and Robin Marantz Henig. It's not by an adoptee, but it goes through a lot of the general psychological issues involved and includes a lot of quotes from adoptees.

I agree with Ann that you don't need to be ashamed of having been an unwed mother who gave a child up for adoption. I was talking with Cara's parents about my relationship with you, and her mother had nothing but compassion for you. "It was such a different time then," she said. "Unmarried women just couldn't keep their babies. It was unheard of." The whole experience was so loaded with shame for you—and so much shame was imposed on you from everyone else—that it's not surprising that you still carry it. I just hope you can conquer it.

Anyway. I have no idea where my friend John Francis got the name Sister Huberjean for me. He just came up with it one day when I was scolding him for something, and it stuck. I hated it at first and got even more Huberjeanian when he'd call me it, but now I have sort of embraced the old biddy.

I'll sign off now. This morning I woke up to find that I'd finally succumbed to the cold Cara's been suffering from all week. My runny nose is so out of control I can't walk anywhere in the house without my roll of toilet paper.

I look forward to your next e-mail. I'm becoming addicted. Cara's new nickname for me is "Computer Geek."

With love,

Katie

DATE: June 15, 1996
SUBJECT: A cheery Saturday morning hello

Dear Katie,

I read the text from the Internet that you sent, about how members of the adoption triad must recognize and work through "seven core issues" to find happiness and serenity. I was fascinated to see all my problems laid bare: loss, rejection, guilt/shame, grief, identity, intimacy and control. I'm a textbook case! And I guess being members of the "triad" is part of what makes us so alike with these issues. It's all so illuminating and fascinating. I am going to run out and get *Being Adopted* today.

Do you subscribe to that publication mentioned in the text, *Adopted Child?* If so, is it any good and where do I get it? I'm thinking I may call CUB to see what they have to offer too. I could use a little strong-minded militancy in dealing with my shame.

I find it cosmic that your father told you about my call back in 1990. At the time, I imagined that I had been vague enough that the call would have been insignificant in his mind and not interesting enough to tell you about. And I really wished he had said where you were, because I spent a lot of time wondering why you did not live at home. I wondered if perhaps you were married and had children, or if you had an apartment on your own, or whether you were hospitalized somewhere—all sorts of crazy stuff.

I'm sorry to hear that you are suffering from a cold and trailing around with toilet paper. Have you tried a little nasal spray? It can really dry up the drip and let you breathe normally. Not that you need my advice, of course.

John is off to karate this morning (he's a third-degree black belt but he hates for people to know it) and then he's going to a computer show to buy, buy, buy: more memory, a faster modem, a CD-ROM and whatever else he feels he must have. Talk about computer addicts! Now he's got a 1996 DEC laptop, two older DEC laptops and the one he has built from scratch himself. *No one* needs so much computing power. But I guess I should be thankful his vices are so innocuous, and that the only cyberlover he has is me.

I'm going to take the kids to a movie today and tomorrow we are going down to Ducky's for a Father's Day cookout with some of the closest relatives. I hope you and Cara have a great weekend.

Love,

El

DATE: June 15, 1996
SUBJECT: Hello back

Dear Ellen,

I'm glad you're excited about reading up on adoption issues. I think that doing that will make the feelings I told you about a lot less scary. Like my tirade about the name Sarah—that wasn't really about the name Sarah at all. I do like that name, and when I was young, I imagined I'd name one of my kids Sarah.

The tirade was actually about my identity. Names are so central to people's sense of self that learning you once were called something else is bound to be disruptive. I think my reaction to the name Sarah is pretty typical among adopted people and, in the grand scheme of things, nothing to worry about. It certainly wasn't a rejection of you as a person. I hadn't even sent off my first letter to you at that point, so I had no sense of you as a person.

It was just that seeing that name made me understand, for the first time ever, that I might not have led the life I've led, might not have become the person I've become, or loved the people I've loved. And that was a frightening thing to realize.

I'd also like to add something to that list of the seven core adoption issues: loyalty. This has been a major one for me. I know now that becoming close to you does not replace or negate my relationship with my adoptive mother. I do know that. And from your very first letter, I knew that you had no intention of trying to do that. But there was an unconscious anxiety that told me I was being disloyal, and this anxiety got inflamed by the overlapping language—that you and my adoptive mother are both called "mother." This is what was going on in the journal entry that mentions eating a burrito at El Farolito. The fierceness of that entry is my loyalty.

Anxieties about loyalty are very common among adopted people. In one book I read about a woman who had wanted to seek out her birthparents but, out of a sense of loyalty, waited until her adoptive parents were both dead before she did it. I think she started searching when she was in her seventies.

Having been in therapy for five months, I know that these anxieties are misplaced. I can be loyal to both you and to my parents at the same time. Love is not a finite resource, and you are not competing with them. But in the beginning, I didn't have a grip on that.

I haven't seen the publication *Adopted Child*. If you get a hold of it, tell me what you think. Being almost twenty-seven years old, I find the title a bit off-putting. I suspect it might be more focused on children than adults.

I want to hear more about Gus and Jack. I have some sense of what they're like, but I want more details. I also want to hear more about Ann before I meet her.

OK. My store of writing energy is spent, so, I'll sign off.
Wishing you good hair days,
Katie

DATE: June 16, 1996
SUBJECT: Yes, it's me

Dear Katie,

Our home computer crashed so I am writing this on John's
work machine. I feel disoriented not being able to get into my own
little mail space.

I understand your struggle with loyalty. I might have had a
loyalty issue myself if John were not so understanding and open-
hearted about you. But he has been his usual terrific self and has
allowed me to pursue my relationship with you without interfer-
ence. (*Allowed* me? Bad word choice. Am I not a liberated woman?
He has offered me, on a *golden platter,* the time to pursue my relationship with you.) He has cooked meals, done dishes and laundry,
taken the kids here and there, whatever . . . so that I could spend the
time I needed writing to you. Never once has he resented my letting
housewifely stuff slide (which tends to happen a lot when I'm in
school anyway). He has always looked forward to meeting you almost as much as I have.

You asked about Jack and Gus: Jack is a very bright kid, a little
short for his age. He looks like he was cloned from one of John's
cells. He's a duplicate, only smaller and with less of a paunch. He's
ten now and a bit of a know-it-all. When we lived in Dracut, he
attended a French Catholic school in Lowell. He won the science
fair competition in kindergarten, beating out seventy-five other

kindergartners with his presentation of "Putting Paper Under Water Without Getting It Wet." In first grade he took the reading, math and overall excellence awards. Jack is a born ham and tends to be melodramatic, crying loudly with a wide open mouth at the slightest provocation, like Lucy Ricardo when Ricky puts the kibosh on her attempts to sing at his club. Jack is outgoing and does dead-on imitations of people. He has a bit of an ego, possibly because he gets such adoring devotion from his little brother, who thinks Jack is the funniest guy on earth.

Gus is my sweet, sensitive, shy boy. He looks like my side of the family with dark hair and eyes. He is tall and skinny, well coordinated, and loves to play outdoors or anyplace where he can explode and run around. He has a terrific, infectious laugh and is John's and Jack's best audience. Gus had a little trouble last year in first grade, so we hired a reading tutor and kept him back this year. He has really bloomed and is now tops in his class academically and socially. His teacher says he is "more popular than Elvis," and Gus absolutely loves school now. He has real artistic ability and has taken to writing his own stories on the computer with me and then illustrating them. He inherited John's loudness so he has a hard time whispering, just like his Dad. The two of them in the morning drive Jack and me up the wall with their screaming, rollicking ticklefests.

Do you realize how many words we have generated to each other just since the beginning of June with our letters and e-mail? We have been writing to each other for five months. You mentioned in your most recent e-mail that you have been in therapy for five months. I thought it must have been longer, because you said you went into it to help you with depression from being subjected to nasty flak resulting from your Lesbian Avenger activism. Does your therapist specialize in adoption issues?

I saw an ad in the paper one time that promoted a lesbian Hispanic comic who was also adopted and was embarking on a search for her birthmother. Are you familiar with her? I wonder if she found her and how it turned out.

I do understand that your initial rejection of the name Sarah had to do with your identity. I sheepishly admit I had a similar kind of reaction when I found out six years ago that your name was Kathleen. All those years I had been thinking of you as Sarah and suddenly I had to accept a whole new name, which I was not particularly fond of either. (But John and I did want to use the name Mary if we had had a girl.) But I *love* the name Katie—I always have. And I certainly love it all the more now. It was not so much the rejection of the name that threw me, it was your saying that you were still trying to find a place for me in your life. Which I extrapolated to mean your maybe not finding a place for me at all: rejection, loss. On an intellectual level, I know that you cannot have a relationship with me without some adjustment and the same is true for me. I just let myself get carried away with glumness and I'm sorry that I put your stomach in knots. But I'm really, really happy that we can discuss these things openly. So please, please do not censor yourself or your feelings when you write to me, OK? I can take it.

This past week was the most shitty week for weather. Ultrahumid and hot. Going outdoors, I felt like I was pickled in the brine of my own sweat, and my hair was a wild, enormous shiitake mushroom–shaped cloud around my head. Every time I looked in a mirror, I felt shocked and depressed. The uglifying humidity coupled with not being in school (where I am able to feed myself with positive, good-student strokes) caused me to be in a rather negative space. Forgive me for having transferred some of that negativity to you in my reaction to your letter.

I hope your weekend was wonderful. I'll try to spend some time on your letter tomorrow. If John can't get my usual computer working, he's going to set up one of the older ones for me.

Lots of love,

Ellen

Dear Katie,

We have been writing and discussing so many things over e-mail that I hardly know where to start as I sit down to write this snail mail letter. I'll just begin by going through your last letter page by page.

More regarding the name Sarah: The most beautiful girl in my high school was named Sarah. She had an ethereal beauty and, yes, she was "thin, pale-skinned, delicate . . . with long, straight hair pulled back into a tasteful ponytail at the nape of her neck." You are so damn perceptive! She was blond and blue-eyed. She was also a very talented artist and one of the most popular girls in her class. She was kind, very bright, and just plain perfect. She seemed very self-assured and somehow above all the horrible teenage angst most of the rest of us suffered. She represented the ideal to me—dark, insecure little chunko that I was. I came to like the name Sarah because it represented beauty, intelligence and accomplishment. I guess I named you Sarah to imbue you with those same qualities, sort of like a fairy godmother. And it worked, didn't it? Bibbidee, bobbidee, boo!

I got to know another Sarah last semester in my political thought class. She was big and tall and comfortable. She had a terrific sense of humor, was a committed feminist and was into women's studies. She was only eighteen but seemed very evolved for such a young woman. I really liked her.

How did you feel about the name Ellen? It is a rather workaday-like name—sturdy, unimaginative. My mother named me after her best childhood friend. I kind of like it when it is paired as Ellen Elizabeth because it sounds more ear-pleasing and musical.

To answer your question about my having told Jack and Gus about you back in 1990. Let's see, Gus would have been about seventeen months old and Jack about three and a half. I would say Gus definitely does not remember and probably Jack does not either. I have no memories from that early in my life. Do you? I can remember small snippets from about age four, but I don't know if I remember them because they have stayed in my memory, or because these snippets are part of family lore that has been repeated over the years. And at the age of three, Jack would not have thought it an unusual circumstance to be told he had a sister, I don't think, because he was too young to question and reason. He probably felt that whatever I told him was the way things were supposed to be. I don't know really.

I do know that I was every bit as snoopy as you and Matt when I was a kid. I know Jack and Gus will be just as snoopy too. I *will* tell them. I really want my joy at being reunited with you out there. I feel like I've been having to hold back in every conversation I have had lately. I hate not being able to talk about you with everybody.

I assume that you have mailed your letter to your parents about me. Have you had a reaction yet? I bet your dad will be fine with it and your mom will have to think on it for a while, but everything will work out well. I'd like to hear what happens.

I have been reading *Being Adopted* and have been learning a lot. I read that they estimate that only 15 percent of adoptees search. That somehow seems like a low figure to me. They do say that open-record advocate groups claim the number is more like 40 percent, but the book bases its figures on a careful study made in Scotland. In any case, I feel pretty fortunate that you searched and found me.

Yesterday, I placed a call to a woman at the Adoption Connection to see if I could hook up with a meeting somewhere, but they, like CUB, do not hold meetings during the summer months. We had a very nice conversation and she told me she was a birthmother who had found her son seventeen years ago. She was very excited for me and thinks that you and I seeing each other will be wonderful. She also said not to worry about telling Jack and Gus because she thinks they will be excited about meeting you too. She says that it's the keeping of secrets that's harmful, and she gave me courage about getting over the shame hurdle. Hopefully, John and I can sit down with the kids this weekend in Maine and tell them.

As for the rest of the relatives, friends, whatever—if they decide the information must somehow change my relationship with them, then so be it. Who needs narrow-minded friends and relatives anyway?

Can you tell me about what it was like for you and your family with Theresa? I asked in a previous letter but you kind of glossed over it. Did you feel you had to be the "good girl" to make up for her behavior? I assume your parents adopted Theresa and Matt sometime after their infancies. Is that right? Do you think I ask too many questions?

Gus brought home all his school-published books yesterday. They are terrific. One is called, "My Brother is Great," which is a tribute to Jack. Another is titled "Frog Things" and is filled with wonderful drawings and frog observations.

I'm going to end and get this off to you.

Lots of love,

Ellen

DATE: June 17, 1996

SUBJECT: Prereunion phone call?

Dear Ellen,

What do you think about talking on the phone before we meet in person? I'm thinking it might make for an easier transition, though it does make me nervous. If you do want to talk on the phone, I'd like to do it while I'm still in San Francisco. I'd feel a lot more comfortable talking here than in my parents' house. Maybe we could schedule a time to talk for the Sunday before I leave? June 23? Let me know what you think.

I'll be checking my e-mail and waiting eagerly for the postman.

Love,

Katie

DATE: June 17, 1996

SUBJECT: Telephone? EEEEEEK!

Dear Katie,

I knew we'd have to consider talking on the phone eventually. Let's make a pact, though, to keep letter writing as our main form of communication—so much more gets said and conveyed to each other, don't you think? I never want to give up our letters, and I hope we never run out of things to write. I sure do love this e-mail though—it's such immediate gratification.

Yes, I'd like to talk to you on the phone and hear your voice. It's OK if we babble at each other incoherently; we are brand new at this, after all. I fear long silent pauses as much as (I imagine) you do, but sooner or later, we will get comfortable.

June 23 for a tel-con is fine. We can arrange the specifics for your visit then. I haven't gotten too far in terms of plans for that. All I know is we are planning on giving each other a great big hug. No need to call me from your parents' house. I hope they take our meeting well and that it will not cause you difficulty with them.

Do you get your e-mail at home or at the office or both? Do I have to censor what I write here?

Love,
Ellen

❧

DATE: June 17, 1996
SUBJECT: Telephone anxieties

Dear Ellen,

The telephone call looms over us, a specter of nervousness and potential awkwardness. I'm glad we'll be talking on the phone, but it's a whole new world, and a much less comfortable one than writing. It's going to be intense if I can hear myself in your voice or speech patterns.

I like people to think I'm unflappable, that there's nothing I can't handle with ease. That's going to be a hard act to carry off in-person and on the phone, when there's no time for me to get a handle on the emotions. For me, this is one of the scariest things about moving away from the letter format and into real-time dialogue.

Like you, I can't stand awkward silences. And I hate crying in front of people. And I hate it when people can tell I'm nervous. So, at least it's on the table that I'll be nervous, and I don't have to put on the unflappable front (which I wouldn't be able to pull off anyway).

And, yes, I want to keep up the letter writing. Phone conversations are totally different than letters, and they don't really facilitate the richness and detail that letters do. It's also harder for me to be as open in person or on the phone. But they have their advantages too, like offering simultaneous conversation, laughter, and the ability to hear each other's reactions.

With all that said, what time do you want to talk on June 23? Since you've got the kids to work around, I'll leave it up to you. Keep in mind that I'm three hours behind you out here in California.

I got your phone number from Catholic Charities in January, but I've never given you mine. I'm including it below, along with my work number. If you want to get used to my voice before we actually talk, it's me on the outgoing message that plays at my work number, and I'm not there Fridays, Saturdays or Sundays. It's also my voice on our outgoing message at home.

You asked about where I get my e-mail. It's only on my home computer, so you don't need to censor yourself.

With love,
Katie

DATE: June 18, 1996
SUBJECT: Continuation

Dear Katie,

In response to your last message, perhaps our voices will be similar in tone, but I bet we will probably have different accents. A midwestern influence (via my mother's Indiana roots) tends to dominate the way I talk. I do not say, "I pahked the cah in Hahvad Yahd." I always pronounce my Rs and do not sound so Boston-like.

Thanks for your phone numbers. I just may call to hear what you sound like on your machines. Or I may call when you least expect it, just so we can get it out of the way. It seems a little silly for us to feel so nervous, doesn't it? Because it does not matter one whit if we babble, talk at the same time or generate some awkward silences—a phone conversation will not change my opinion of you. I will like you no matter what—that's a given. I just want you to be completely you and I will be me, warts and all.

I've been wondering what prompted you to move way out to San Francisco. You wrote that you did not have a job when you moved out there. Was it because you perceived it as a haven and knew you'd be accepted? Or was it because you wanted to more fully investigate gayness? Or because you figured there would be more opportunity for dating? (Just a joke!) Have you ever thought of settling here, in Northampton? (I think that's the town with a large lesbian community, isn't it?)

Looking forward to hearing your voice.

Love,

Ellen

DATE: June 18, 1996
SUBJECT: More continuation

Dear Ellen,

Maybe a surprise call would be a good idea. The nervousness
does seem silly, given all the letters that have gone back and forth.
Still, it's there. But it's not because I think anything's going to change,
or that you'll suddenly realize I'm a raving lunatic with an intoler-
ably screeching, nasal voice. I do know that it will be fine, even if
awkward at first.

To answer your questions, I moved to San Francisco for the
queers. I didn't have a job out here, didn't have a place to live, didn't
know a soul, but I knew I'd be happy. There'd be less bigotry, less
compulsion to conceal my identity and more fun. And, yes, I knew
that the dating options would be much choicer here than they were
in Bowling Green, Ohio. I had also researched the opportunities for
freelance journalism and found that the Bay Area had several alter-
native weeklies that I could write for (though, in the end, I didn't
really pursue that too fervently). But that was a distant second as far
as motivators go.

I haven't thought about living in Northampton. From what
I've heard, the dyke community there is a lot less open and free than
San Francisco (pretty much any place in this country is less open
and free). And it certainly is smaller than San Francisco and doesn't
have the Northern California coastline surrounding it.

A big part of me would like to live in San Francisco for the rest
of my life. But who knows? I do know that I'll be here for a good
long while, though.

Have I told you that one of my cousins gave up a kid for adoption when she was an unmarried teenager? She's a doctor now, with

two young daughters, and I've never spoken to her about her experience. I only heard about it from a reference dropped in a conversation a few years back. Now I wonder how she feels about the whole thing and if she's thought about searching. Her kid might be as old as eighteen or nineteen now. Maybe I'll try to talk to her at our family reunion in July.

Say hello to John for me—or, if you're reading this, John, hello to you.

I'll see you soon. And don't you dare diet.

With love,

Katie

DATE: June 18, 1996
SUBJECT: I heard your voice!

Dear Ellen,

Just picked up your message. Your voice sounds very different from mine. More raspy-throaty. I wish I'd gotten that trait rather than the bunions. Oh well.

I will be working this Friday to catch up on all the work I have to do before I leave, but we can talk while I'm there. I have my own office and nobody bothers me. Let's set a time to be sure that I'm there—I've been working in somebody else's office because his computer is better than the dinosaur I have at work. Anytime between ten and four pacific time is great.

Write back. Or call, if you feel like surprising me.

Love,

Katie

DATE: June 18, 1996
SUBJECT: We survived

Dear Ellen,

So that wasn't too bad, huh?

I did feel shy, and I could barely hear myself speaking. It was like there was background noise going on in my brain—the nervousness, I guess. But for our first phone conversation, I think we did admirably. Nervous, yes, but still coherent. Most of our sentences were intelligible, and there was no major trauma.

I'll sign off now.

Love,

Katie

DATE: June 18, 1996
SUBJECT: Queeries

Dear Katie,

Your sentences during our phone conversation were definitely more intelligent than mine. Unbeknownst to me, some of John's blatheriness has apparently crept into my personality during these past eleven years. I was so nervous I felt like I had to keep chattering away, therefore my end of our conversation verged on inane. I simply could not think! But that's OK because I am a writer, not a thinker. I loved hearing your voice. It's lovely.

"I moved to San Francisco for the queers" is a great opening line for a story. I really admire your sense of adventure and chutzpah—

to move to a city where you knew no one, had no job and no place to live. Where did you stay when you first got there and how did you find the job at JFKU? John has been to San Francisco a few times on business and to visit a friend who lives in San Jose, but I have never been out to California. It looks like a beautiful place, and it seems like such an exciting place to live from what you tell me. I'm glad you don't live in a place where you'd have to be repressed or inhibited.

I'd like to ask a couple more questions about queerness, if you don't mind. You refer to yourself sometimes as a "dyke." I have seen the term femme used in the personals section of the *Boston Globe*. Is it only preferences in attire that distinguishes the two? Probably not, I think, but I don't know why one would prefer one name rather than the other. Is a dyke always butch? Does "butch" mean the way a person dresses and "dyke" refer to the role played in one's relationship? It used to be that the word "queer" had a very negative meaning, but now it seems to be an encompassing term that runs the sexual gamut and includes everyone who is not hetero. Is that true?

Lots of love,

Ellen

DATE: June 19, 1996
SUBJECT: Queer studies 201

Dear Ellen,

So you've got a fundamental understanding of queer issues and now it's time for the more complex issues, like the butch-femme debates and the reclaiming of derogatory language.

First, your definition of queer is correct. It was a disparaging term for a long time, but in the late eighties and early nineties radical queers reclaimed it, under the theory that it stops being a term of derision if we joyfully call ourselves by that name. After all, it's merely another word for our sexual identity, so why should we run away from it? The same logic goes for formerly derogatory words like "fag," "dyke," "lesbo," "homo," etc. Cara and I have matching T-shirts that say, simply, "HOMO" on the front. She also has a "FRUIT" shirt.

I am one of the many inclusive-minded queers who prefer the word "queer" because, as you noted, it does span the spectrum of all of us nonheteros. I also like the word because it still has a bit of a rebel connotation. Another definition of queer, after all, is "not normal."

As far as the word "dyke" goes, your interpretation is a bit off. It isn't usually used as a synonym for butch (although I have occasionally heard it used that way). A more common definition is that dyke means "lesbian." But that is changing, especially among younger queer women. More and more lesbian and bisexual women are using the word dyke as an umbrella term to include all lesbos and bis, especially those who are out, proud and nonapologetic about their sexuality. It has a snarling, take-no-bullshit quality to it that I love.

That still leaves us with "butch" and "femme." You have no idea what a can of worms that one is. I have sat through more dinner-party debates on the subject than I could count. Some people think it's an inherent and unchangeable identity. You are born either butch or femme, and you stay that way until you die. Some say it's about the sexual role you take: whether you are a "doer" or a "done-to" (which would mean that there are very few bona fide butches and femmes out there, since on any given night, most people are both "doer" and "done-to").

I'll give you my take, which would be hotly contested at any dyke potluck you might attend. I think it is less about sexual role than it is about style—not just style of dress, but style of *being*. How you walk, how you sit, how you laugh and talk, what you wear, and sometimes how you act in bed. To me, butch-femme styles are about the use of gender symbols. Butch style uses the symbolism that in the heterosexual world would be called masculine—like a strutting walk, calm confidence, men's clothing. Femme style uses symbols that would be called feminine—like makeup, longer hair, skirts. Your brother John would probably refer to this as one person "trying to be the man." But this is obviously not what I'm saying.

Butch-femme doesn't really break down so easily as masculine-feminine. There are all sorts of permutations of these categories: There are vixen femmes, girly girls and clean-scrubbed natural femmes (which is what I would call Cara, though she doesn't call herself a femme). I know a glamour-femme (long, platinum hair, ice-blue eyes, low-cut dresses when she steps out for the night) who is also an auto mechanic. There are stone butches, soft butches, biker butches, faggot butches (who like gay male style). Back when I still carried a pocketbook, one of my friends referred to me as "butch with a purse."

Sometimes the use of gender symbols is conscious. I dated a woman once who, I swear, practiced her suave butch smirk in the mirror. She smoked Marlboros, scrunched up her face like James Dean and walked weight-lifter style, with her arms held out from her sides. Our relationship lasted about a week. Sometimes the use of the symbols is unconscious, like the women who, even when they were six years old, looked like truck drivers if their mothers forced them into a dress. Most of the time it's a combination of the two: People naturally lean one way or the other and then cultivate their style accordingly.

Some people classify themselves as "switches," going from one role to another depending on their mood. Right now I'd say I'm more butch than anything, but just two years ago I wore makeup almost every day and some of my favorite outfits were colorful dresses I'd bought at thrift shops. So, historically speaking, I guess I'm a switch.

There's also androgynous, a category that doesn't really go too far in either gender direction. And then there are people who aren't any of the above, people who would never even imagine playing with gender symbols and people who think this whole discussion is remarkably tedious. There are also women who think butch-femme is inherently oppressive because it is "mimicking heterosexuality." I think it's just a fun and interesting (if overanalyzed) part of queer history and culture.

Does that answer your question? I think it's a riot that you are reading the women-seeking-women personal ads. What other extracurricular research are you doing on queer stuff?

By the way, you were not all "blathery" on the phone (though Cara and I both got a big kick out of the fact that you were so quick to blame John for it).

Love,

Katie

DATE: June 19, 1996
SUBJECT: Tutti Fruitti

Dear Katie,

Who else could I blame for my faults and inadequacies but John? I certainly did not have *any* before I met him. John and I had lunch together yesterday and I said to him, *"Will* you stop fidgeting! You're driving me nuts." He said, "Lots of women would *love* to have a guy who fidgets."

Thank you for the "Katie Hern Speed Course in Homo Dynamics." I had no idea that the word "dyke" was used to cover both lesbians and bis. At one time, I had thought it represented the butchest of the butch, but since getting to know you, I could see that I was wrong. It is a rather harsh-sounding word, "snarling" as you say. I much prefer the term "fruit." It sounds so succulent and delicious. Reminds me of *Rubyfruit Jungle* by Rita Mae Brown, which I read way back in the seventies, I think. I remember really liking the book because she made lesbianism sound so wonderfully erotic, exotic and sensual. I should look into it again to see how I'd feel about it now because I have completely forgotten the plot.

I like the word "queer" too. It sounds kind of eighteenth-century British, sort of foppish yet aristocratic. It's a good word. In fact, I like some of these old-new word choices a lot better than "gay," which doesn't have the mellifluous and euphonious qualities of "fruit" or "queer." Anyway, it's nice to have a whole department store of labels with which to outfit oneself proudly. A name for every mood. I agree with you that it all seems fun and interesting. And I would add comfortable, proud and evolved.

I sort of knew that the terms "butch" and "femme" did not designate sexual roles. Why would any woman want to limit herself during intimacy with a particular style? But I am still unclear on some terms: "faggot butches who like gay male style"—what might that be, if I may be so bold as to ask? And "stone butches" (they only do it on concrete, perhaps?). And "vixen femmes" and "girly girls"—are they called those names because they like to flirt and wear dresses?

About personal ads: the *Boston Globe* runs two pages of personal ads every Sunday in the Arts section, which I always read for
book reviews. Occasionally I will browse to see if I might be missing
something. There are many hetero ads, fewer "male-seeking-male"
ads, and fewer still "women-seeking-women" ads. They all sound
pretty much the same, though, hetero or queer. The men always
describe themselves as "tall, handsome and intelligent" looking for
"slim, very fit, attractive" partners—no ugly fatties need apply. The
women say they are "sensitive, romantic" and seek "soulmate for long-
term relationship." Some are upbeat, others plaintive, lots just pathetic.

I published a personal ad for myself once on a dare from a
friend. He had placed an ad himself and was happily culling the
wheat from the chaff of his seven responses. He was dating one very
intelligent music professor and his experience seemed pleasant and
fun. So he and I made up a very amusing ad for me—I wish I still
had a copy of it. We put it in the *Want Advertiser* to percolate, and
in a matter of a few days, I had literally hundreds of responses.
I was just overwhelmed! They ranged from the truly bizarre and
psychotic to the sickeningly needy. I got a photo of a headless
fellow standing stark naked in front of his bookcase so I could "see his
taste in reading." I got many letters proclaiming fervid love and
devotion—they fell madly in love with me just from my ad. Imagine!

I eventually made first dates with two of the more apparently
"normal" fellows: One was pleasant and good-looking but not for
me, and the other found out my address and phone number and
called me for two years afterward. He also was able to breach the
security system in my apartment building to slip a sick mash note
under my door, which scared the shit out of me. I finally told him
that the police were monitoring my calls and if he bothered me
any more, I would have him arrested. So I do not recommend the

personal ads as a way to meet people, but I do find them interesting on a sociological level.

You asked about my extracurricular studies: Last night I watched a program called *In the Life* on PBS. Are you familiar with it? It's for queers, by queers, and I found it really interesting. It ran excerpts from short films, like *Shaving the Castro* about a barbershop in SF, and one called *Both My Mothers Are Named Judy,* narrated by a little girl with dyke moms. It must be homo week on PBS because two nights before I had watched a program about gay WWII vets, male and female, who had suffered horribly at the hands of the military both during and after the war. One old guy talked about being harassed and drummed out of the army with a dishonorable discharge, which he was still lobbying to get rescinded. These people had their lives ruined by military and congressional idiots and by the prejudice in society that was so rampant in those days. It's scary that this kind of virulent prejudice has now been taken up by conservative right-wingers who feel so threatened by homosexuality. I hate that prejudice even exists and that you might suffer at its grimy, infected hands too.

Write soon.

Love,

Ellen

DATE: June 20, 1996
SUBJECT: Free at last

Dear Katie,

I feel liberated! I told John's mother about you and she is very, very happy that you and I are in touch. She's very excited for me. What a load off.

John and I will tell Jack and Gus tomorrow on the ride up to Maine. (We'd tell them tonight but John will be at karate until after they go to bed.)

All this week I have been working on my wimpy self to get over the shame and let it go. I feel so much better having taken the first step to opening my life up to scrutiny. And I am so very excited that I will be able to be honest and open with Jack and Gus and have them share my joy at seeing you again.

Anyway, I just wanted to share it with you.

Send me some mail.

Love,

Ellen

⌒⧑⌒

DATE: June 20, 1996
SUBJECT: Re: Free at last

Dear Ellen,

I'm thrilled that you told your mother-in-law and that you're planning to tell Jack and Gus. That's really great news. I think it will be a lot easier for me to meet them if they know who I am, and it will certainly be easier for you not to have to keep hiding it from them. (Or at least that's my guess, having been in the closet myself and finding it hard to conceal things that were important to me.)

I think my parents got their letter today because there was a message on my voicemail from my mother asking me to call home. The reassuring thing is that her voice was very cheerful. She couldn't conceal an emotion if she tried, and if she was unhappy, I would be able to tell. Her tone of voice was really upbeat, a big relief for me. Anyway, by the time I got home tonight it was too late to call them, but I'll talk to them tomorrow and I'll let you know how it goes.

So, back to your questions about my "Speed Course in Homo Dynamics." A lot of the terms I threw into my e-mail were invented on the spot—vixen femmes, girly girls. They're not really anything in particular. That's the beauty of it—you can make up identities as you go along, sort of mixing and matching different elements you like. Vixen femmes might wear spike heels and tight dresses, or they might wear combat boots and T-shirts but be really seductive and bitchy, or they might just be bitchy. Or just seductive. The identities are really fluid, but you've got the basic idea. A girly girl is bound to be more girly-girlish, wearing short dresses, batting her lashes and maybe giggling. But then on certain nights she might feel more like a vixen femme.

I did not make up the term stone butch—these are very, very butch women (they pass for men in the streets) who don't like to be touched sexually. They do the touching, and sometimes they refuse even to take their clothes off. I've never been with a stone butch, and I don't know how many there are out there.

Faggot butches. That's a harder one to explain, but their butchness is more like a gay male than a hetero guy. To take it to an extreme, they'd prefer interior decorating and a gossip session with the girls to watching a ball game in their underwear.

To really understand all this, you'd need a guided tour of the Castro district here in San Francisco. I'd be happy to give it, if you'd like to visit sometime. And Cara and I just bought a guest futon, so there's a place for you to sleep. But maybe we need to get past our first meeting before we start planning that.

I'll sign off now. Have a great weekend in Maine.

Love,

Katie

DATE: June 21, 1996
SUBJECT: Happy Friday

Dear Katie,

I am not the least bit apprehensive anymore about telling Jack and Gus—or the rest of the world, for that matter. I'm really looking forward to the ride up to Maine, and I'm excited that I will finally be able to put pictures of you all over the house if I want.

We will be coming back from Maine earlier than usual on Sunday because Jack is going to a friend's birthday party at 11:30 a.m. So I will write to you then and let you know what they had to say.

I still don't get faggot butches. It seems to me like a girl acting like a guy who acts like a girl. I would love a tour of the Castro district someday to get a firsthand view. And I want to extend the welcome mat to you and Cara to stay here anytime in our recently redecorated and sumptuous guest suite (Jack's bedroom).

I'm dying to hear how it goes with your mom and dad. E-mail today.

Love,
El

DATE: June 21, 1996
SUBJECT: Out of the closet, again

Dear Ellen,

I spoke with my parents today, and it went well. As I suspected, my mom was very willing to talk about it. She said she was shocked but that she didn't feel threatened or have any negative feelings about it.

The best thing was that she had a lot of questions and was genuinely interested in hearing about you and what the experience has been like for me. "Does she draw?" was one of her first questions, since I am good at drawing. Then, "Isn't it amazing that she's studying creative writing!"

She wanted to know why I'd waited so long to tell them and seemed to understand when I told her that it was a lot to take in and that I needed to let myself get used to it before I talked with them. She also seemed to understand when I told her that although I had never consciously felt ungrounded, this experience was making me feel a lot more grounded. "I'm sure there was probably a big void for you," she said.

My dad was more closed-lipped about it. He simply said that he knew it was the right thing for me to be doing and that I'd handle it in my own time, in my own way. I tried to get him to talk about his reaction to it, but he didn't have anything else to say. He might be more willing to talk when we're together in person—he hates the phone—or it might take him some time to want to talk about it.

Anyway, I'm not worried about either of them. It's fine, even if it does take some getting used to.

I did find out some bad news during that phone conversation, though. Apparently Theresa's marriage is over, and she's pregnant with another man's baby, probably twins. I feel like I should call her to see how she is, but talking to Theresa while she's in the middle of a trauma is like trying to plant seedlings during a tornado. I know I'll leave the experience feeling like I've been picked up and hurled against the side of a garage.

Write back soon. I'm eager to hear how things went with Gus and Jack.

Love,
Katie

DATE: June 22, 1996
SUBJECT: Hello from Jack and Gus

Dear Katie,

Hey, Sis. Did you know that I like Legos and other stuff that you can build with? How does it feel to have little brothers? It feels weird to have a sister.

From Jack

Dear Katie,

Can you stay overnight at our house? I like to draw. Will you draw with me? I can't wait to meet you.

Love, Gus

Dear Katie,

Enormous, titanic sigh of relief. The kids are excited, especially Gus, who asked, "Can she come live with us?" When I told him that you have your own house now, he said, "Well, can she come for a sleepover—for two weeks?"

Both boys were confused at first and had lots of questions about adoption. They couldn't understand your having another family or how you could be their half sister. But they were very happy to hear your father is a dentist and your mom is a teacher. Jack said, "Boy, she must have great teeth." Gus said, "She never even had to go to school!"

We talked about you nearly the entire three-hour ride, and I feel that they have a firm grip on all the relationships. I am typing on John's laptop and having a *really* hard time with it because the keyboard is so small. I wish I were home so I could type a few pages of their reactions and observations.

When I first told them, Jack was sure I was only kidding. A little later, he eyed me warily and said, "Do I have any *other* brothers or sisters that I didn't know about?"

I am relieved that your parents reacted well and that my relationship with you will not be a source of discomfort between you and them.

I promise to write a lot more when I get home. This keyboard really sucks. I keep typing stray letters and making tons of mistakes, plus the kids keep trying to read over my shoulder, so I feel somewhat inhibited in what I can write.

Send me mail.

Love and big hug,

Ellen

DATE: June 22, 1996
SUBJECT: Hello to Jack

Hey, Jack—

Thanks for the note. Your mom had told me that you like to build things. I preferred Lincoln Logs to Legos when I was a kid, but Legos do have their advantages.

Right now the games I like are Pictionary and the computer game Spin Doctor. I am the absolute champion at Spin Doctor. Do you have that for your home computer?

It feels weird to me too, suddenly having two little brothers. I've known about it for five months, though, so I'm a bit more used to it than you and Gus probably are. One of the things that's weirdest for me is that you are both so young. In the family I grew up in, I was the youngest. My brother Matt is three years older than me, and my sister Theresa is four and a half years older. But now, with you and Gus, I'm the oldest. And *way* older too—I'll be twenty-seven in July.

Anyway, I'm thrilled to meet you both next week. See you then.

Love,

Katie

DATE: June 22, 1996
SUBJECT: Hello to Gus

Hey, Gus—

It was great to get an e-mail from you. I'd like to be able to sleep over at your house. I'll talk with your mom about it.

And I'd love to draw with you when we meet next week. I'm drawing pictures for you and Jack right now, as a matter of fact, and I'll mail them to you on Monday.

Your mom tells me that you've been writing stories and illustrating them. I hope I get to see some of them next week.

So, I can't wait to see you. Only a week to go.

Love,

Katie

DATE: June 22, 1996
SUBJECT: Wow

Dear Ellen,

I was really moved by the messages from Gus and Jack, especially when Jack wrote "Hey, Sis." And I'm delighted that Gus asked if I could come live with you. It's really tremendous to receive such an immediate outpouring of love.

I don't know if a sleepover is going to be possible on this trip, but it does sound like fun. Would you be comfortable with that at this point? I think I would. I guess we can see how we both feel on the Monday we meet. And I'd love to come up to Maine for a night with Cara, but our schedule is so tight for the few days that she's here that I'm not sure we'd be able to. She's coming in on Thursday, we're getting together with you and Ann on Friday, and then we're planning to see my cousins down the Cape on Saturday.

Anyway, I can't wait to hear more about the conversation you had with the kids on the way to Maine.

I'm making drawings for Gus and Jack. For Gus I've already started a dragon. Any ideas about what Jack might like?

Oh, I realized in going through some of our past e-mails that I didn't answer a couple of your questions. I've been in therapy only since the beginning of January. I should have gone in last spring, when the depression hit, but I wasn't too keen on the idea at first. It was a wonderful and much-needed coincidence that my therapy started up right after I got your name from Catholic Charities. My therapist is not a specialist in adoption issues, but since we've been working together, she's gone to a conference and done some reading. She's great and very insightful. And she makes jokes and offers her own opinions during our sessions. I wouldn't be able to stomach a dead-serious dolt sitting across from me and just nodding for an hour while I struggled to find things to say.

Looking forward to your next e-mail.

With love,

Katie

DATE: June 23, 1996
SUBJECT: To our sister

Dear Katie,

I'm drawing pictures for you too with my glitter crayons. I'll give them to you when you come, and I'll give you one of my books I wrote in school.

So what kind of pictures did you draw for me? Do you want to play games with me too? Mom will go out and buy Pictionary so we can play it.

Love,

Gus

Dear Katie,

It's Jack. No, I don't have Spin Doctors, maybe you can bring over a copy of it. I have a game called Sim City 2000; it is a city simulator. You build these huge cities and when you get enough "sims" (people) you get rewards (such as archologies at 120,000 sims). If you have it, I know cheats for it.

Well, see you on Monday!

Love,

Jack

DATE: June 23, 1996
SUBJECT: Happy Sunday morning!

Dear Katie,

We came home from Maine late yesterday afternoon, arriving here around 8:30 p.m. It had been raining buckets all day and the atmosphere was not conducive to family harmony. The rain in Maine can make us all insane. Normally placid John turns into snarling Jack Nicholson from *The Shining*. (Just a slight exaggeration.) Being in the dark, damp and deep piney woods always calls to mind axe murderers, serial killers and social deviants.

The kids were thrilled to get your e-mail. You never saw such delighted eyes and smiles! Gus has not stopped talking about you. We would all love it if you could stay overnight with us while you are here. But, like you say, we'll meet first and talk about it later.

I am so glad I told them about you. Their knowing will make your visit all the more joyous for us.

On the ride up to Maine, many of Gus's questions focused on why you grew up with another family and not with us. He wanted to know why you did not call me "Mom," like he does. I explained that you have another mother for whom you have the same feelings as he does for me. He had never heard of adoption before, so the concept was a little difficult for him to grasp. He'd say, "But are you her *real* mother?" I'd say, "I'm Katie's biological mother." He'd say, "What's biological?" "Is Katie your oldest child?" (Gus's aside to Jack: "Jack, you're not the oldest anymore.") "Am I still the youngest?"

Jack had a firmer grasp on adoption, and after his initial barrage of questions related to our various familial relationships, he tended to be more self-focused with his queries. "Did you tell Katie I like to build things?" "Does she know I like computers?" (Jack's aside to Gus: "I'm still the oldest in *our* family—I'm Daddy's oldest!")

I wish I'd had a tape recorder on the trip. They were so curious, open and direct, and always totally accepting. They are terrific kids. Just like you.

I was really touched that you are drawing pictures for them. Gus will love a dragon—nothing makes him happier than monsters, aliens and creepy-crawlies. Jack would probably like a drawing that has something to do with outer space: space ships, space creatures and planets.

Did you get my letter yet? Please don't feel you have to write back before your trip here. We are getting so much said on e-mail anyway that a letter would just be redundant.

Write back immediately, if not sooner.

Love,

Ellen

⟡

Date: June 25, 1996
Subject: Last e-mail for a while

Dear Ellen,

I'm scurrying around with one hour to go before the Super Shuttle picks me up. I still need to do laundry, finish packing and go to the bank.

I packed up a bunch of photos to show you, Gus and Jack's drawings, and your photo to show my mom (and maybe my dad, if he'd like to see it). I had mentioned to Cara's father a while back that I was looking for a frame for your picture, and last night her family gave me a beautiful frame with a note that said "Have a great reunion."

OK, I've got to run. Call my parents' number if you need to reach me. Won't be long now before we see each other. Send my love to Gus and Jack.

Love,
Katie

DATE: June 25, 1996
SUBJECT: Par avion

Dear Katie,

Just wanted to wish you a safe and wonderful trip. I'm wondering if you will have access to e-mail in Brockton. If not, I'll see you July 1! We are all so excited.

Love,
Ellen

DATE: June 25, 1996
SUBJECT: NOW it's the last e-mail

Dear Ellen,

I picked up your last e-mail as I sent mine off to you. Unfortunately, I won't have e-mail access in Brockton. We'll have to go cold turkey for a while.

Love,
Katie

Ellen, approximately age 7.

Ellen, age 21, soon after Katie's birth.

Ellen, age 45, in the first photo she sent to Katie.

Katie, approximately age 5.

Katie as a high school senior.

Katie, age 25, in the first photo she sent to Ellen.

July 1996

DATE: July 9, 1996
SUBJECT: Welcome home!

Dear Katie,

It feels so good to be home in your own space, doesn't it? The finest accommodations elsewhere cannot compare to being surrounded with your own things. When we go away to Maine for longer than a few days, I really climb the walls. Our times there usually come to an end when I say, "Get me out of this hell hole!"

Maine was particularly hellish this past weekend. I drove up soon after you and Cara left here and the ride was pretty pleasant. I was cruising along with the radio on full blast, singing at the top of my lungs (which the kids never let me do when they are with me because my voice is so bad). Then I hit Naples, a lakeside resort, where it was a bumper-to-bumper crawl for five miles—upwards of one hundred thousand people had gathered for a fireworks display. Cars were parked on both sides of the road, making for a narrow passageway barely wide enough for through traffic. And people were swarming like ants, coming at my car from every direction. Normally a two-and-a-half-hour ride, this trip took three hours and fifteen minutes.

Saturday was unseasonably chilly, overcast, rainy and gloomy, with only occasional flickers of sunshine. Lousy weather never deters the kids from enjoying the outdoors, but I prefer the warming rays of the sun.

On Sunday, which was a gorgeous day (always the case on the day we go home), we got up to have breakfast and opened the cabinet—the cereal boxes were accompanied by a few big black ants. John noted that the ants seemed to be coming from the vent above the stove leading to the attic. He hied himself up to the attic armed with a can of bug spray in each hand to seek out and destroy the enemy colony. A few seconds later, we witnessed the colony's retreat: Hundreds and hundreds of half-inch-long black ants poured forth from the vent, out from the cabinet, down the front of the stove, and dispersed themselves all over the floor, which was soon writhing with their revolting black bodies.

The kids screamed, I screamed, John's mother screamed. John yelled from the attic, "Step on them!" as he scrambled down the attic stairs with his spray cans cocked. We crunched those little suckers underfoot and John let them have it with his chemicals. Eventually we stemmed the tide of ants but were left with a rather grizzly scene—a shiny wet and slippery carpet of black antennae, appendages and eviscerated bug bodies.

It's normal to have to cope with a variety of in-house livestock up in Maine, like spiders, mice, mosquitoes, the occasional beetle, even a frog once last year. But I draw the line with ants. I don't want anything walking over my food or eating the floorboards out from under me (we think they were carpenter ants). Anyway, I couldn't get out of there fast enough.

I wonder what time you'll be home today. I hope your flight is good (uneventful). I can't wait to have e-mail going back and forth again.

I've said to John a hundred times that I wish you lived closer so I could see you more often. I so enjoyed the time we spent together and I miss you.

I think Cara is really, really lovely and sweet. I'm so glad I was able to meet her. I can see why you love her so much. I can also see why she loves you. You are terrific, Katie. I love your laugh and the way you tell a story. And I love your sensitivity. And your sense of humor. And your intelligence. I guess I love everything about you. You are just perfect.

Anyway, I've got to run out to dinner. Write ASAP.

Love,

Ellen

Date: July 10, 1996

Subject: Decompressing in San Francisco

Dear Ellen,

It was nice to have an e-mail waiting for me when I got back yesterday.

This reply is going to have to be a short one, I'm afraid. After two emotionally exhausting weeks in Massachusetts, I'm drained. I'm having trouble squeezing out even a few quick paragraphs. My friends have eagerly asked me to tell them all about my trip, and I've had to say, "I'll tell you about it another time."

Being back in my own home, in my own life, in my own bed, is exactly what I need. And I need a good span of alone-time to unwind and sort through everything that happened back East. It was impossible for me to do that while staying at my parents' house, and the strain of not being able to has been incredibly hard on me. It has also been hard dealing with the fears that my relationship with you has triggered for my parents. I feel stretched thin, like Silly Putty pulled until it's transparent, just before holes start opening up.

So be patient for the next few days while I burrow inside myself. I'll be in better shape to talk when I come out.

I'll send you another e-mail before too long.

With love,

Katie

DATE: July 10, 1996
SUBJECT: 'nuff said

Dear Katie,

You sound spent. Take all the time you need to replenish yourself.

Love,

Ellen

DATE: July 15, 1996
SUBJECT: Still decompressing

Dear Ellen,

I slept twelve hours last night and spent this afternoon cooking a good meal. I also took Thursday off from work, spent Friday getting a deep-tissue massage and napping, and barely left the house all weekend. I'm still not back to my old self, though. The trip really took a lot out of me.

So that's all for now. I just wanted to let you know that I'm still here and still replenishing myself. I hope you're well. Say hello to Gus, Jack and John for me.

    With love,

    Katie

DATE: July 15, 1996

SUBJECT: A thousand good wishes for your happiness

Dear Katie,

    Now I am worried about you. What happened to throw you so off balance? Is there anything I can do for you? Please write and tell me what has upset you so.

    Love,

    Ellen

DATE: July 15, 1996

SUBJECT: Not yet, be patient

Dear Ellen,

    Thanks for your concern. I'll talk about what happened on the trip before too long, but I haven't had enough time to sit with it yet.

    The short version: I've been overloaded. Flooded like a town that tapes the windows for a hurricane but still doesn't think it's going to be as bad as the weathermen predicted. Right now, I'm surveying the area from a rooftop, trying to see where the lawn chairs have swept off to. The good news is that all the valuables stayed dry in a second-story room, and with some time and a few open windows, the carpets will dry out just fine. Until then, I'm wearing rubber boots in the house.

I had a lot to deal with those two weeks in Massachusetts: the anxieties around meeting you and the kids, the panic my relationship with you has ignited in my parents, bringing a female lover home to meet the family for the first time. And I had to deal with it thousands of miles away from my home, my friends and my massage-therapist roommate.

So I don't think there's really anything you can do for me, but thanks for offering. I just need to sit calmly while the floodwaters recede. The house is pretty much above water now, but the neighbors keep floating across the front lawn in inner tubes. I'll write a more substantial letter when I can see the yellow lines in the street.

Love,
Katie

⌒⟩⟨⌒

DATE: July 16, 1996
SUBJECT: Some background

Dear Ellen,

I was just lying in bed trying to sleep and a letter to you started writing itself in my head. It started like this: Let me tell you more about Theresa.

She was on the other side of the country the whole time, but Theresa has everything to do with why my stay in Massachusetts was so difficult. Some of my earliest memories of Theresa are of the chaos that swirled around her growing up. She fought constantly with my parents, and not just little fights either. I remember one fight in particular, when I was about seven. Coming home from an errand, my mother and Theresa screamed at each other while I sat silently in the back seat, picking at the skin on my fingers. I don't remember what they were fighting about. As soon as my mother shut off the car, Theresa lunged at her across the seat, clawing and kicking and calling her a bitch. I clutched the door handle, afraid to move, screaming "Stop it! *Just stop it!*"

Theresa started smoking pot in sixth or seventh grade, and eventually got into heavier drugs and stole money from everybody in the family. We shared a room until I was about eleven, and I used to move the roll of money I was saving from one hiding place to another in the room—pinned inside the back of Snoopy's shirt, tucked in the space between my desk and the wall, balled inconspicuously into a sock in my drawer. And wrapped around the roll with three or four rubber bands was always the same note: *"Theresa!!!* I know exactly how much money is here, Theresa!!!"

When she was a teenager, Theresa ran away more times than I could count, staying with friends or in run-down apartments in the worst part of Brockton. And when she wasn't there to have screaming matches with my parents, they just had them *about* Theresa with each other. After they thought I'd gone to sleep, I would sit at the top of the stairs and monitor the fights. And I would focus, with all the energy in my body, on keeping the family together. I'd pray, I'd make bargains, I'd peel skin off the bottoms of my bare feet until they bled—"I promise to never play with matches again if it will just be OK."

And, I'm not sure how much of this was conscious, but I made a commitment to never be anything like her. I would never bring so much pain into the house, never make my parents cry, never run away or wear feather roach clips in my hair. I wouldn't even be in the drama club because that was Theresa's thing—calling attention to herself, being dramatic.

As a teenager, where Theresa had worn skin-tight velvet pants, I wore pearls and red plaid kilts. Where Theresa got suspended from high school for drug use, I got straight As and delivered sermons to my friends about the dangers of drugs. I didn't even take a puff off a joint until my junior year of college. Where Theresa got kicked out of college for drugs, I had a scholarship and earned my room and board as a resident advisor, organizing finger-painting parties in the dorm during exams.

The picture I'm painting is a lot more black and white than the reality. I drank in high school, drove like a maniac in the family cars and had a wicked angry streak coursing beneath those kilts and pearls.

Still, there's a lot of truth to the black and white. The way Theresa has phrased the dynamic: I am the "golden child" and she's the "step-child." The way my mother put it in a recent conversation about Theresa: "If things hadn't gone well with *you,* I would have felt like a complete failure." And the way my father phrased it last week: "There was nobody who was more wanted than Theresa, nobody who received more love and affection. Mum was a schoolteacher and wanted to have kids so badly. And then, when it was clear that things just weren't going the way we'd hoped, all the stock got placed in you."

None of this is a complaint: "Poor me. I got straight As and a scholarship to one of the top universities in the country. Waaaaah." No, I'm telling you this to help you understand why the past few weeks have been so hard for me.

I asked both of my parents last week, "Did you think we kids might seek out our birthparents?" And, in separate conversations, they had the same response: "Theresa, always. But you . . . ," then they trailed off.

Matt was absent from a lot of the discussions last week

because he's always been right in the middle, in both age and family dynamics. Theresa and I get discussed most because we are the poles. She is the manic-depressive who changed her name back to the one her birthmother gave her. And I'm the one they could always count on. Always.

Given that history, it's hard to watch my parents worry that they might lose me. Hard to watch them feel so much pain, to see them feeling so insecure and helpless. And even harder to try to shoulder all of that for them, which is what I spent a lot of energy trying to do last week.

That's about as far as I can go with this tonight. But I do have another book recommendation for you about adoption. It's called *The Primal Wound: Understanding the Adopted Child* and despite having a title that makes me cringe, it's got the best discussion I've seen of the lasting reverberations of adoption. Interestingly, it talks about two distinct reactions kids have to being adopted: the problem child who acts out constantly to test the parents, and the people-pleaser who never causes any trouble. I can't remember the author's name, but I'll ask Matt. (I lent the book to him.)

With love,
Katie

DATE: July 16, 1996
SUBJECT: Patience is a virtue and I am a fallen woman

Dear Katie,

First, let me just say I loved your letter likening your emotional overload to a flood. Excellent writing! You have such a gift.

Second, I am so sorry that you are straining under the weight of so much emotional luggage. You seem to be trying to carry the load for everyone. I guess load-bearing has been your assigned role in the family too. When Theresa made a mess, you were the cleanup girl. Since she made your parents miserable, you were determined to make them happy. It must have hurt you enormously to see them suffer. You are so sensitive and compassionate.

But you suffered too. Being responsible for everybody's happiness is an overwhelming burden to carry. It leaves you with little energy left over for yourself. And you were not able to realize your true self until you moved away from home to go to college.

Yet when you went home to visit, your parents wanted you to be the same perfect, answer-to-their-prayers daughter you had always been. I guess our parents always see us as the children we were, and as the children of their hopes and dreams for us.

Knowing you, I am certain you will always love and cherish your parents. Their fears of losing you are groundless and once they sit with their emotions for a while, I'm sure they will get a grip on their insecurities. You are still the one they can always count on—they can't help but know that. Searching me out is not a condemnation of their parenting skills.

Tell me what you felt in meeting me and my family. Express yourself and don't worry about my feelings.

The kids were talking in the back seat of the car today about what a good time they had with you. Totally unsolicited and impromptu praise for you. I hadn't even mentioned your name.

I hope your parents made Cara comfortable. But maybe it was like walking on eggshells staying in their house because you felt like you had to restrain yourself and put a lid on your affectionate feelings for Cara around them. I can see where that might have been a strain.

I will seek out *The Primal Wound.*

Don't feel you have to write back immediately. I can be patient when necessary, though I do tend to be much more into immediate gratification.

Love you,
Ellen

P.S. I got the pictures back and I will send you copies.

DATE: July 18, 1996
SUBJECT: Using the active voice

Dear Ellen,

So it's 11:04 p.m. on July 17, which means it's 2:04 a.m., July 18, on the East Coast. You were just going into labor with me exactly twenty-seven years ago.

It's a strange thing, growing up adopted. I never realized it before. Seemed completely natural to me. But then, I never had anything to compare it to.

I've always been a huge birthday freak. Growing up I had big birthday parties—miniature golf, Carvel ice-cream cakes, slumber parties with nighttime hide-and-seek in the yard. I even celebrate my half-birthday, January 18. In high school, with enough prodding, I got my parents and my boyfriend to give me cards and gifts to honor my turning whatever-and-a-half. They'd just insert "half" before the word birthday on the cards.

But somehow my birthday was never about being born. It was more like the day I became one year older. Birthdays happened in the passive voice: "I was born." I teach my students that you use the passive voice if you want to conceal the person who did the action. Like, instead of saying, "I lost the file," you say, "the file has been misplaced." Now I can use the active voice. As any English teacher will tell you, the active voice is preferable.

It's 11:16/2:16. Twenty-seven years ago at this time, you were probably in the shower. Why did you take a shower anyway? Because your water had broken? And because, like a good Catholic girl, you were freaked out by any and all bodily fluids? That's just a guess. If it were me at age twenty, that would have been the reason.

Were you sleeping when your labor started? Did you have any warning beforehand? And had you carried me the full nine months or was I premature? The year 1969 was way before yuppies, I know, but had you done any yuppie-type pregnancy things? Putting headphones around your belly and playing classical music, or reading to me from your favorite authors? I'm just wondering.

So it's almost my birthday on this coast. Last year I celebrated with a huge party. It was called "Katie Hern's Vengeful Birthday Bash," and between fifty and seventy-five people came. This was not long after all the trouble with the Radical Right, so I put up a huge piece of butcher paper in the hallway—six feet across—and encouraged my guests to write and illustrate their revenge fantasies on it.

This year I'm having a quieter birthday. Just me, Cara, Matt and Jane going out for garlicky Italian food in North Beach. Then Friday I'm picking Cara up at work and speeding us off to Clear Lake, located in wine country a couple of hours north of the city and just a few miles from the Old Faithful geyser. We're spending the weekend in a cabin right on the lake, and I am going to relax.

You asked in your last e-mail about how it felt to meet you and your family. It's a question I can't answer, and not because I'm protecting you. I just don't have access to those feelings yet. I tried to write in my journal about it a couple of times while I was in Massachusetts, but that part of myself was sealed shut. I couldn't squeeze out even a drop. It's all in there, and I'll reach it at some point, but right now the door's still swollen shut from the flood.

It's 12:03 a.m., July 18. The day—to use the active voice— that *you* gave birth to me.

Happy birthday to me. I'm sure glad you did.

Love,
Katie

DATE: July 18, 1996
SUBJECT: Happy 27th

Dear Katie,
Happy birthday to you,
Happy birthday to you,
Happy birthday, dear Katie,
Happy birthday to you.
Lots of love,
Ellen, John, Jack and Gus

DATE: July 18, 1996
SUBJECT: Thanks for the flowers

Dear Ellen, John, Jack and Gus,
I loved the flowers you sent. It was such a nice surprise. The florist called to find out when he could deliver them, and I tried to

get him to tell me who sent them.

"We don't give out that information, ma'am," he told me, like I'd asked for someone's FBI files. So on top of the flowers, I had a few good hours of suspense too.

It's a bonus I hadn't thought of when I sent off my first letter to Ellen—an expanded family means more birthday presents.

Oh, and I've finished one of the books you gave me and will start using my new journal as soon as I fill up my current one.

Thanks again, and I'll write more soon.

With love,

Katie

DATE: July 19, 1996

SUBJECT: You're welcome!

Dear Katie,

Hope your birthday was terrific and that you got everything you wanted.

I have not been able to find *The Primal Wound*, but I did pick up two other books to try and help me understand why you are blocking your visit with me. They talk about anger, depression, reality not living up to the fantasy image, etc.

So I will wait until you can talk. No more pushing.

I love you.

Ellen

DATE: July 19, 1996
SUBJECT: Did you get the "active voice" message?

Dear Ellen,

I sent a message to you at about 1:00 a.m. on my birthday called "Using the active voice." You haven't mentioned it or
responded, so I'm wondering if you even got it. If you didn't, I'll
resend today before we leave for our weekend at the lake.

The name of the author of *The Primal Wound* is Nancy Newton Verrier. She was a JFKU student, and the book grew out of her
master's thesis. It was published in 1993 by Gateway Press in Baltimore, Maryland, and Lafayette, California. It's really worth a read.
Maybe a bookstore could order it for you?

It's Friday morning and I'm not working today. I'm going to
spend some time with my journal to see if I can sort some things
out for myself. I can feel the logjam starting to break up and maybe
I'll be able to write my way through it today, or at least through part
of it.

But thank you for saying you wouldn't push on this anymore. It makes me a lot more relaxed to know that you'll be fine,
even if it takes me a while to open back up. I'm trying to get around
my crippling tendency to be an emotional broker for other
people. If I fall into that trap with you (the way I did with my
parents in Massachusetts), I'm afraid I might never get into those
sealed rooms.

So let me know if you got the "active voice" e-mail.
I love you.
Katie

DATE: July 19, 1996
SUBJECT: I'm a little inactive on the "active voice."

Dear Katie,

Yes, I did get your e-mail. Now don't get upset, but it made me feel shut out. I felt like you were going all around the mulberry bush with filler, stuffing the page, so to speak, with not much in the way of substance that I could sink my teeth into. You were only pretending to have an "active voice." Keeping in touch for the sake of keeping in touch with a bit of pedantic English-teacher instruction thrown in, but avoiding a connection, as you have been doing since you left here.

My initial reaction was "Yah, OK, but where's the beef?" Then I started to feel sorry for myself. Lucky for me, I have a great support system here in John and the kids, and I also knew enough to try and determine from where you came. Don't ever feel you must be my emotional broker. I just want complete honesty from you and I will try to give you the same, along with my love. I know it's natural for you to want to make the tough meat of emotion palatable for everyone. But it is much better to savor its full flavor, without any tenderizer. (Gee, great metaphor, Ellen.)

So I am relaxed now and reading like crazy.

To answer your in-utero questions, I took a shower because the day of your birth was the hottest day of the year. I had not even been sleeping in my room but had dragged my mattress into the common room (the only room with an air conditioner) and was sleeping cheek to jowl with all the other girls on my floor. When labor awakened me, I was sweaty, and of course I needed to shave my legs—2:00 a.m. shadow, dontcha know.

Are you insinuating that only yuppies listen to classical music? I had not yet developed an appreciation for classical music back then so, no, I did not try to pass my good taste on to you via headphones. And I read silently—I don't even have to move my lips. No darlin', I transmitted my thoughts to you via electric brainwaves, which is why you have always loved to read and write, and why you are an aficionado of excellent literature. I also wrote a ton of really bad poetry. And I spent a lot of time caressing you as you moved about inside of me.

The kids and I just got home from seeing *Kazaam,* Shaquille O'Neal's movie in which he plays a genie. I have to admit I enjoyed it, though I went to see it under some protest: I really object big time to his making such huge gobs of money as a basketball player. He just signed a $123-million contract to play in L.A. I hated the idea of adding my $12.75 to his bloated coffers. But man, he is big and good-looking. I admit I engaged in a little fantasy as I watched his 7'1" glistening body. OK, so I'm a pervert—having sexual fantasies in a kid's movie.

I hope you and Cara have a lovely weekend at Clear Lake. It sounds like just the ticket for rest and relaxation.

A warm hello to Cara. Have a hell of a good time.

Love,

Ellen

DATE: July 24, 1996
SUBJECT: Reply to inactive on active voice

Dear Ellen,

I was very upset by your last e-mail. It surprised and hurt me to see so much hostility and judgment threaded through the message, and I'm angry that you would call the things I've written to you "filler." It felt like an air strike on my most vulnerable territory.

By an allied country. And I hadn't even realized I was at war.

I would like to talk with you about all of this, but I am not ready to do that right now. I'm still overloaded, and I haven't been able to carve out a quiet enough space for myself to sort through all my feelings. Until I can do that, I can't write about them. I am *unable* to write about them.

I feel stretched between two poles—you on one side and my parents on the other, with each of you holding a set of expectations and wishes that I can't meet. The strain of this is tremendous. As much as I love all of you, I need time to unstretch myself. By myself.

I hope that we can start writing again within a few weeks and that when we do, we'll both be ready to talk seriously about the difficult things going on, as well as the joyful things. And I hope that we'll be able to respect where each other is coming from.

Until then, I won't be checking my e-mail.

With love through hard times,

Katie

DATE: July 24, 1996
SUBJECT: I am sorry

Dear Katie,

I am very, very sorry that I hurt you with my insensitivity and obtuseness. I did not write that message to intentionally offend you and I am truly sorry for doing so.

Anything else I try to write here sounds like a pile of shit.

I hope you can forgive me for not recognizing and respecting your need to process our reunion. I have come to understand that my needs are different from yours at this point in our relationship.

My pushing was a need for feedback and reassurance, while your need was to retreat into a sort of limbo to deal with being overwhelmed. I interpreted your retreat as a wall, which was extremely stupid of me, since you really have been quite clear in explaining your need for processing time to me.

Again, I'm sorry. Write when you can.

Love,

Ellen

August 1996

DATE: August 16, 1996
SUBJECT: You still out there?

Dear Ellen,

I appreciated your apology for the e-mail you had written when you were feeling shut out. It really helped to soothe the sting that e-mail had left, and I was relieved to hear you say that you know we have different needs right now.

I'm in a much better space than I was when we last wrote. I've spent a lot of time writing in my journal and doing things at home—stringing a beaded necklace, painting two bookcases, repotting plants.

My trip back to Massachusetts was so emotionally overwhelming that I shut down almost completely. Over the past couple of weeks, a lot of the feelings the trip brought up for me have been surfacing. I'd like to talk to you about them, but I think a lot of it might be difficult for you to hear. Is now a good time for you to get some intense e-mail from me?

Love,
Katie

DATE: August 17, 1996
SUBJECT: Hello

Dear Katie,

I am happy to hear from you.

Difficult or not, I want to hear what you are (have been) feeling. Let 'er rip. I will cope.

Love,
Ellen

DATE: August 18, 1996
SUBJECT: I'm edgy

Dear Ellen,

It's hard to know where to start. I've got a few pages of a draft together, but I don't really feel comfortable diving right into it. I think that after your "inactive" e-mail, I'm still a bit nervous about what's going on at your end. Before I can really talk about my feelings, I need to know that you're able to be open and receptive to them.

Can you fill me in a bit more about what's going on with you?

Edgy in San Francisco,
Katie

DATE: August 19, 1996
SUBJECT: I'm OK, you're OK

Dear Katie,

Perhaps I was too quick to apologize so profusely for my "inactive" e-mail to you. When I wrote it, I was feeling lighthearted and happy and not the least bit insecure. There really was no malice intended in that letter. I had thought I was being amusing. While it is true that I felt a bit shut out, I had not taken out any big guns to blast my way through your wall. All I was trying to say was that I needed a little feedback from you about how you felt about me. I never intended my message to say that I was declaring war, or that your writing was anything less than brilliant.

I am still very sorry that my e-mail hurt you, of course, but I want you to understand that no hostility or judgment was in my heart when I wrote it. I still love you and want you to be happy.

I am also not competing with your parents to try to get you to love me more than you love them, nor am I trying to take their place in any way. You can give me what you can. Even if it's nothing. For now.

I am still the well-adjusted, reasonably happy person you first met in our letters. It has been wonderful getting to know you and I have enjoyed our correspondence tremendously. Whatever you want this relationship with me to be, I am open and receptive to it. I don't know what can be so terrible that you feel you can't talk about it with me. Whatever you want to say, I assure you I can deal with it. If what you have to say is hard for me to swallow, I will just chew on it until it becomes digestible. Whatever. I want honesty.

I have read *Birthright* by Jean Strauss, and *Lost & Found* by Betty Jean Lifton. I understand that it is quite normal for postreunion rifts to occur. The same reunion that filled me with love and happiness caused you to shut down emotionally. We just came at the meeting from different places.

I hope this letter gives you what you need, that it makes you comfortable and eases your edginess.

Love,
Ellen

⌒∞⌒

Date: August 24, 1996
Subject: Fallout from reunion

Dear Ellen,

So many feelings have surfaced since July, I barely know where to begin.

One of the things that has become clear to me over the past few weeks is how I dealt with being adopted growing up. Until about a year ago, I denied that being adopted was in any way significant. And I constructed a very tight story around it, closely regulating the information I would allow in about the circumstances of my birth.

I used only certain language—thought of myself as "adopted," never as having been "given up for adoption"; thought of my parents as my *parents,* my real parents, my only parents, not as my "adoptive parents." If someone were foolish enough to ask if I wanted to meet my "real parents," every muscle in my face would harden and I would inform them, with a shivering calm, that I knew my real parents.

I also focused on how lucky I was. Lucky to have such a good life, such loving parents, my neighbor Joe Hymoff taking me to

Producer's Dairy every Thursday night and meticulously peeling the skin off my hotdogs. I thought about how lucky I was to have my brother Matt, even if he did used to pin me to the floor, lean over me and let big gobs of drool hang from his mouth until they dropped into my face. I thought about being taught to read while I was still in preschool. And about receiving such a good education at a private school, even if the Catholic brainwashing did take years to overcome. I thought about all the wonderful people who wouldn't have been in my life if I wasn't adopted. I focused on all that I had to be grateful for.

I did not think about my other set of parents. On the rare occasions when I did, the phrase was "biological parents": impersonal, scientific, mechanical. And I would become furious when people would use emotional words like "roots" or "original," "family" or "mother" to describe the "biological" side. I hated the significance these words gave to what I was so intent on shutting out.

I never thought about being carried inside someone's womb, never thought about being born and never thought about the tremendous bond that occurs between a mother and her child during pregnancy. I absolutely did not think about that.

As a rabid pro-lifer in high school, I advocated adoption as an easy solution to the problem of unintended pregnancies. When someone would try to reason with me, gently pointing out that it is unfair to require that a woman carry a child for nine months and then have to give it up, they'd run into a brick wall: "OK," I'd say, stiffening, "so labor is painful. But a few hours of pain is not so much to ask."

Of course, at the time I wasn't aware that I was protecting myself from anything. Until maybe four months ago, I believed my own story: "I'm adopted. Big deal. It's not like an afterschool special or anything." But that story was actually a fallout shelter I had sealed myself into. It protected me from what I couldn't acknowledge: that my mother had given me away. Even now that's a sentence I can barely bring myself to write.

To cope, I created a massive distance between myself and my birth roots, a distance so vast that when I read the report from Catholic Charities in January, I felt like I was reading an interesting document from someone else's life. Even though they were speaking directly to me—"You were born July 18"—I couldn't connect it to myself.

For a month or two after receiving your name from Catholic Charities, I referred to you as "this woman, Ellen." I talked about reuniting with you as "making contact." (Matt pointed this out to me one night in a restaurant, "God, Kate, she's not an alien.") I couldn't use the word "reunion" because that would mean we'd met before, which was just too much for me to take in.

Gradually, with all the letters we've exchanged, the distance I so carefully constructed has shrunk. It shrunk to about half its size when I read your letter about my birth, which smashed a gaping hole in the roof of the fallout shelter. I felt raw and vulnerable for weeks after that, like a molted crab between shells, with none of the protection I had relied on for so long. It wasn't pretty, but I recovered, and like the crab, I was able to grow.

Meeting you in person magnified that experience by about a hundred times. The distance shrunk so fast it practically made a sucking sound. Seeing myself in Gus, looking over photo albums as you gently pointed out my relation to the people in them—"This is your grandfather"—having Ann respond to one of my stories with the comment, "Yup, you sure are Ellen's daughter"; it broke down at least half the walls in the shelter. Once the dust cleared, I could only blink and squint past the shattered concrete, trying to make out the vague shapes of the landscape outside.

When I got back from my trip, someone at work asked me where I'd gone.

"Visiting family in Massachusetts," I said.

"Really? Whereabouts?"

"Some in Brockton and some in Chelmsford."

About a week later I was talking with someone about a group of Bay Area organizations she works with. She named a few—the city of Danville, the city of Walnut Creek, and a corporation I hadn't heard of.

"You know," she told me. "They make that computer game Sim City?"

"Oh, right," I said. "My little brother loves that game."

I've let myself acknowledge my connection to you and the rest of the family, let myself think of you as my mother and Gus and Jack as my brothers. And in the process, I've been overwhelmed with a sense of loss. Growing up, by telling myself that you didn't matter to me, I was able to keep these feelings at bay. I held them back for twenty-seven years.

But since my trip back East, sadness has seeped over me with the steadiness of a spill on a thin paper towel. A couple of weeks ago, while Cara and I drove to the grocery store for cherry tomatoes and red peppers, I broke down crying in the passenger seat. What set me off was thinking about a picture of Cara's brother Owen holding his newborn son.

Elliott, who was premature, is tiny in the photo, and Owen is looking down into his face, oblivious to the camera. The tenderness of Owen's spread fingers, the love in his face and the protective lift of his shoulder as he cradles Elliott—even writing about it, I've had to stop to cry.

Meeting you in person, I felt the connection I've felt all through our letters. You were incredibly warm and so were John, Ann, Gus and Jack. I loved that Gus was so eager to spend time with me, and one of my favorite moments was when, after Gus had spilled the surprise about the birthday cake you'd made for me, Jack clarified that it was "from a box."

At the same time, I realized how profoundly we've been disconnected my whole life, how thoroughly the family ties were severed. I was someone to mow the lawn for, a guest whose glass is refilled as soon as it's empty. Visiting you, I carefully watched what I said. During dinner, after declaring that I hate *3rd Rock from the Sun,* I was mortified to realize that I'd just trashed one of your favorite television shows.

Back in San Francisco, as my feelings started surfacing, one of the first to arise was grief that I am a stranger to the people I now consider family.

This is the scariest letter I've written so far. All along I've been so feverishly upbeat, repeating how great it is to get to know you, how happy I am, what a great life I've led. All of this is true. Having been adopted into the Hern family has given me a life I love and a whole set of people I wouldn't trade for the world.

But there's also a lot more going on, a rawness torn open by getting to know you. I'm telling you about this because it's what I'm dealing with. I can't pretend it doesn't exist, can't keep being so terminally upbeat.

I'm not sure how you're going to react to this letter, and I've spent a lot of time worrying about it. Even with all your assurances that you want honesty from me, I've gotten the impression that you're reluctant to talk about the pain that I might feel as a result of having been given up for adoption. In a previous letter I brought up my fears of losing people and said that these were related to my being adopted; in your response you said you didn't think the two were related. And in Massachusetts, when I told you that reading about adoption has given me insights into why Theresa has behaved the way she has, you quickly moved away from the subject of adoption and attributed her behavior to her genes.

I can understand why you might not want to think about the difficult repercussions of adoption for adoptees. It was a painful enough experience for you, without adding the pain it has caused me. And you've already shouldered too much shame and guilt for one human being.

But it's the reality we're working with. Being adopted has been a difficult thing for me to deal with. In addition to all the good it brought, there's also a lot of pain. And it has had far-reaching effects throughout my personality, not all of them positive.

I've said a lot in this e-mail, and I've gone back and forth over whether to send it to you. Telling you this feels like a huge risk, so I'd like to ask you not to respond to it right away. Please take at least a week to just sit with it before replying.

Until then, with love,

Katie

DATE: August 26, 1996
SUBJECT: It's not radioactive after all

Dear Katie,

I know you asked me to wait a week to reply, but I've been thinking that you might need a little reassurance until I can write a more complete reply to you.

I just want to say that I was very happy to get your letter because you opened the lines of communication again. I'm glad you took the risk to tell me how you feel. I thank you for your honesty. I sincerely do not want you to ever have to wear a mask with me, or hide what you are feeling for fear that you might hurt me. We need to feel those painful feelings in order to get through them. Nothing gets resolved by avoiding or stuffing away or carefully hiding those emotions.

I also want you to know that there is absolutely nothing you can say that will make me love you less than I do.

I am working on a more complete reply.

Love,

Ellen

⌐❧⌐

DATE: August 29, 1996
SUBJECT: RE: Fallout from reunion

Dear Katie,

I spoke with Nancy Newton Verrier on the phone today (August 27) and ordered a copy of her book, *The Primal Wound.* After much searching, I discovered that the only way to get the book was directly through her. It may take a few weeks for me to get it, but I sent off a check this afternoon. I promise to read it when it comes.

I do know that your adoption has caused you pain and that your pain is different from the pain and shame that I have felt. I also know that each adoptee experiences being adopted differently and struggles with many issues along the way in life. I worry about talking to you about these issues but not because I am afraid of the emotion. I'm afraid I will be inadequate in articulating my thoughts, or that I will say the wrong thing and cause you more pain instead of helping.

I was very moved by your letter and I am so sorry that you've had to suffer as a result of my relinquishing you for adoption. I take full blame for the consequences of giving you away and you have every right to be angry with me (although anger was not what you expressed in your letter, you have alluded to your anger in previous letters). I have been very angry at myself for being me twenty-seven years ago. You can write to me about your anger and I will answer you as best I can.

Yes, our family ties were thoroughly severed six days after your birth. I too have felt overwhelmed with loss when I have allowed myself to really connect with it. Losing you, giving you up, was horrific. We lost so much. But I have had so many more years than you to stare that loss in the face. I have learned to cope, recognizing just as you have, that avoiding the pain, or trying to toss it off, does not work. Eventually, I was able to temper my pain and loss with hope. Hope that we would reconnect some day.

I harbor the hope that our reconnection will hold tight and flourish. I know the possibility exists that our connection will fail to take root, but I hope with all my heart that, with time, we will no longer feel like strangers to each other. I don't ever want you to feel bad again that you have somehow offended me by not liking the same television programs that I do. I don't want you to worry about offending me with your opinions, preferences or dislikes. We are different people with differing tastes. Neither do I want you to have to weigh every word you write to me, nor hide your real feelings as they surface.

God, why is this letter so hard to write? All I want to say is, Katie, tell me what you are feeling and I will tell you what I feel. As long as we talk, everything will be fine. It's when we try to protect each other or hide our true selves from each other that we will fail. You can hate me or dislike my personality traits. And you can hate what I have passed on to you. Just talk to me. Feelings are not set in concrete. They change and evolve over time and we can deal with them day to day.

Tell me about your pain and the effects adoption has had on your personality. I have read so many different stories by adoptees. Lifton's book says every adoptee feels persistent guilt about adoptive parents, has a fear of abandonment, feels shy and withdrawn, feels like a loner, is afraid of rejection or conflict, is anxious to please and is submissive but filled with rage. You told me that Theresa is the classic "bad adoptee" and you were the "good adoptee." Lifton says this stems from a "state of confusion about the strength of their bond with the adoptive parents" and "a sense of a lack of connection."

One thing that I am curious about is why you and Matt and Theresa all moved clear across the country from your parents. Perhaps your moving was an effort to get away from having to play a role, a breaking away from having to meet other people's expectations, a need to discover who the real you was. This search for identity is universal in all of us, but it is magnified exponentially when one does not exercise those muscles until adulthood.

But let me get back to your letter specifically and what you wrote to me. In never allowing yourself to think about your own birth and birthparents, you thought you had convinced yourself that being adopted was perfectly desirable, even advocating adoption as an easy solution to an unwanted pregnancy. You protected yourself from that "lack of connection" by refusing to admit it existed. Do you fear now that you have taken on more than you can handle? Having one family is hard enough and now you have opened the door to a whole new set of family members to complicate your life.

Gus asked the other day if he was now related to your parents and could he get to meet them. Which got me thinking that maybe our meeting your parents would not be such a bad idea. Are they still very upset? I read somewhere about an adoptive mother whose fears and insecurities were immediately alleviated by having met the birthmother in person. Just a suggestion. I would be scared to death to meet your parents myself, but I would be willing to do so if you thought it would help.

Anyway, talk to me. I am in this with you for the long haul. I love you.

Ellen

September 1996

◦◦❧◦◦

DATE: September 1, 1996
SUBJECT: A quick note

Dear Ellen,

Thanks for your e-mails. It's a tremendous relief to be able to start talking about these things.

I'm three pages into my next e-mail to you. It's exhausting to look at this stuff, and I have to give myself breaks along the way. Depending on how busy my week is, you should have the e-mail by next weekend.

I do want to say one thing here, though. In several of your e-mails since my trip back East, you've spoken of the possibility that we won't be able to maintain a relationship long term. I guess that's the big fear in a situation like ours. But I pretty much take for granted that we will remain in each other's lives from now on. For me, what's on the table now is the *kind* of relationship we'll have. If we don't get the difficult things out in the open, I think we'll settle into a friendly but distant relationship, one that can never move beyond the superficial. On the other hand, if we are able to talk honestly about these things, even if it is incredibly painful, we'll be able to be genuinely close.

I, for one, am rooting for the latter. I can't stand the thought of being on my best behavior with you forever. Politeness wears me out.

That's all for now.
Love,
Katie

DATE: September 5, 1996
SUBJECT: Unbarricading the basement

Dear Ellen,

In the emotional fallout from our reunion, something else clicked into place for me. It has to do with the "chosen baby" story my parents told me about being adopted. The way I remember it, it went something like this: "You were adopted, and what that means is that you are special. We chose you to be our baby."

When I was very young, the story had the desired effect. It made me feel proud of being adopted rather than ashamed, and I used to strut around nursery school gloating about it: "I was adopted, so my parents *chose* me. Yours just got stuck with you." And then I'd flounce away, clearly superior, my ponytails swinging.

But there was something terrifying about the story too, which lingered close to the surface as I got older. Whenever I think about the "chosen baby" story, I always think of that song "How much is that doggy in the window?" It's like the two are synonymous in my mind—one always conjures up the other.

I'm sure you know the song:

How much is that doggy in the window?
The one with the waggly tail.
How much is that doggy in the window?
I do hope that doggy's for sale.

When I hear the song, I imagine a frisky puppy—a golden retriever or yellow lab—with huge paws and a big doggy smile, clamoring against the storefront window, flirting with all the people passing by on the sidewalk.

And I imagine long rows of incubators filled with babies wrapped in pink and blue blankets, watched over by anonymous nurses and fluorescent lighting. My parents browse the rows, my father with his big hands clasped behind his back, my mother exclaiming at each baby they pass, "Oh! Look at *this* one, David." And I'm the waggly-tailed puppy, cooing in my incubator, flirting, being just so irresistible that they simply *had* to take me home.

The image of it still makes my stomach drop. I was chosen, thank god. But the never-spoken fear the story inspired was that I might not have been. What would have happened if, as they browsed past, I'd been sleeping or scrunching up my face and shitting my diaper? And what happened to all those other babies who didn't flirt and coo as successfully as I did? Orphanages? Foster homes? Lingering under the fluorescent lighting with those anonymous nurses?

Of course, as I got older I realized that it didn't really happen like that. There was no row of incubators, and my parents had no choice in the matter. Catholic Charities assigned me to them, and they picked me up on July 25 and brought me home. But those disturbing what-ifs lodged themselves someplace deep in me, like parasites clamped to my intestines.

I developed a much more grisly set of what-ifs by the time I reached junior year of high school, the year dominated by the rabid Iowan's "morality" class. No single teacher fucked me up as much as this woman with her righteous right-wing Catholicism. In that class any nascent potential for sexuality that I might have had shriveled up like an apple blasted in a microwave for a whole afternoon.

Premarital sex was always sneered at, in her harsh Midwest accent, as "getting horny in the backseat of some car with some guy"; homosexuality was something to be pitied.

The biggest impact this teacher had was through her ceaseless preaching about abortion. I think I told you about this in one of my earlier letters, about how if you didn't spout the pro-life dogma you failed your tests. What I didn't tell you about was how the months we spent learning about abortion affected me at a personal level.

In a lot of ways, abortion was pretty far removed from my life. After all of her ranting, I certainly wasn't going to have sex until I was married, and when I did finally get married and have sex, I planned to use birth control. As a sixteen-year-old virgin, I believed that abortion was something I'd never have to confront for myself.

Despite all that, abortion felt more central and relevant than any subject I'd studied at Ursuline. One of the first things we learned was that abortion was legalized in this country in 1973, a fact I absorbed instantly. As the rabid Iowan wrote "1973, *Roe v. Wade*" on the board, all I could think about was that I had been an unwanted pregnancy. If I had been conceived just four years later, I realized, I might not have been born at all. Actually, I didn't think I "might not" have been born. I felt certain that I wouldn't have been born, certain that I would have been aborted.

When the teacher showed us graphic footage of actual abortions and made us take detailed notes about what the different forms of abortion did to the fetus—saline solution burning off its skin, a D and C slicing it from the womb, the suction method tearing it apart and sucking it out in pieces, which sometimes got jammed in the tubing and had to be knocked loose—it was all intensely personal. I didn't imagine myself being pregnant before I was ready to have a child. I imagined myself as the fetus.

Looking back on my childhood, I can see how unstable my existence felt. It seemed like I'd come perilously close to not making it. Everything felt tenuous, like there was nothing I could count on.

When people talk about how living through the Depression affected them, it sounds incredibly familiar. I'm always guarding against hard times, even in the way I purchase toiletries. I like to have at least two boxes of tampons in the house and no less than a dozen rolls of toilet paper, just in case. When supplies start dipping low, I move into a mild state of distress and act quickly to bring the stockpile back up.

When I do have something stable in my life, like my relationship with Cara, I worry that it isn't going to last. I *expect* that something horrible will happen to tear it apart, something beyond my control, like she'll die or we'll wake up one day and find that everything between us is withered and dry and there's nothing we can do to replenish it.

This sense of tenuousness is one of the lasting repercussions of adoption. You said in your last letter that you take full blame for the consequences of giving me up, but that's not what I'm looking for. I've spent a lot of time going over that, wondering if what I subconsciously want, in telling you all this, is to punish you for giving me up. But I really don't think that's what's going on. It isn't about blame.

I don't want you to assume responsibility for all this, and I'm not looking for you to solve it for me or make it better. It wouldn't be possible anyway. These things have been with me my whole life, and even if you constructed the most perfect, eloquent response, I'd still need two boxes of tampons under the sink. What I'm looking for is to get all this into the open so that I can stop playing the role of adoption poster child.

I don't have an idealized, romantic image about what it would have been like if I hadn't been adopted, that I'd be trouble free and calm as a Buddhist monk. People who grow up in their natural families have plenty of shit to deal with too, and a lot of them probably have the same shit I have. And, like I've said before, I wouldn't have wanted it to go any differently than it did. That was one of the scariest things, initially, about getting your name from Catholic Charities; it made me realize that I might have become a very different person if I hadn't been adopted into my family, something that still makes me nervous. The way I explained it to my father in July was this: "Having led the life I've led, I've grown quite attached to it."

Being at your house did show me, though, that at least one thing would have been better if I'd grown up with you. It happened during the Scrabble game we played with Gus and Jack. We were playing the big-kid version of the game, so Gus was at a disadvantage. You and Jack helped him out, but he did come up with three words without anyone's assistance. Two of them were "nude" and "sex."

After he laid out his letters, he looked around to make sure everyone was OK with what he'd come up with, but beyond that he was absolutely calm, like it was perfectly normal for him to be eight and spelling the word "nude" in front of his mother. If I were playing Scrabble with my parents tomorrow and "nude" was the only word I could create from my letter tray, I'd probably pass my turn. I'm twenty-seven.

My last two e-mails to you have been about the ugly, unspeakable aspects of myself, the things that feel like mutant hostages I've kept trapped in the cellar all my life. While I'm letting them into the open, it feels like they're going to take over the house, cackling and wiping their dirty feet on the walls. I worry that I'm never going to be calm again, that I'm never going to stop being hurled around by all the unleashed emotion. So, to answer your question more directly: Yes, it does at times feel like I've taken on more than I can handle.

Opening myself up to a relationship with you has forced me to become acquainted with those ghastly, foul-smelling people in the basement. And the thing is, in my calmer moments I can see that once I get these things onto paper, they stop looking so grotesque. I looked over my last e-mail to you yesterday and actually said to myself, "Oh, is that all?" And in those calmer moments (which I hope will become more frequent), I can see how much energy is freed up by bringing it all into the open. It's like I don't have to spend my days barricading myself against the cellar door anymore.

The material you included from Betty Jean Lifton made me smile, though it isn't the least bit funny. I warned you, not long ago, against taking Lifton too seriously. When I first started thinking about being adopted, I hated her guts. I would lie on the couch on a Saturday morning and stage sarcastic readings from her books for my roommates: "Listen to *this* one."

Soon after sending off to Catholic Charities for my records, I read the first chapter of her autobiography, and it actually inspired me to write a poem, one of only three I've written in my adult life. It was a rant poem, asserting with every bit of my defensiveness that I am not fucked up like Betty Jean Lifton, there's nothing wrong with me, and there's nothing wrong with adoption, and would she please just shut her fucking mouth. This is a paraphrase.

Now that I've dismantled some of that defensiveness, the things you included from her book sounded like they could have been written about me specifically—persistent guilt about adoptive parents, a fear of abandonment, feeling shy and withdrawn, being afraid of rejection and conflict, anxious to please. These are some of the central hostages in the cellar—pleased to meet you, charmed I'm sure.

You asked about the anger I might have toward you, but that isn't something I'm in touch with right now. If it *is* there, it's stowed away someplace even more dark and isolated than the cellar.

I know that I have been incredibly angry for a long time. In college my male friends received the brunt of it. In grad school it was my lover Martin. The tiniest of infractions from them brought swift retribution. Once, my first year at NYU, I was walking around the dorm in my pajamas, and my friend John Francis thought it would be cute to yank down my pants as I walked out of his room. His tug got them to about mid-thigh, not really exposing anything because the top of the pajamas hung past my butt and I was wearing underwear anyway. But I inflated with fury and spun around so quickly that he looked for an escape route. I was standing in the doorway, so there wasn't any escape, and before either of us knew it, I was blindly swinging my fists and pummeling him. I stopped not too long after he was curled up on his bed and calling out, "Katie! I think you broke my tooth! Katie!"

When John Francis visited me in Massachusetts in July, he and I reminisced about the way I tormented him, and I couldn't believe the picture of myself that was emerging. "Why did you hang out with me?" I asked. He just shrugged and replied, "It was funny when you did it to someone else."

I can't tell you too much more than this because my anger has always been a floating anger, not rooted to anything I can name. I don't know if it springs from being adopted or something totally different. I do know that it has subsided over the past couple of years. Before John Francis drove to see me in Massachusetts, another college friend asked him, "Is Katie still so angry?" And I'm pretty certain that when he got back to New York, he reported that

I'm not. That's what I instructed him to do anyway.

I need to wrap this up. If I go over this e-mail one more time, I'll need to enter a behavioral modification program for compulsives.

I'm touched that Gus is asking if he'll get to meet my parents, and I'm glad that you'd be willing to do it. That's more than I can handle thinking about right now, though. I think they've gotten past some of the panic that gripped them in July, and my mother did tell me recently on the phone that she would like to meet you someday. But "someday" felt like the key word of her sentence. Let's talk about this again in a little while.

So write back, and take your time. I know that I can't process this sort of material at the e-mail pace we had been maintaining before my trip, so please don't feel like you have to either.

I love you,
Katie

⁓⧉⁓

DATE: September 15, 1996
SUBJECT: Going away for a week

Dear Ellen,

I just wanted to let you know that I'm leaving Wednesday morning to visit friends in Washington, D.C., for a week. I'd love to hear from you before that if you get time to write.

Having released a few of the hostages from their basement confinement, it's been more unnerving than I would have thought to wait for a response. After four days I started checking the e-mail twice a day. At six days it moved to three or four times. This weekend I've checked for mail anytime I'm near the computer. I hate being so neurotic, but in this situation, I can't seem to avoid it.

Say hello to everyone for me. I think about Gus and Jack a lot.
Love,
Katie

DATE: September 17, 1996
SUBJECT: Sorry for the delay

Dear Katie,

I hate to think of you waiting by the computer for my reply. I also hate that it is taking me so long to answer your letter, but I really have been squeezed for time. My schedule this year sucks big time. Today I have to tutor for four hours at school, but I am hoping that since it is the beginning of the year, no students will show up. And then I will be able to spend some time replying to your last e-mail.

I'm sorry for making you wait, but I want my reply to be thoughtful and not just dashed off. Have a wonderful time in Washington.

Love and hugs,
Ellen

September 21, 1996

Dear Katie,

I can't believe this letter is taking me so long to write. I feel like a slug for not getting it off to you sooner, but I simply could not find the time. If this letter seems choppy and incoherent, it's because I've written it in snitches and snatches of little stolen snippets of time. Forgive me. I'll try to do better in the future.

Today, because no students showed up to be tutored, I was able to delve again into *The Primal Wound* and write down some of my thoughts to share with you. First, thank you so much for recommending it to me. Nancy Newton Verrier is so sympathetic, understanding and insightful. It was very helpful to me to have all the issues and causes laid out so plainly. But it was also painful learning that this "primal wound" caused by your being separated from me cannot ever really be healed good as new. There will always be scar tissue even when it heals over.

Wouldn't I love to be able to write you the most perfect, eloquent response and make all your pain go away. If only that were possible! All I can do is read your letters and try to understand. As usual, you are very eloquent in expressing yourself. You've made your feelings come alive for me, likening the "ugly, unspeakable" aspects of yourself to malodorous mutant hostages locked away in the basement. Yet now that you've let some of those feelings out and you are no longer your idea of the perfect "adoption poster child," you have not transformed into a monster, only a normal human being with normal reactions and feelings. I think you have handled your life admirably.

And let me just say this: There is no aspect of your personality that I will reject. My love for you is unconditional. I welcome whatever revelations you care to make to me. I will always love you. I realize this is much easier for me to say than for you to believe, but the passage of time will add to my credibility.

That said, I'd like to make some comments and ask some questions, if I may. Verrier explains the "false self" as a behavioral facade put on by those children who shut down as a way of adjusting to their adoptions. It was very helpful to me to understand the reasons behind this because I had thought that perhaps you had not been able to be your real self (or your fully integrated self) because of your parents' expectations. I found myself blaming them a little bit for not allowing you to be you. Now I see that your being the perfect adoption poster child was a defensive reaction to the primal wound and to fears of abandonment and rejection. And I also see that there is really no one to blame, not even myself, for the situation we find ourselves in. No one then had any idea that giving up a child for adoption would have such lasting repercussions for everyone involved. Now at least some people do.

I wonder if you have recommended this book to your parents. Since Verrier is an adoptive mother herself, she offers excellent insights and is not judgmental or blaming. She does not inspire guilt, rather a feeling that all the problems are surmountable and can foster closeness. If your parents have read it, have they shared with you how they feel?

Verrier mentions psychosomatic illnesses manifesting in those adoptees who were compliant, yet not in those who acted out. Is this true in your case? I wonder for myself if all the health problems I had in my early twenties after I gave you up were caused by our separation and my repressing my grief. More than likely. I had my appendix removed, I had the pilonidal cyst removed, I had Bell's palsy, I had migraine headaches and I had horrendously severe eczema.

Some of the things that Verrier talks about are bone-chillingly sad. Like the fact that some adoptees cannot bond with their adoptive mothers, nor feel true joy or intimacy. It must be truly awful to go through life feeling disconnected and alienated. Are these things that you have felt?

I really like Verrier's chapter on empowerment. She takes the fact that sometimes life sucks and gives us hope that it can be made better through our own attitudes and actions.

Back to your e-mail. Re: Gus and sex, I am hoping that a liberal attitude will have better results with Jack and Gus than the repressed sexuality that I grew up with, but I can't be sure. Ann was very liberal with her kids, yet her daughter Elizabeth is also an unwed mother. The big difference between Elizabeth and me, though, is that she kept her child. Ann and her husband Don gave Elizabeth unwavering emotional and financial support so that she and her baby, Justin, and the baby's father, Paul, can live decent lives. They live in a house in Natick that Don owns, Paul has a job and Elizabeth is on her way to completing college.

I am appalled that you were subjected to such graphic and horrible images of abortions in your "morality" class, and that everything about human sexuality was treated like it was filthy and degrading. Geez, silence is preferable to storm-trooper methods like that teacher's. I guess the rationale was that the uglier and more disgusting they made sexuality seem, the less likely you girls would test your sexual wings. It's hard to shake off that kind of brainwashing. God knows, it has taken me decades and mine wasn't nearly as nastily subversive as yours was. How do you feel about abortion now? Were you ever faced with an unwanted pregnancy yourself?

On a lighter note, what did you do in Washington? Did you just see friends or was there a protest about the recent ruling on same-sex marriages? I haven't seen anything on the news. The kids and I went to Washington two years ago with John on one of his business trips. While John worked, we toured the museums (Gus loved the nude sculptures in the park outside the Hirshhorn Museum and Sculpture Garden) and rode the tour trolleys all over town. But the kids' favorite memories of the trip were the hotel pool, room service and living squalidly squashed with all four of us in one room with two queen-size beds.

I'm going to end now. Write as soon as you can and I will try to be quicker with my reply. Wish you were here in person so I could give you a hug.

Love,
Ellen

DATE: September 24, 1996
SUBJECT: Hi

Dear Ellen,

I got back from Washington today and it feels good to be home. I wasn't there for anything political, just visiting a couple of friends. My good friend Tara from NYU lives there, and I stayed with her. Also, my friend and ex-lover Martin was visiting the East Coast from Scotland, so I spent a couple of days hanging out with him and his girlfriend.

The trip was a blast—salsa dancing, an Irish festival, a ghost tour in Harpers Ferry, West Virginia. At one of the Smithsonian museums, I saw an exhibit of things that have been left at the Vietnam Memorial, like mementos and letters to the dead; it was incredibly powerful, probably the most moving museum exhibit I've ever seen.

I've had a long day of traveling, so I'm going to go sit on the couch and do nothing until Cara gets home from work. I'll write back this week.

I missed you. Send my love to Gus, Jack and John.

Love,

Katie

DATE: September 26, 1996
SUBJECT: Quick note

Ellen,

Just a quick note—I have sent the photos as I said I would. Of the ones from my house, the only rooms not shown are Jo's bedroom and the study Cara and I share, which was a mess when I took these pictures. I love the photo of me and Matt in my backyard.

Of the photos of you and me together in Massachusetts, my favorite is the one on top, the two of us at the restaurant looking at the camera. I framed it.

Will you send me some recent photos of Gus and Jack? In all the activity of our first visit, I didn't take any.

I'll write a longer e-mail soon.

Until then,

Katie

❧

DATE: September 30, 1996
SUBJECT: *Buenas noches. Qué tal?*

Dear Katie,

Got your packet of photos and writing stuff in the mail this afternoon. *Muchas gracias.* I like seeing pictures of where you live. Your house looks almost the same color as mine. Is it? Does your section of the city have a particular name?

I showed the photos to Jack and Gus and John. Gus saw your living room and said, "Ooh, pretty!" He also likes your old-fashioned bathtub. Jack likes your cat. John wants to know if you are safe there (he notes the bars on the windows and door). I like your built-in cabinet in the dining room, all your books and your cozy-looking backyard with the little pink flowers twining around.

Anyway, I just wanted to drop you a little note to tell you I got your package and to thank you for the pictures.

So write soon.

Love,

El

DATE: September 30, 1996
SUBJECT: Hello

Dear Ellen,

I got your letters in the mail today too.

I'm glad to have the photos, but there are only about two that I like of myself—the one of Cara and me at your kitchen table, and the out-of-focus one of you and me at the restaurant. In the rest I look like the wreck I was that week—sleep deprived, bad hair, a little out of my head. Cara doesn't look quite herself either—she had a horrible cold while she was visiting Massachusetts.

Oh well. Next time the photos will be more flattering.

I think that my house is actually very similar in color to yours, but my circuits were so jammed during my visits to Chelmsford that I don't have a clear memory of the exact color. Sensory overload.

The name of our part of the city is the Mission district, and it's pretty safe. We do need bars on the windows, since it's very easy to slide a knife into a window lock and open it from the outside (that's how they broke into our last apartment). There's quite a bit of gang activity in the neighborhood, and I've seen some ugly scenes while living here, but for the most part those rivalries don't really affect outsiders. As a bespectacled white person in chinos and oxford shirts, I'm pretty far removed from the fray.

Oh, I wanted to tell you about a dream I had a few nights ago. I dreamed that I met my biological father and other siblings. I met the kids first, and they were all African American, some of them very light-skinned and others very dark. At one point while we were getting to know each other, our father walked by on the other side of the room, and the kids pointed him out to me. He was a tall, lanky, dark-skinned African-American man, and when I saw him, I looked around at the rest of the kids and said, "What happened to all *my* melanin?"

A big part of the dream involved coming to terms with a new identity. "I am African American," I kept repeating to myself, "I'm a person of color." It was perplexing, because at some level I remembered that Doug's background is Irish and English, but in the dream I just thought, "Well, there are Black people in Ireland and England."

The dream was very vivid and I think pretty straightforward in its meaning. As the thunderclouds have started receding around my relationship with you, I've been able to think more about Doug, and I'm increasingly aware that I know nothing about that side of my roots. I think the dream was signifying the enormity of that unknown: that I could actually be African American and not even know it. It's interesting that I never actually met or spoke with my father in the dream. In real life I don't think I can envision doing that yet.

I guess that's it for now. I need to go to sleep.

Love,

Katie

October 1996

DATE: October 1, 1996
SUBJECT: Quick note

Dear Katie,

I sent you another envelope in the mail today. Lots of photos of Jack and Gus. I will also send you their school pictures when they come out, probably in November.

Interesting dream you had about being African American. I used to always dream about animals, or plagues of bugs, or water leaks in my walls and ceilings. One really vivid dream I had right before I married John was about you, I think. I was at the bottom of a great winding staircase with beautiful crystal chandeliers hanging down from a high ceiling. I looked up and saw a headless child wearing a pretty ruffled dress and carrying a candle in her hands. What the hell it means, I have no idea, but then seldom can I interpret my dreams because most are so bizarre.

Anyway, write soon. Love that e-mail, keep it coming (but only if you can spare the time—don't feel obligated).

Love,
El

DATE: October 7, 1996
SUBJECT: Can't think of a title

Dear Ellen,

Thanks for all the photos of Gus and Jack. I love the ones in their Cub Scout uniforms, and I framed the one of them with their tongues sticking out.

I didn't have as much free time to write as I thought I would last week, because I had a lot of revision and rehearsing to do on a story I was preparing for a coffeehouse reading. It went fine, by the way. People liked the story and laughed in all the right places. I sent you a copy today. The main character is obviously based on me, and you'll be able to see that I drew upon a lot of the things we've discussed in our letters to create the story.

One of the women in the audience came up to me afterward and told me that she was adopted too. She had joined ALMA and found her birthmother after a long search, but it didn't go well. Her mother didn't want anything to do with her, and when she asked her birthmother how she could have given her up, the woman responded, "Just remember, you could have been aborted."

Jesus Christ. My experience has been as easy as an afternoon nap compared to that.

I was interested to read that you've dreamed a lot about bugs and leaks in the ceilings. These have been some of my most vivid dreams too. Once, while I was sleeping at Martin's apartment in Bowling Green, I dreamed that there was a huge gaping hole in the ceiling directly above my face, and crawling around the crumbling plaster were thousands and thousands of white maggots. Convinced it was real, I screamed and sat up in the bed. Martin tried to tell me it was a dream, but I threw his hand off me, jumped out of bed and ran into his closet, feeling desperately along the wall for a light switch (of course, there had never been a light switch in his closet). The dream was so real that even when he turned on the light and I saw that the ceiling was fine, it took several minutes to come out of my panic.

I want to hear more about that dream you described of the girl on the stairs. Did she have no head at all, or could you just not see her head? And why did you think it was about me? It's interesting that you had it right before you and John got married—what do you make of that?

Anyway, back to your letter from a while back. I'm so relieved that we've been able to talk about the hostages in the basement. The strain of being a poster child was getting to be too much to bear. It was at the point where unless we talked about these things, everything we might say to each other would feel false and hollow to me.

The phrase "adoption poster child" came to me while I was in Massachusetts. My cousin Jeanne, who's also my godmother, has adopted two kids from Romania. She and her husband Andreas adopted the first girl, Maria, directly from the mother, who was so poor and already had so many children that she just couldn't take care of her (apparently, there is no access to birth control there). Maria was three months old when they adopted her and I think she's five now. After they brought her home, Romania tightened up its rules about international adoption, so they couldn't adopt the next child this woman had. Instead, they had to go through one of the orphanages there.

Jeanne told me that even though there were hundreds of kids at the orphanage they visited, the halls were absolutely silent. The kids sat quietly by themselves, careful not to cause the slightest bit of trouble. American charities had shipped truckloads of toys there, but they were all locked up in a storage room, never even opened for the kids to play with, probably about to be shipped off to the black market or taken home by the staff.

Jeanne and Andreas adopted a three-year-old named Alexandra, whose mother had abandoned her on the steps of the orphanage. I met her for the first time down the Cape, after she'd been with them for about eight months. She was absolutely adorable. She followed Maria around, smiling and laughing and mimicking everything she did, and she was charming and friendly to everyone, no matter how many hordes of strangers came traipsing through. My father, Cara and I took her for a walk down to the beach, and she climbed onto our shoulders without a second thought and clapped her hands when we bought her an ice cream.

Everyone complimented Jeanne and Andreas about how cute and well-adjusted Alexandra seemed, and they just shook their heads. Andreas said, "she would lie in her own excrement for hours without saying anything." Jeanne explained that the officials at the orphanage used to trot Alexandra out when people visited, and she would smile and dance and delight them. "She was the orphanage poster child," Jeanne said, "It was what she did to survive."

She and Andreas have spent months trying to convince Alexandra that she doesn't have to do that anymore, that she doesn't have to be cute and charming all the time, but it's going to be a very slow process.

It is probably the most extreme example of the behavioral facade Verrier writes about. Alexandra's situation is very different from mine and far more traumatic, but seeing her and talking with Jeanne about it, I understood myself a little better. I understood that, like her, I never felt there was room to screw up. I still carry that with me, not just with my parents but also with my friends, my job, Cara, you, Matt and Jane.

As you said in your last letter, this isn't anybody's fault: It's just the way things are for me as an adopted person who has always felt her existence was tenuous and conditional. I'm glad that you're not blaming my parents for this anymore. From some of your previous e-mails and letters I had sensed that you were feeling that way, and it put me in the awkward position of feeling like I had to protect my parents (a role I'm slowly moving away from). They're not responsible for my playing the role of poster child. I don't think they even know I've done this. I didn't know it myself until very recently; it's not like I sat down and decided one day that I would put on a false self. It was just instinctive.

My parents think of me as someone who always speaks my mind and does what I want, even if other people won't like it. My father is especially proud of me for this. And they're right. I came out to them as queer even though I knew it would be hard for them; I've developed a relationship with you even though that violated the code of the closed-adoption system. I do what I want and I speak my mind, but to do it, I always have to battle the Good Girl inside who wants everyone to like me. And she fights dirty—pulling hair, scratching, name-calling. It isn't pretty.

My parents haven't read *The Primal Wound.* I bought a copy for them, but when I reread it to see if it would be something I could send them, it didn't seem quite right. I think they might be as defensive about this stuff as I was for so long. I'll probably first send them a book that gives more of an overview of the issues and doesn't talk so much about "wounding." That would probably be an easier way for them to start understanding it all.

But I'm not sure when I'll actually do that. We're operating on a mutual avoidance policy right now. I don't mention anything about adoption or reuniting with you, and they don't either. After the incredibly difficult things that came up when I was with them in Massachusetts, it's not something I'm eager to dive into again, and they seem just as happy to pretend it doesn't exist. Not a healthy strategy for the long-term, but for now it gives me the space to handle one difficult thing at a time.

You asked if I had psychosomatic illnesses growing up. I'm not sure. I've had stress-related illnesses, but how do you isolate whether they were caused by adoption or something else? I've always been adopted, so it's not like I could compare my pre-relinquished self to the adopted version.

I did throw up pretty often as a kid, and my skin has always been hypersensitive, with bad eczema flaring up now and again. In Bowling Green, where I felt like I was suffocating emotionally, I developed severe allergies and asthma. And a few months after moving to San Francisco, a time when I was working as an office temp and really stressed-out about whether I'd be able to make it here, I got that pilonidal cyst. It was so huge that as I lay there bare-assed on the table, the doctors brought in groups of medical students to view it. I was particularly delighted about that. For the past few months I've been able to feel my heart leaping around in my chest sometimes, especially when I'm stressed-out.

So I guess the point is that my body does react to my emotional states, and thinking about it now, I bet that having been given up for adoption has been a factor in my illnesses. As I wrote in my last long letter, it has given me a constant, base-level anxiety, so I guess that when you add on extra stresses like coming out of the closet in Bowling Green, Ohio, and being in an oppressive relationship for six months, it would be harder for my body to ward off illnesses as successfully.

In your case the link to our separation is more clear-cut. You can compare your state of health before the pregnancy to your health after you gave me away, and there you have it. Lots of stress-related illnesses. What is Bell's palsy, by the way?

I hate the phrase "primal wound," but that's just my own defensiveness talking. On the one hand, I do believe that our separation did a lot of damage, which was then magnified throughout my life. So I believe there *is* a wound, but I hate it too. I hate to think of myself as permanently, primally fucked up. In my more rational moments I can accept it and know that, even with the damage, I'm still pretty OK. I remind myself that my therapist called me "one of the worried well," worried about some things in my life but fundamentally well. Then something will happen that sets off my fears of loss, or rejection, or some other part of the wound, and I go into a panic that I'm always going to be damaged, that I'll never just be fine.

I need to wrap this up. I can't tell how long this letter is, but I suspect it's a whopper. I just reread some of what I've written and I can see that I'm doing what is called "intellectualizing," talking about painful things as if they're just some interesting cerebral problem to dissect. Oh well. I figure I deserve a little bit of reassuring intellectualization after all the difficult emotions I've faced recently.

I hope your tutoring work is going well.

Love,

Katie

DATE: October 10, 1996
SUBJECT: Lots of stuff

Dear Katie,

Congratulations on the successful debut of your adoption story.

I have not yet gotten it in the mail—maybe today. (Later—nope, it did not come in today's mail either.)

My Spanish teacher is a big flaming asshole who spontaneously combusts nearly every day over some minor transgression by a student in class. Yesterday he screamed at a girl when he perceived that she had been snickering at him as his back was turned. This was not true, of course—just a paranoid delusion on his part—but he accepts no explanations or excuses: only *he* is right, like he has some kind of God-granted infallibility. She asked him why he was screaming and he said, "Another word from you and I will forcibly remove you from this class!" She felt at that point it was best to leave.

Anyway, I still love the Spanish language and hope that I can really learn it despite my professor. Jack is also taking his first year of Spanish. So far, all we can do is greet one another and count together, but we get a real kick out of it. Sometimes Gus tries to join in by making up his own words, which he then asks me to translate: "Squirdufo buffadas," he says. "Mom, what does squirdufo mean?"

Dreams. Wow, I am amazed that you've had bug dreams and water-leak dreams. Are dreams genetic, being passed from one generation to the next? I've had bug dreams all my life but never maggots. Just swarms of black crawly bugs—centipedes, slimy-looking millipedes, dime-sized trilobite-type bugs, and ants, ants, ants. I recall being awakened with a jolt from bug dreams too, absolutely positive that bugs were all over my bed.

My water-leak dreams started while I was married to Jim and stopped after I married John. I used to dream the ceiling and walls of my apartment were bulging and undulating with wavelike movement, seeping trickles of water and ready to burst from the pressure of water behind them. Now that I think about it, perhaps they started after we had an actual leak in the living room ceiling, which damaged my bookcases and some of my books. In that apartment we also had a problem with the area around the sliding glass door. We were on the top floor and somehow water dripped down from the roof into the wall around and over the door. It was so damp that mushrooms sprouted out of the carpet. Imagine my shock when my persnickety housekeeping self moved the drapes one day and discovered a thriving colony of fungi!

About my dream of the girl on the stairs, my perception is that the top of the stairs was shrouded in mist. As I looked up in the dim light, I saw her legs descending and then the bottom of her dress, then her torso appeared. As I watched, her whole body came out from the mist, but she had no head. The reason I think she was you is simply because she was headless, translating into no face and not recognizable. You were always in my thoughts but everything about your life was unknown to me. I did not know where you lived, or what your life was like or even what you looked like. The dream itself was not at all terrifying to me; I inhabited the dream more like I was an observer than a participant.

About having the dream right before I married John, I had a rich and incredibly active dream life before marrying him. I think this was because of the emotional upheaval I was going through at the time. Scared shitless to get married again, even to make a commitment, to let myself fall in love (key word: *fall*). Loss of control, vulnerability to being hurt. My dreams always become more plentiful, memorable and lush when I am experiencing big emotion in my life. I had lots of vivid dreams after my mother died too.

And some of my dreams simply cannot be explained or even related to what is going on in my life. Like my dream that a family of coatimundis in gray-and-white-striped flannel pajamas was living in my apartment. Or my dream that as I was driving down Route 9 in my yellow, sunroofed Volkswagen bug, I was being followed by a large and noisy circus parade, out of which charged an elephant. Luckily, I saw him coming toward me and I sailed out through the sunroof just before he jumped through the roof into my car and drove off.

Your cousin Jeanne and her husband Andreas sound like they might be familiar with Verrier's work. Have they read a lot about adoption issues? I remember when the Romanian dictator Ceausescu was ousted, there was lots of TV coverage about the horrors in Romanian orphanages. His policy had been to forbid birth control so as to encourage a huge birth rate—more people to squeeze for money to support his decadently opulent lifestyle maybe, I don't know. It was horrifying to see the conditions under which those children had to live. It's even more awful to think that the situation for these children has improved only marginally since.

When I reread the section in *The Primal Wound* directed toward adoptive parents, Verrier did seem a little more harsh in tone. She seemed to express less sympathy and more admonition toward them. I think this is because she was coming from that point in the triangle herself and fully realized after much trial and error what needed to be done to help her own child. But she was also very encouraging about fostering closeness and an open, loving and honest relationship. I think you are right to start your parents off with an overview so they won't get drowned with guilt for not instinctively knowing what to do. How could they have known?

Re: your heart leaping around in your chest. That is genetic, I'm afraid. My mother, my aunt, my sisters, me. We all get tappity heart spasms every once in a while. To me, it feels like my heart stops and then starts up again suddenly. My spasms have nothing to do with stress (I think), because I sometimes feel my heart chugging and lurching when I'm just relaxing in bed. Barbara says she has them more often when she's lying down. My mother and my aunt eventually had to take medication for palpitations and fibrillation, but I don't think the condition was life threatening.

Bell's palsy is paralysis on one side of the face. In my case I first noticed that one eyelid was not blinking in concert with its sister, then that my tongue felt somewhat numb. I mentioned this to a co-worker who delighted in telling me all about how Bell's palsy had transformed a woman she knew into a permanent gargoyle. Then I recalled that I had once seen a Ben Casey episode on TV, where a beautiful woman was disfigured by facial paralysis and not even Ben's skillful surgery helped her. I rushed to my doctor, who referred me to a neurosurgeon. He gave me massive doses via needle of cortisone and vitamin B-something and told me to upwardly massage my face as often as possible.

But before I got better, I got a lot worse. The right side of my face fell so when I smiled it was a lopsided grimace. I drooled when I ate. I had to wear a patch on my eye because my eyelid would no longer close. I was a twenty-four-year-old grotesquerie married to a man who felt he deserved nothing less than womanly perfection. Luckily, my face improved and by three to four weeks I was back to normal. Which does not happen in all cases, particularly when the person is older. I don't know if medical science has definitively established what causes Bell's palsy but I was told at the time it could simply be caused by a nerve near the ear being adversely affected by cold temperature. Best to wear a hat from now on, perhaps.

My tutoring at The Write Place is going OK. I've had a few return customers who feel I've helped them. I don't know if I will ever feel really confident about teaching writing. A lot of the stuff about theories of teaching writing that I've been reading as part of my class is astounding to me. I never realized there was such a science to it—actual blueprints for making writing work well, even for getting students to invent.

I have been able to write a long letter today because it is my day off from classes and tutoring, and I do not have any other urgent business to attend to other than bill paying, changing beds, packing for Maine and doing laundry. It feels really great to be able to write a long letter to you without interruption.

Love,
Ellen

⌐✖◌ე

DATE: October 19, 1996
SUBJECT: Would the *Boston Globe* lie?

Dear Katie,

My horoscope for today said, "You will receive a letter from a loved one far away. It may not be a really long letter because she is very busy, but she will surely write to you today."

And guess what your horoscope said? The horoscope for Cancers stated, "Someone far away is feeling a distinct need for a few words from you. Write as soon as possible." Yup, *es verdad*. You can trust the *Boston Globe*.

Just thought you would like to know.

Love and a hug,
Ellen

⌐✖◌ე

DATE: October 19, 1996
SUBJECT: A whole bunch of things

Dear Ellen,

I'm sorry to hear that your Spanish teacher is such a big wanker. I took three years of Spanish in high school and over the past year or so I've been trying to resurrect it. The Mission district is the Latino section of the city, so I hear and see Spanish every day. Plus, Cara is fluent, so we have conversations in remedial Spanish and she gives me tips about what I'm doing wrong. My accent is good, but I have a tiny vocabulary and only know the present tense of verbs.

My friend Tara in D.C. also speaks Spanish, so during my visit she and I spoke in broken, present-tense sentences. While we were salsa dancing, I drank two beers more quickly than I should have, and it started interfering with my ability to lead. I wanted to tell Tara I was drunk, only I didn't know the word for that. What I came up with was, *"Tengo cerveza en mis sesos"*—I have beer in my brains. It might actually mean "I have beer in my beef brains," since *sesos* is a word I picked up from the burrito menus at local taquerias.

So. On to more about dreams.

Like you, I also have vivid dreams during stressful or intensely emotional times, and sometimes they're so vivid that I get up and start acting them out in my sleep. I was a bank teller during summer vacations in college, and it was incredibly stressful, always having to be vigilant or else you might give away a bunch of extra money or screw up somebody's account. Plus, it involved doing the same movements over and over all day long—counting out bills, running deposit slips through the printer, checking things on the adding machine.

So at least three times a week for the whole summer, I'd have what I called bank dreams. I'd dream that I was searching for a manila envelope for the customer service rep, or trying to balance my accounts at the end of the day; I would actually start doing the work in my sleep, like sorting through my bed sheets for slips of paper. Sometimes I'd even get out of bed and walk over to my bureau as if it were the printer. Most of the time I woke up during the dreams and then went back to nonbanking sleep, but sometimes the only evidence that I'd had bank dreams was that, when I got up in the morning, the light was on or there were scribbled numbers on a piece of scrap paper on my desk. Waking up in the morning to go to work, I often felt like I'd already put in a full shift at the bank.

My most vivid anxiety dream was during my senior year of college, when I served as a resident advisor in one of the dorms. I took my job very seriously and worried that I wouldn't handle it well, and one night early in the fall there was a crisis. The father of one of my residents died suddenly, and he lived in India, so the kid, named Rajiv, couldn't go to the funeral. I didn't know what to say or do for him and felt like a failure as an R.A. That same night I started dating one of the residents on my floor (not Rajiv, of course), and I felt anxious about the ethics of that (though clearly not so anxious that I didn't do it, huh?).

I didn't get to sleep until about 3:00 a.m., and when I did, I dreamed that I had told Rajiv that I would meet him in the lobby, but that I'd stupidly missed our meeting because I fell asleep. I leaped out of my bed and went running out of my room. I took the elevator down to the ground level and wandered around the lobby in my pajamas looking for Rajiv. The security guard asked if I needed help, and I just kept repeating, "Have you seen my resident? I was supposed to meet him. Have you seen my resident?"

At one point the desk attendant looked at me and said, "Are you an R.A.?" I woke up out of the dream, shook my head clear and wandered back to my room. Afterward all I could think was, "Thank god I don't sleep naked."

You asked if my cousin Jeanne is familiar with *The Primal Wound.* I'm not sure about that, but I know that she and her husband have done a lot of reading and talking to people about adoption, and they seem to have a very clear understanding of what is involved. Jeanne was excited to hear that I'd been in touch with you. She tried to talk to my mother about it too, but she wasn't able to get very far with that.

Jeanne is one of the seven kids of my Uncle Kelley and Auntie Kath, and she's sister to my cousin Susan, who gave up a daughter for adoption when she got pregnant as a teenager.

Anyway, Jeanne told my Auntie Kath about it, and she had a very touching reaction. It was the night of the Fourth, and we were down the Cape, gathered around the big kitchen table after the fireworks. I was standing beside Kath's chair, and while everyone else was talking and joking, Kath took hold of my wrist and said quietly, "I hear you had a big reunion this week."

I nodded and hoped my parents weren't hearing this across the table.

"I think that's wonderful. You're brave to break the bonds like that, I know that was hard to do."

I nodded again, stunned that she would know how hard it was to go against the unspoken mandate that adopted kids forget their original family, and even more stunned that she'd say this with my parents in the room. I couldn't speak because I didn't want to start crying in front of everyone.

"I hope it happens to our family someday," she said and let go of my wrist.

That conversation has really stayed with me. I had never thought of myself as a lost member of an extended family, but what Kath said drove that home. I could see so clearly that there was a missing member of the clan, Susan's first daughter, whom I may never meet. And when Kath said that, I saw how much she feels that loss too.

This is a piece of my own situation that's come to me very slowly. My sense of your extended family as being *my* extended family came in bits during my trip back to Massachusetts. One time when that awareness broke through was when you told me that I was your parents' first grandchild. A voice in my head responded, "I wasn't *really* their first grandchild. It doesn't count." But another part of me registered the hole my adoption represented in the family. Another moment when this registered was when I came in your kitchen door on our second meeting and was introduced to Ann. I think that I said, "Nice to meet you," and went to shake her hand, the way one does when meeting a stranger. She responded, "Can I give you a hug?"

Sometimes when I'm writing to you I get tremendously frustrated because there's so much to say. No matter how many eight-page letters I send off, there's still a whole lifetime of experience that we didn't share. Writing about my bank dreams, I wanted to tell you about the bank robbery I had when I was a teller, but that's a long story and there's all this other important stuff to talk about—questions you've asked that I haven't answered yet, adoption stuff I need to talk about—and there's only so much time to write. I feel like we'll never catch up. The reasonable voice inside my head says, "No, you'll never catch up. Those twenty-seven years have passed and you can't get them back. You can only move forward." But sometimes I wish that voice would just shut the fuck up.

I felt the irredeemable loss this week when I saw a little boy, maybe five years old, riding along on a skateboard with what looked like his older brother. The five-year-old was standing between his brother's legs, hanging on to the older boy's hands and leaning out from the skateboard like a windsurfer. They zoomed along the sidewalk, laughing, and I thought about how nice it would be to be able to play like that with Gus and Jack. But then I realized that both of them are already older than that kid. I missed the times when they were five years old and could windsurf on a skateboard with me. And living so far away, I'm missing the time when they're eight and ten too.

You asked in an earlier letter if I've ever faced an unwanted pregnancy, and the answer is no. When I finally overcame enough of my Catholic school brainwashing to become sexually active, I was compulsive about birth control. My boyfriend and I used spermicides and condoms and kept an eye on the calendar to avoid the times I was most likely to be ovulating. When I got on the pill, I never missed a day and always took my tablet at the same time, 6:00 p.m., to make certain that no rogue eggs would slip out and become a decision I'd have to live with for the rest of my life.

I've read about how some adopted girls get pregnant very young as an unconscious way to connect to their birthmothers, but I was the opposite. There was no way in hell that I was going to get pregnant. No way. When I thought about that possibility, a nauseating vision of shame would grip me. I imagined myself eight months pregnant and huge, walking down one of the busy streets in the neighborhood to go to the drugstore for something, with everyone watching and judging me. People passing in cars, the Ledermans who owned the drugstore, their daughter who managed the store and gave me shitty schedules when I worked there. That's David and Mary Hern's daughter. Pregnant. Not married. And everyone, including my parents, would know that I'd had sex.

You also asked about my views on abortion. I'm not sure that I could ever have one because, knowing that I was an unwanted pregnancy myself, it would probably be traumatic. I don't think it's an easy subject, abortion. At the same time, I believe that women need to be in charge of their own bodies and that the decision needs to be in individual women's hands, not in the hands of Jesse Helms or my "morality" teacher. Once I started looking at the subject from the perspective of the woman rather than the fetus, I couldn't be pro-life anymore. (Which doesn't mean I'm not breathing a sigh of relief that you didn't have one. I still feel like I was lucky to make it through.)

I had an incredibly interesting lunch with an adopted woman I met recently named Emily. On the way to the restaurant we talked about our jobs and other day-to-day small talk, but before we even got out of the car, we were talking about some of the most intense, personal aspects of our experience as adopted people. And though we'd never really spoken to each other before that day, we could talk in shorthand and finish each other's sentences because our experiences were so similar.

What was most amazing to me was that even though she hadn't been told that she was adopted until she was twenty-three, she had a lot of the same personality effects that I have—having her self-esteem be completely dependent on her external achievements, feeling a pervasive sense of tenuousness, not being able to trust people or let people get close to her, being the trouble-free child of her family (in contrast to her older brother, the trouble-filled parallel to Theresa).

Before our lunch I had wondered if maybe Verrier's theory wasn't quite right. I'd thought that it might not be the initial separation that caused the damage, but rather the knowledge that you were given away. But this woman's personality was firmly in place by the time she found out she was adopted, and she still had the same repercussions that I have.

Her birthmother had been fifteen when she got pregnant, and her parents were mortified Roman Catholics who tried to make her miscarry. They sent her horseback riding for hours, and when she started hemorrhaging, they refused to call the doctor. She somehow carried the baby, Emily, to term and gave her up for adoption.

Emily said that for the first year after learning she was adopted, she ignored the information. Just didn't deal with it. (I had her beat on that one—I'd done it for more than two decades.) Then she decided she needed to find her birthmother. She contacted various search agencies and, after years of looking, finally found her. Her birthmother had changed her name to Cinnamon; she was homeless and staying at a shelter. She'd had two more children after Emily, and she kept them both but later abandoned them when they were eleven and thirteen.

Emily said that it was incredibly painful to meet her mother, and that she spent the first year of the experience crying all the time. I told her about how all my emotions shut down when I met you, and she said the same thing had happened to her, like she wasn't really in her body but was just watching it from the outside.

Their reunion was about five years ago, I think. Meeting Emily again was very healing for Cinnamon, and now she has a job and her own place to live. They still write to each other, but I got the sense that they aren't very close. I know that she told me she met both of her birthparents, but during lunch we didn't talk at all about her father. I don't know the story on that.

It's been a long time since Emily's reunion with Cinnamon, but there's still a lot of pain there and the repercussions are still powerful. Emily is six months pregnant herself, and the pregnancy has been an intensely ambivalent experience for her. She doesn't feel connected to the baby at all, resents it sometimes and feels a lot of shame about being pregnant (even though she's married and in her thirties). She even found herself reenacting her birthmother's experience by unconsciously doing things that put the baby at risk, like martial arts exercises in which she dove onto the floor mats while five months pregnant.

When Emily started talking about her ambivalence, I said, "I wondered about that. As soon as you said you were pregnant, I thought, 'God, that must be hard.'" And I could see relief wash through her body. She said that no one around her understands that. She's surrounded by pregnancy police who monitor what she eats and keep bullying her to be the glowing mother-to-be.

But I understood it immediately—birth isn't usually the wonderful, joyful experience for adopted people that it is for other people. We're disconnected from it, as if birth is something that didn't happen to us. It's also the source of a lot of pain, since it's so closely related to being given away.

I think that this is another thing I was dealing with in July after our visits together. It was the first time in my whole life that I'd thought about having been born, and I had to confront all the pain associated with that. I was numb and shut down, but at some deep level it was affecting me. Throughout the week of my birthday I thought about what was happening at that time in 1969—twenty-seven years ago you were going into labor, you were recovering from the delivery, you were holding me while the astronauts walked on the moon, it was our last day together, I was being given to my parents while you were being driven around by yours until you could get control over yourself and stop crying.

I'll sign off now. I look forward to your next letter.

With love,

Katie

November 1996

DATE: November 4, 1996
SUBJECT: Gus and Jack's Halloween stuff

Dear Ellen,

I wanted to thank Gus and Jack for the stuff they sent. I put the pictures and story up on the refrigerator so that everyone at our Halloween party could see them. I was particularly impressed with Jack's story. Do you have any sense of how they teach writing at his school? Do they emphasize the creative process of it, or do they drill them on grammatical correctness at the expense of creativity and development? The second option is too common, I suspect.

Anyway, I'd like to thank them directly. Do Gus and Jack have their own e-mail accounts where I can write to them?

OK. I'm going to make myself some dinner. I look forward to your next letter.

With love,
Katie

DATE: November 7, 1996
SUBJECT: Greetings from Chelmsford

Dear Katie,

Jack and Gus do not yet have e-mail addresses, but John plans to give them one (or two) as soon as he repairs our computer.

Anyway, the kids really appreciated the fact that you displayed their work. And Jack says he would like to send you the revised version of his story—he works on it a few hours every week. His school does not spend any time, as far as I can detect, on grammar so, no, I don't think they are stunting his creativity with lots of rules. Maybe I am though. What happens is that Jack spends his allotted time (he usually is required to write in one-hour segments two or three times a week at home) at the computer inventing and writing his ideas and then I go over it with him.

I try to help him make the story more coherent by asking him lots of questions about it. Does this event follow that, does this make sense with what you've said before—that kind of stuff. And along the way, I tell him he needs a period or a comma to make the language flow. I don't pound it into his head the way the nuns did with me back in elementary school. His teacher sees how he writes in school (without my help), and she thinks he is a gifted writer with great imagination. Tell me what you think. Am I approaching this wrong with him?

To your letter of October 18, I love your Aunt Kath. I was very moved by the way she talked to you about our reunion. It made me think of my own mother not having been able to meet you and how your existence was such a difficult subject for us to discuss. And it also made me think how lucky you are to have such a big, loving family.

And speaking of family, I want to tell you again that you are welcome here anytime you can get away. If you change your plans for Christmas, we would love for you to come and spend a little time with us. But I know how hard it is to juggle family time. We spend Christmas Eve until 8:30 at Ann's with all of my clan, then we go to John's mother, where she has a traditional Swedish smorgasbord for fifty relatives and close friends. After they leave, we open presents and stay up until after midnight. We don't get home until 2:00 a.m. Then it's up at the crack of dawn for the kids to open their presents from Santa. It's fun but also exhausting.

I was surprised to read about your friend Emily's reaction to her pregnancy. I had no idea that being adopted could cause such ambivalence. I find it so sad that she feels disconnected from her baby and, further, that no one understands her feelings. I wonder how she will feel when her baby is born. I hope she is well supported by her husband and friends.

Feel free to write to the kids at my e-mail address or John's. They would be truly thrilled to get letters from you and to write to you themselves.

Hello to Cara.

Love you,

Ellen

❧

DATE: November 17, 1996
SUBJECT: 1:00 a.m., Monday morning

Dear Ellen,

I hope that all is going well with you and that your schedule has eased up a bit.

Mine has been consistently jam-packed this quarter. JFKU used to have two different locations in Orinda (northeast of Oakland), but one of them recently closed. We've built a bunch of new buildings, and since September three of the five schools have been located on my campus.

What this has meant is that huge numbers of people who might not have been motivated to travel to another campus to see me have now found the motivation. I'm swamped. One week I saw 120 students—just me, in four days. 120 different students. I'm keeping thorough records of the increase in usage and am planning to use them to push for a midyear budget increase to hire more staff for the Academic Support Center. Until then, though, I'll be missing a lot of lunch breaks.

Thank you for the invitation to spend Christmas with you. It still looks like I'll be spending it with Cara's family on a trip—probably Japan or Mexico—but it feels good to be asked anyway. I've been thinking that I'd really like to spend a chunk of nonpressurized time with you, John and the kids. It was just too much to try to cram all that getting-to-know-you into two days in July, and I'd love to have relaxed hanging-out time with you all. I might try to get away in the spring, in between winter and spring quarters. Or even for a long weekend during the quarter. And I think I'll skip the family juggling all together and just make it a visit to see you all. How does this sound to you?

I would especially like to get to know Gus and Jack better in person. I've started a couple of e-mails to them, but I never get very far, probably because we don't really know each other. I think of them as my little brothers, but I hardly know what to say to them. Will you fill me in a little more about how they are doing with the sudden advent of an older sister? What sorts of things have they been saying and asking? What are their feelings about it?

Also, how are you feeling about it all lately? Rolling that boulder up the hill this semester, there probably hasn't been enough time to feel much of anything. Still, I don't have much sense of how things are going for you.

Have you been to any adoption group meetings? Matt has sent money to a search agency to find his birthmother for him. I don't think it will take too long, since he already has his birthname and the number of his original birth certificate. He's also been going to therapy to deal with all the stuff that has come up about being adopted.

But his life is a bit tumultuous right now. Things had been rocky between him and Jane for the past couple of years, and last week she moved out of the apartment. He seems OK, but I worry about what's going to happen in the near future. Like if he gets his birthmother's information on December 22 and realizes that he's alone, at Christmas.

One last thing: Jack's lucky to have you helping him learn to write. Grammar should be taught in the context of producing a work, as part of the broader process of writing, and it sounds like that's exactly the way you're handling it. Has he sent me his revisions yet? I'm dying to see the new version. And for the future, you should send me anything and everything they want to send me. I'm thrilled to get stuff from them.

Another thing: I strongly recommend *Secrets and Lies,* a British film about a reunion between a birthmother and daughter. It is incredibly good. Emotionally wrenching, but hopeful too. I left the theater feeling like I'd had a catharsis.

It's almost 1:00 a.m., and I want to get this off to you before my work week starts.

I'm looking forward to your next letter. Say hello to everyone for me.

With love,
Katie

DATE: November 18, 1996
SUBJECT: Happy happy, joy joy

Noviembre diez y ocho, mil novecientos noventa y seis
Dear Katie,

    Yo estoy muy contenta hoy porque su carta. I think that's how I'm supposed to say it but maybe I left out the word "of" and I'm too lazy to look it up right *ahora.* Who cares. Anyway, I am delighted and so happy that you want to come for a visit. It will be so wonderful to sit with you awhile and talk. Letters are nice, but I crave some face-to-face interaction and contact. So, Katie, anytime you can get away is fine. (Just give me a little notice so I can clean this pigpen of a house.)

    Yes, my house *is* a pigpen these days. My school schedule has not permitted *contemplation* of the dirt, let alone cleaning it up. The other day, as I was deeply immersed in a paper, John said, "Can you put these dirty dishes in the dishwasher before you come upstairs?" I said, "What dirty dishes?" Then I politely pointed out that they were not bothering me and they could sit in the sink until morning, which prompted a rather huffy and dish-rattling response from him as he decided to put them in the dishwasher himself.

    Jack and Gus are *extatico* to know that you are coming for a visit. I told Gus after I got your letter this morning and his eyes got wide with excitement. He said, *"Yeah!!!* When is she coming?" I said probably sometime after Christmas, and he said, "Can't she come before that?" Later, I asked Jack what he thought about your coming for a visit and he said, "Boy, that would be great, I can't wait!" He says he really likes you and you are his sister, so he's very happy that you are coming. Jack hopes you are able to stay for at least a few days, and he offers you his room. Gus thinks a few days is not quite enough time—"Can't she stay for a week?"

The kids are really happy that you are their sister and in their lives. You made a huge impression on them when you were here. The fact that you played with them and interacted with them on their level was just the right thing to do to endear yourself to them. They are hoping we can all take a trip out to see you sometime too. So, if you have any worries whatsoever about them, don't. At this age they are very open, loving and accepting. You *are* their sister and they do not question that fact.

Sounds as though you are very busy too—120 students in one week! That's almost half of the number you said you see in a year! At our center we have fourteen writing tutors and we only see an average of fifty students a week.

No, I haven't been to any adoption group meetings. I tend to have a one-track mind, so it kind of slipped from my consciousness. I haven't felt any particular need for "support" lately, either. I think our relationship is evolving really well. There are times when I feel insecure, but then I get a letter from you and I feel heartened again.

I hope Matt will not be disappointed in his search. It's good that he's seeing someone to help him cope with all the stuff that's bound to come up. I'm really sorry to hear that Jane and he split. The holidays looming ahead won't make it any easier for him. Will you and he get together for Thanksgiving? Is he coming home for Christmas? I hate to think of him alone and lonely. But maybe he has a circle of friends who can boost him up. Let me know how it goes for him.

And how are your parents? Will Theresa come home for the holidays?

I'll try to see *Secrets and Lies,* or maybe rent it when it comes out. I haven't heard or read anything about it. Is it new? The movie houses around here don't show anything but blockbusters. Maybe it's in Boston somewhere.

One more thing: How can you function in the morning when you get so little sleep? I am a bear without my seven to eight hours.

Gotta run. Bedtime for the kids.

Love you,

Ellen

DATE: November 28, 1996
SUBJECT: Happy Thanksgiving

Dear Katie,

Happy Thanksgiving to you and Cara and Matt. We hope you have a lovely holiday.

Do vegetarians do turkey on Thanksgiving?

Gus has a couple of jokes for you: What do you call a turkey's shoemaker? A gobbler cobbler. Why didn't the turkey eat Thanksgiving dinner? He was already stuffed.

Lots of love,

Ellen, John, Jack and Gus

December 1996

DATE: December 5, 1996
SUBJECT: Hello

Dear Katie,

It seems like forever since I've heard from you, and I have been thinking about you a lot. *Qué tal?* Is everything OK? Are you still very busy at work?

I read something interesting the other day. Joni Mitchell—a singer very popular in the hippie era who has made more than twenty albums—as a twenty-year-old art student gave up a daughter for adoption. Since Joni is now fifty-three, that would make her daughter thirty-three. Joni is searching but has not yet found her daughter.

This semester is nearing the end for me. My last day of classes is December 11, but I have finals on the eighteenth and nineteenth. Still have one paper left to do and I am way behind on my *Español.* I have not done *any* Christmas shopping yet but will go out tonight with my sister-in-law, Diane, to try to make at least a small dent on the list for John's side of the family.

Write to me when you can.

How was your Thanksgiving?

Love,

Ellen

DATE: December 6, 1996
SUBJECT: Hi

Dear Ellen,

Things here are fine, no need to worry. I got tangled up in my life during the past couple of weeks and didn't get a chance to sit down and write.

My friend Tara from D.C. visited for a week with a friend of hers from work. They were here for Thanksgiving, and Matt, Cara, my friends and I went out to a restaurant for dinner. (The vegetarians at the table didn't eat turkey, to answer your question from before. Cara had a mushroom and Swiss crepe, and I had pumpkin ricotta ravioli and a salad. Not exactly traditional, but even when I did eat meat, turkey was just too damn dry for me.)

The day after Thanksgiving, Cara and I drove up to Lake Tahoe to celebrate our anniversary—it's two years since our first awkward date. We stayed at a gay bed and breakfast right on the lake, and it was so relaxing and perfect that we barely left the room the whole weekend.

I'm still very busy at work, but things have lightened up a little. I've started planning the request for a midyear budget increase, and I will hopefully be able to hire an assistant early next quarter, but my morale is lower than it's been in a while. I've started thinking about going back for a Ph.D. I've called the major universities in the Bay Area and asked them to send me information about their programs.

Matt's having a hard time and feeling very alone. We talked yesterday on the phone while we were both at work, and he read me a journal entry he'd written. It was about adoption, his relationship with our parents, his fears about what's going to happen with his birthmother and his feelings of rejection about being given up. It was so raw and painful, we both ended up crying. In the middle of the conversation I had to stretch out the phone cord so that I could close the blinds and lock the door to my office.

The week Jane moved out, he became involved with a friend of his named Mindy and he says he loves her and is really happy about the way things are going between them. My main desire is to support him, but quietly I wonder if he's plunged into this new relationship to avoid feeling the pain of his breakup with Jane. And more important, to avoid being alone. He's told me that one of the lasting repercussions of adoption for him has been a pervasive loneliness; he has a hard time being alone even for an evening, and in the past he's always moved directly from one relationship into another.

I spoke with my sister Theresa on Thanksgiving, and even though things are pretty messed up in her world, she sounded calm. The baby is due soon after Christmas—it isn't twins after all. She's still in contact with her husband, but she's living with Miguel, the baby's father. Matt is planning on going down to L.A. for a visit after she has the baby. I might try to do that too.

Neither one of them is planning to go to Massachusetts for Christmas. My parents will spend the day with Aunt Kath and some of the cousins. Matt is going to stick around here, and Theresa will be in L.A. getting ready to have her baby.

She and my parents don't get along, so even if she weren't pregnant, she wouldn't go home for the holidays. Last Christmas, when my parents visited San Francisco, it was the first time in four years that they'd been together, and it was a nightmare. The night Theresa arrived from Los Angeles, we all went out for dinner—Theresa wearing a miniskirt, high heels and an animal-print blouse, my parents in their Talbots and Brooks Brothers outfits. Theresa/Courette was more manic than I'd seen her in years, and she didn't stop speaking the whole evening. Everyone at the table winced each time she referred to herself as Courette, and she was so high strung she screamed at her son Georgie every few minutes. My parents were thrilled to spend time with their grandson and pained to spend time with their daughter. I tried to mediate and hold things together and then, when it was over, I went to Cara's apartment and stood under a blistering shower before crawling into bed and bursting into tears. I felt like a suitcase packed way too full, my compressed insides about to split me apart.

Matt doesn't have finalized plans for this Christmas, but he says he wants to spend the day volunteering someplace. On Thanksgiving he bussed tables at a home for the elderly. He might also try to go away snowboarding, but money is pretty tight for him right now. Jane and he used to split the rent, but now he's paying the whole thing himself, along with all the car expenses.

The plans for Christmas with Cara's family are solidifying. We're going to Amsterdam and probably Paris, and Cara's brother was able to get me a discount fare from United, so I won't have to pay any more than four or five hundred for my flight. I'm really looking forward to it, except for having to mingle with the French. In college I went to Paris on a school trip, and everyone in the city had the attitude of a drag queen working the door of a New York nightclub, determining with a haughty flick of the wrist who is, and is not, worthy.

Do you have any ideas about what I could get Gus and Jack for Christmas?

Good luck on your finals, and say hello to everyone for me.

With love,

Katie

DATE: December 8, 1996
SUBJECT: Christmas shopping

Dear Ellen,

Cara and I went to the mall today and spent a bunch of time in Learningsmith, a cool educational toy store. I got some ideas for Jack and Gus, but I wanted to check to see if they already have some of the things I've been thinking about.

Have they seen the Wallace and Gromit Claymation videos?

Do you have Spin Doctor yet?

Has Jack got the Brick by Brick design set?

Any writing or art supplies they need or want?

I'm just at the brainstorming stage right now, but Learningsmith got me excited. I bought myself a creative writing book there that looks really good.

OK. I'm off. We're making Indian food tonight and then watching *Terminator 2*.

I'm looking forward to your next letter.

Love,

Katie

DATE: December 9, 1996
SUBJECT: Pre-Christmas greetings

Dear Katie,

We had twenty-two inches of snow this past weekend, which knocked out our power for three days. Now Gus wants us to have another blackout every Sunday to ensure more TV-less "family time."

To get to your questions from yesterday's e-mail, we recently added all three Wallace and Gromit videos to our collection—they are Gus's favorites. We do not have Spin Doctor. Jack is very into Sim stuff (this is the game he showed you when you were here). We are giving him Sim Park and Sim Tune for Christmas, but computer stuff is too expensive for you to give them.

We love Learningsmith too. We went there Friday night after the first storm abated. Jack liked some of the puzzles (those triangle ones where all the pieces are the same and must be matched on all sides, and the puzzles that are 3-D). Jack likes science stuff, building stuff and computer games. He does not have the Brick by Brick set. Gus liked the motorized K'nex "wormoid" and "beetle." He also liked a myriad of small toys and craft kits. He is very easy to please, so you could get him just about anything. Please do not spend a lot of money, Katie. They will be thrilled just to get a package from you.

I tried to see *Secrets and Lies* the Friday after Thanksgiving. According to the newspaper, it was playing at 3:30 at a small theater in Littleton along with the new *Star Trek.* John, Jack and Gus would go to *Star Trek,* and I would see *Secrets.* But when we got there, I discovered the assholes had left the previous week's listing in the paper, and they were showing *Romeo and Juliet* instead. I guess I'll have to wait for it to come out on video.

It feels like Sunday to me. My sense of time is all screwed up. Tomorrow I will tutor for the last time at The Write Place. I did not sign on for next semester because it is too time consuming and not worth the paltry sum they'll pay me ($6 per hour). I have, however, picked up a small job tutoring a Korean student in English.

Happy anniversary to you and Cara. Hope you have many more

happy anniversaries together.

I've been thinking about Matt. I worry about him being alone at Christmas—the worst time of the year to feel lonely. Will he be with Mindy, at least? Is he not going home because he doesn't have the money? You haven't said much about Matt's relationship with your parents. Wouldn't he like to spend Christmas with them?

Does Theresa work? Did she ever find her birthmother?

When are you leaving for Europe? You lucky girl, you. Cara's family sounds terrific and I'm sure you'll have a wonderful time. It will be so nice for you to see the sights with the woman you love. And love will take the sting out of having to interact with those Parisians. They were nasty way back in the early seventies when I visited Paris. I think it has something to do with having to speak French, because I found the denizens of Montreal to be equally as obnoxious—maybe it's because they have to work so hard at understanding each other, what with all the dropped consonants and vowels at the end of practically every word.

John is calling me so I must end. I wanted to get a quick note off to you.

Write soon.

Lots of love,

Ellen

DATE: December 23, 1996
SUBJECT: Merry Christmas

Hi Ellen,

It was nice to talk with you on the phone last night.

I'm doing all my last-minute things before the trip, and I wanted to wish you all a Merry Christmas. I sent Gus and Jack their own personalized greetings.

It looks like I'll be coming for a visit on Friday, after my trip, if that's OK. Let me know.

Let me know too if the package I sent arrived in time. I'll be wicked pissed if it doesn't get there by the twenty-fourth. I sent it on the sixteenth for God's sake. Yours didn't arrive today, I'm sorry to say, but it will be a nice bonus to come home to in January.

That's all. I just wanted to say I'll be thinking of you and the kids. Now I need to pack and finish my laundry.

Have a wonderful Christmas and New Year, and send my regards to John.

Love,
Katie

DATE: December 24, 1996
SUBJECT: Christmas joy

Dear Katie,

We can't wait to see you!

We got your package and are all very pleased with our presents. Jack and I played Brick by Brick all day, and John had a delicious cup of coffee (he's saving some for you to have when you come). Gus has been investigating things with his combination microscope-telescope and is anxious for me to do the clay mask with him. I have enjoyed saying dirty things in Spanish to John, and I love the CD— lovely music. Thank you, Katie.

It's too bad our package did not get to you yet. The post office said it would be there by Monday. Phooey.

We hope you have a wonderful trip and a very merry Christmas and New Year's.

Your coming to visit on Friday will be terrific. We are planning to take you out to dinner. There are lots of really good restaurants in Lowell that will offer you a more savory gustatory experience than we can. I am a truly terrible cook (being that I have no culinary imagination) and John is worse (though he sold himself as a great cook before I married him). I can, however, make you some brownies. In fact, I am famous for my brownies—everyone loves them.

We are so excited.

Have a safe and happy trip.

Love,

Ellen, John, Jack and Gus

January 1997

DATE: January 6, 1997
SUBJECT: We love you.

Dear Katie,

Just want to tell you how much we all enjoyed your visit here. The kids are really crazy about you and can't wait for you to come see us again. I hope you did not get too exhausted by their demands on you—you were such a good sport to play games with them and draw pictures for them. Gus told me the next day that he thinks you are a much better artist than I am. (His previous opinion was that I was the best in the whole world!)

I was filled with happiness and joy to see you again and have been experiencing residual elation these past few days. I hope you got as much happiness out of our visit as I did.

Write and tell me how it was for you (and be honest, please).

I keep wishing I had said this to you while you were here: I love you.

Ellen

DATE: January 8, 1997
SUBJECT: A post-visit hello

Dear Ellen,

I had a wonderful time with you as well, and I can hardly wait to come for a longer visit. It would have been nice to have more time for just the two of us, but I thoroughly enjoyed spending time with Gus and Jack. There were so many funny or touching moments with them.

I think that while I was there, Jack got a glimpse of one of the differences between being adopted and growing up with your biological mom. It was when he and I were playing that computer game together and the glass of ice got knocked over on the computer table. You demanded, "Who said you could bring a drink in here, Jack?!" And then, when we all realized I was the one who'd brought it in there, you and I just laughed.

I was wondering what Jack thought about that obviously different response, and I got my answer in the car on the way home from the restaurant. He and Gus were talking about something, I can't remember what, and I heard him grumble, "Well, Katie won't get in trouble for anything anyway."

Did you notice this? It makes sense, of course, that if you didn't raise me you wouldn't scold me too frequently, especially since I'm twenty-seven years old with a head full of gray hair. But I think Jack felt himself the recipient of a grave injustice.

Another moment that stood out was when Gus, coloring on the kitchen floor, paused to say that he felt like he'd seen me before. "Before July?" I asked. "Yeah, way before. Like when I was in heaven before I was born, I saw your face."

It was such an intense thing to hear that my first instinct was to make a joke—"What did my hair look like?"—but it's really stayed with me. What did you think of Gus's saying that? Has he said anything else like that?

I'm thrilled that Gus and Jack have taken to me, and I enjoyed seeing John again. And of course it was wonderful to see you in person again. This trip was such a dramatic contrast to the first one. In July I barely slept for days beforehand and then had to spend months afterward processing all the suppressed grief that came up. But this time was just undiluted pleasure. What a relief.

Did you know that it's one year since I got your name from Catholic Charities?

I loved all the things you gave me for Christmas. I'm wearing the blue and white shirt as I write this, as a matter of fact. After I finish the book I'm reading, I plan to start one of the books you gave me. I also loved coming home to that box of stocking stuffers. It was probably the third thing I did after coming into the house— I put my bags down, went to the bathroom and then opened that box.

Tell Gus that Fling Flang, the king alien, is prominently hung on the wall beside the refrigerator. I tried to put Jack's No Farting sign up in the bedroom, but Cara objected. I think it's the Southern woman in her that doesn't like to acknowledge bodily functions like farting.

Does John know the dates of his trip to San Jose yet? It will be great to see him, even if you and the kids aren't able to come. Maybe I'll make dinner for him here and he can meet Cara, Matt and Jo. (Unlike you, I do enjoy cooking. Indian food is my specialty.)

OK. I need to wrap up. Cara came home a few minutes ago with our friend Amber, and I'm going to go be social. Amber's mother, by the way, gave up a daughter for adoption a few years before you did. They reunited eight or ten years ago, and Amber says that the daughter has become just a regular member of the family.

Write soon.

I love you,

Katie

⚮

DATE: January 12, 1997
SUBJECT: Sunday

Dear Katie,

So how has it been, getting back to everyday living after your European vacation and visit home? What's happening at work?

My vacation has been terrific—the high point being your visit here, of course. I am so happy to hear that you had a good time with us—"undiluted pleasure"—symphonic to my ears.

I have been having a marvelous time seeing friends I neglected while I was in school. The Saturday after you left, the kids and I met my friend Patty and her daughter for a roller-blading date. Patty and I were able to visit for three hours while the kids skated. Jack and Gus really got into blading and improved their skills to the point where they have been clamoring for as much rink time as they can squeeze out of us. John and I took them to the rink after school this past Friday too.

I had lunch with Ann on Thursday at a new little restaurant I discovered in Lowell called Luna D'Oro. Mediterranean cuisine, coral-painted tin walls, antiques, warmth, really cute waiters, reasonable prices for lunch. The menu offered lots of vegetarian choices, so maybe we can go there together when you come for your next visit.

Ann and I talked about arranging some kind of family gathering, since you'd like to meet everyone and put faces to all the names. I also suggested it would be fun to go see "Late Night Catechism," which is a play whose central character is a nun teaching a catechism class (the audience)—an apt entertainment choice for us byproducts of a Catholic school education. Therefore, let me know as soon as you can when you plan to come so I can get all my ducks in a row.

I met my friend Marie for lunch on Wednesday. John and I became friends with her and her husband, Richard, when we lived in the condos in Dracut (they live in Lowell now). I had never told her about you because, while she's one of the sweetest people I know, she was also one of the most central grapes on the condo grapevine. I did not want my personal data spread to the forty-three other units in our association (where we were privy to the most personal information about each of the other dwellers, living in such close quarters). Anyway, I did tell her all about you over lunch and she was thrilled. So thrilled that when I talked to her the next day, she had already shared the news with her neighbor across the street, who then revealed that her sister had also given up a child for adoption; therefore the neighbor can "really relate" to me. I had every expectation that Marie would be a conduit for my happy news, but I was a bit taken aback by the swiftness with which tales travel.

Jack and Gus broke out in huge, proud smiles at the news that you've again displayed their work. Jack thought it was hilarious that Cara objected to his No Farting sign. He knows (via my conditioning) that "ladies do not fart"—in fact, I have told him we are functionally incapable of producing any flatulence other than the most delicate and inoffensive sort. Having not seen (or heard) evidence to the contrary, he still believes me.

Regarding the ice spill in the office, Jack often feels that he has been "the recipient of a grave injustice." Don't be too concerned that he was somehow traumatized. You were witness to his skill at dramatizing for the school nurse and magnifying what may have been a small headache into a variety of very serious, school-dismissable ills. Jack is good at squeezing tears for effect; he can turn them on and off like tap water. I have tried to encourage him to join the drama club and have told him he can have a great career on the stage. He's just honing his skills. Both Jack and Gus get really bent if my yelling at them is too one-sided and perceived as un-equal. Jack was just confirming that he thinks of you as one of the family, equally worthy of being reprimanded by me.

Speaking of drama, Jack had his first ski lesson on Thursday. It was the first of six classes, which will take place after school once a week. As he descended from the bus after a hard four hours on the slopes, his face reminded me of the picture you sent me of the face you made at your mother during your seventh birthday party. Man, he was really pissed that I had subjected him to such torture and indignity, and he vowed he was not ever going back. However, after a solid hour of complaining, he admitted that there's a learning curve involved and maybe he could give it another try. I have to give him a lot of credit for his persistence—he did not give up on roller blading either. He fell down a hundred times and was thoroughly bruised and battered but kept pushing until he could stay on his feet. I'm very proud of him.

Gus is a more natural athlete than Jack, and it takes him a lot less time to master things like this. But Jack is also very competitive and wants to be as good as (or better than) Gus, so he'll keep at it until he gets it.

Gus possesses an absolutely sparkling innocence and imagination, which is why he could make that comment about seeing you before in heaven. He has asked questions about his whereabouts before he was born, wondering how come Jack lived with us for two years before he came along. I'm sure we gave him the standard answer, "You were up in heaven," and he has somehow extrapolated that out to explain why you seem so familiar (familial).

Though he has been told by Jack and others that there is no such thing as Santa Claus, Gus clings to the shards of his belief. This year he was sure that Santa stuffed the stockings even if he did not bring the other presents. He had Jack convinced of it too.

I'm not sure when John's going to be in San Jose, but I think it's the beginning of February. I'll let you know.

Did Theresa have her baby yet? How is Matt? How did the rest of your visit with your parents go?

Write me a long letter.

Lots of love,

Ellen

DATE: January 16, 1997
SUBJECT: Integration

Dear Ellen,

I talked with my sister yesterday. The baby is a week overdue, and when I called, Theresa/Courette was feeling shitty—painful joints, swollen feet, constant heartburn and depression.

We ended up having a really good conversation about growing up and the dynamics of the family, probably the best conversation we've ever had. She acknowledged how difficult it must have been for me to have the role of keeping the family together, and she apologized for how much pain she caused me growing up.

I told her that after so many years resenting her and blaming her, I'm finally starting to understand what she was going through. I also told her that I recognize that at some point, years ago, the family closed in on itself with her on the outside and she became the family scapegoat.

It was all amazingly easy to talk about. Neither of us was defensive or blaming, and I was stunned at her capacity for honest self-examination. She had tried to talk with me about all this last Christmas during the two crazy days she stayed in San Francisco, but we didn't get very far. She was talking a hundred miles an hour and popping anti-anxiety tablets, and all my energy was devoted to maintaining the family peace. Every time she tried to talk about growing up, I'd deflect it with the suggestion that we light candles and make a pot of herbal tea: "Let's just relax, OK?"

I've been thinking a lot about severed bonds recently, and how they're a pattern in my family. Each of us kids was severed from our biological families, and a trail of broken relationships litters the family history, especially on my mother's side.

I'd like to break this pattern. Reuniting with you has got me thinking about integration—first integrating my biological side with my adoptive side, and now mending some of the other weak or broken relationships in my life. Over the past year Matt and I have been able to share deeper and deeper things with each other, and now it seems like the severed relationship with Theresa/Courette may be mendable.

Theresa and I talked a lot about adoption in our conversation yesterday, and I passed along some of the insights I've gained from my reading. I was surprised that she hadn't made the connections

I've made about how adoption has shaped our family dynamics. I'm going to give her copies of Betty Jean Lifton's *Journey of the Adopted Self* and Verrier's *Primal Wound,* and she said she would also like to read the letters you and I have been exchanging. I told her some of them might be hard for her because they talk about the chaos of our house growing up, and she responded simply, "That's fine, Katie. It's all true."

She hasn't gone any further in trying to find her birthparents. She said she still might, but she's afraid of what she might find; that they're in jail, or worse, that they don't want to have anything to do with her.

She's also afraid that she'll find them and learn that she's nothing like them. Throughout her childhood people told Theresa that she must take after her birthfamily. She didn't take after either of our parents, that was obvious. She always felt like an outsider, and she has a fantasy that somewhere out there is a family where she would fit in. If she finds her real-life biological family and learns that she doesn't even fit in with *them,* she's afraid that she'll be crushed.

So far I've written to you about the difficult sides of Theresa/ Courette because for decades those have been the only things I could see. But there is a lot about her that I really admire. She's always been very open with affection, and even during the years when I refused to speak to her, she often told me that she loved me. Cara and I took a trip down to L.A. about a year and a half ago, and she made both of us feel incredibly welcome, cooking an enormous Thai feast complete with dozens of handrolled spring rolls.

I'm also awed by her survival skills. She's had a harder life than me and Matt put together, but her resourcefulness always gets her through. She told me once that while she was pregnant with Georgie, her boyfriend, Georgie's father, doused her in gasoline and tried to light her on fire. Her next relationship ended when her lover came to her house, tied her up with telephone wire, beat her with a frying pan and stabbed her. Georgie was at daycare, thank god. She still keeps her phone number listed under a false name, just in case either of them should try to come after her.

Through all this she took care of Georgie and put herself through college, with honors. She moved to Los Angeles with everything she could fit into her suitcases and somehow managed to finagle her way into a nice apartment and a new car.

I guess that's it for now about Theresa/Courette. I'm going to visit her in mid-to-late February with Matt and Mindy. The baby should have become a little less alien-looking by then.

Thank you for the vest you sent. I got it in the mail today and it fits really nicely.

Write back soon.

Love,

Katie

~∞~

DATE: January 21, 1997
SUBJECT: Vague/fluid identities

Dear Ellen,

I just got up from bed, kept from sleeping by a floating anxiety. I've had a long weekend, and tomorrow is my first day back at work in several days, a prospect that makes me irrationally nervous.

I think this goes back to the sense of tenuousness I told you about a while back. It makes me feel like I'm on a precipice when, realistically, I'm not. I *should* feel great about going back to work tomorrow. I just got my long-awaited raise, and I'll be hiring some-body to assist in the Academic Support Center, both unambiguous signs that things are going well. But somehow, I'm even more wor-ried that it's about to fall apart.

I get a similar feeling when I teach. I've been teaching for more than five years, and from student evaluations and the progress I see in student writing, I know that I do it well. But every time I finish a workshop or a class, I feel like I've gotten away with something. Always under the surface is the fear that I'll be exposed—as a fraud, incompetent, bigoted, whatever—that some concealed ugliness will show itself, for everyone to see.

The positive side of this insecurity is that I push myself to be a better teacher, writer, person. The negative side is the pointless in-somnia on nights like this.

Anyway, I've been doing a kind of personal year-in-review, and I realized that 1996 was a breakthrough year in understanding both my family and myself. I think a lot of this has to do with our re-union. It forced me to be introspective and examine fears and pain I'd been shielding myself from for so long, and to get a clearer per-spective on my life.

At certain moments, like pretty much all of July and August, it was hell. But now, looking back, I feel like a different person from who I was twelve months ago. I'd spent so long compressed in on myself, like that Indian guru from *That's Incredible* who could fold up his long, lanky body and squeeze into tiny Plexiglas boxes. But this year I've finally started to unfold myself and stretch, opening myself up to you and, in the process, becoming more open to the other people in my life. In the realm of massive turnabouts, these changes rank up there with coming out as queer.

My propensity for 180-degree shifts is another thing I'd say is related to being adopted. My friend Emily, who is having a hard time with adoption stuff now, calls the quality a "vague sense of identity." I prefer the more positive word "fluid," but either way there's a lot of shifting involved.

Each of the kids in my family has a vague/fluid sense of self, or seems to anyway. Matt is working on an art project right now in which he fills small jars with images or words that represent some part of his personality or history. He says it's about trying to capture and store the different pieces of himself. If they're sealed in airtight jars, he can't lose them.

In Theresa/Courette this quality is most obvious in how she assimilates into whatever culture she is part of at the moment. Georgie's father was from Laos, so when they were together she learned his language and cooked Laotian food. Her next lover was from Vietnam, and she did the same thing again, only in Vietnamese. Her husband and her current lover are both Mexican, and she's become practically fluent in Spanish, had a big Mexican baptism for Georgie (whose name she now spells "Jorge"), and addresses cards to "Katie y Cara." She grew up in white, middle-class Massachusetts, but now even her English has a Mexican intonation.

A few months ago I was lying in bed with Cara talking about something or other, and she said, "Ten years ago, when you were at Ursuline, what would you have said if someone told you that in 1996 you'd be a left-wing vegetarian living in San Francisco, in bed with your female lover?"

Sometimes I worry about what I'm going to be like in five or ten years—maybe living on a nudist commune in Oregon and weaving tapestries from marijuana fibers? Or running Christian Right conversion programs that turn sinful lesbians into docile housewives for the Lord? Blowing up banks and government offices in a communist insurgency group? Or *working* for banks or the government and worrying about capital gains taxes?

The fluidity can be scary, and at times it's difficult not having a solid sense of who I am. This is partly why I appreciate our letters so much. For me, they're the equivalent of Matt's jars—pieces of myself captured and saved on the page, to go back to anytime I want. Sometimes, if I'm feeling unmoored, sitting down with the letters is all it takes to ground me again.

On the positive side, having a fluid sense of self makes me more open to growth. That's what I tell myself anyway. I know people who approach life with their feet planted and their arms crossed: "This is how I *am,* and it's not going to change." I couldn't achieve that kind of inflexibility if I tried, because "who I am" is so very slippery.

It also gives me a handy chameleon quality, and I can fit in almost anywhere. At JFKU, I work with students from the five different schools, and I have to be able to talk about writing in ways that make sense to each of them. I teach mostly the same material, but with law and management students I explain it in terms of "efficiency" or "goals"; whereas with holistic studies people I say things like "It's a process" and "Where you are is exactly where you need to be." Mostly I listen to the language people use when they describe their own writing and then adopt it when explaining something to them.

I've written a lot to you about the ways adoption has affected me, and I'd be interested to hear more about the ways you think it has affected you. Did it have anything to do with your decision not to have other kids for so long? Or your fears of letting people get close to you, before John? Do you think it has shaped the way you've raised Gus and Jack?

I'd also like to hear about any changes you've experienced over the past year. Have the effects of our reunion been as dramatic for you as they have been for me?

I was interested to read that you'd told your friend from your old neighborhood about our reunion. This seems like a major step away from your shame. What's the status of your coming-out process? Does everyone in your extended family know by now? All your siblings? How are you feeling compared to, say, six months ago? And what are the reactions you've gotten?

I realized during my last visit, when you and I were walking into Jack's school together, that I might be in for what some adoptees call a "bastard moment," when you're confronted with the fact that your existence is a source of shame for your birthparents. We walked into the office together, and while you dealt with the process for getting Jack out of school early, I wondered if I'd be introduced to the school nurse. You asked what had been going on with him, and she told you that she'd given him a cough drop, even though according to the law she shouldn't because that's diagnosing, but she felt that she knew Jack well enough to give him one. And then came that pause in the conversation, when the nurse turned toward me.

I didn't realize I'd been holding my breath until she said, "You must be Jack's sister from San Francisco. He talks about you all the time." God, it was such a relief to be acknowledged so openly. I felt that relief again when Jack's friend called to see if he could go over to play and he responded, "I can't, my sister's here." It's like every time I'm acknowledged the shame dissipates a little bit more.

OK, on to more of the details from daily life: I've applied for a novel writing workshop in UC Berkeley's extension program. It's taught by a man named James N. Frey, who does mostly mysteries, I think. He's also written a couple of how-to books: *How to Write a*

Damn Good Novel is one of them. I'm not sure when I'll know if I'm accepted or not, but I'll be mortified if I'm not, especially now that I've told a bunch of people that I'm planning to take this course.

I guess that's about it for now. I was planning to wait until I got your next letter before I sent this one, but my insomnia has inspired me to just finish it up and get it out.

Send my love to everyone.

Love,

Katie

DATE: January 24, 1997
SUBJECT: Composed

Dear Katie,

Your last two letters were phenomenal. So moving and insightful, and incredible for me to read.

"Integration": It is truly wonderful that you and Theresa are working your way back toward each other. She is part of your family and is one of the people who has known you longest. Shared history is a very strong bond, and I'm betting that you'll be able to overcome past hurts to form a strong relationship with each other just as you have done with Matt. In my own experience with various family members, I may not always like one or another of them, but they'll always be my brothers and sisters and I love them, despite their shortcomings or (what I perceive as) the pain they may have caused me. Heck, I'm sure they find me lacking and think I've caused them pain, too. (They're wrong, of course, but I'm not here to quibble.) We still continue to speak with one another, and it would be unthinkable for me to cut any one of them out of my life.

Sometimes my relationships with them are hard work, but not one of them has done anything unforgivable either, so I haven't really been faced with the decision to sever contact.

Sometimes people do unforgivable things to one another. Sometimes it can be practically impossible to maintain family relationships. Or like what happened to us, sometimes circumstances force people apart. And sometimes people themselves use up all the love and good graces of family members, so their families can no longer abide them. This often happens with alcoholics and drug addicts because relationships tainted by these addictions are so much more painful and complicated. The rest of us are just not equipped to deal with them.

My father was an alcoholic, as I told you before. He too was hell to live with when he was drinking. Some drunks get happy and sappy, my father just got mean and nasty. His problem was not apparent to me until I was in high school, although my mother said he always used to be an embarrassment at the parties they went to when they were younger; he was the cause of their not being invited to parties as they got older. As I think about it, I remember always having to be keenly aware of my father's "moods," taking note of his mien and conducting myself accordingly. I recall doing this as a youngster, and also being concerned about having friends over to the house if he was around. So I guess even though I just said his problem was not apparent until I was in high school, his alcoholism was a problem during my earlier childhood too.

My father's gin and tonics made him mutate into a raging dictatorial martinet. He spouted German phrases at us staccato-style and became our commandant, ordering us around like prisoners of war. When he was not raging, alcohol often sent him into maudlin remembrances of his army career; I think he felt his time in the army was the apex of his life. He felt a big need to control us and some of his rules were quite insane. For instance, curfew lateness merited grounding—no excuses—and one minute was considered late. One of my most heinous crimes was leaving my razor on the side of the bathtub instead of removing it to my room after I showered. I was confined to the house many, many weekends because of that sin. Another capital offense was failing to answer properly and formally when he addressed me: "Ellen," he'd call. I could not say, "What?" I had to answer always, "Yes, Daddy?" "Who is in the bathroom?" he'd say. I'd have to answer, "It is I, Ellen."

Sometimes he would make a sneak attack as I sat in my boyfriend's car saying goodnight after a date. He would bang on the car window and demand that I go immediately into the house. He was terrifying. I would avoid all confrontations with him, even striving to avoid any contact with him, if I could. I spent a lot of time in my room so our paths would not cross.

What I dreaded most of all were the fights my parents would have. I would lie cowering in my bed with the covers pulled over my head, listening to every screaming word as they battled each other. Two times my father got violent enough that my mother had to call the cops to cart him off. After especially awful episodes, she banished him from the house and threatened divorce, which then would prompt him to reevaluate his life and he'd try AA for however long he could make it work for himself. These times were peaceful and the family would slowly stitch itself back together, although eventually my mother's love for my father was damaged through erosion and broken trust.

He was a loving, intelligent, reasonable man when he was not drinking. I think the longest he stayed with AA was about three years, but he was in and out on a regular basis in the late sixties and early seventies. He had been doing pretty well until the final year of his life when he again started drinking. But by then (1974–75) he'd lost most of his rage, seemed slightly wet-brained and was just mostly depressed and despondent to be back on the bottle again.

The final night of his life, my father was raging at my brother Jed. Jed, disgusted, went upstairs to his room and closed the door. My father banged around in the kitchen, making himself some peanut butter and crackers. Then he came up the stairs and banged on Jed's door. Jed tried to ignore him. When the banging stopped, Jed opened the door and discovered that my father had been banging on the door because he had been choking. Jed tried to revive him but it was too late. He died at the age of sixty-one.

Pretty awful story, isn't it? Maybe every family has awful stories to tell (or keep secret). I hope it's not true for *all* families. I hope Jack and Gus will never have ugly stories to tell about their childhoods.

"Fluid identities": I can identify with the sense of tenuousness you describe in resuming work after being away from it for a little while. I feel the same way in going back to school each semester. I don't suffer from insomnia, though. I am more apt to crave vast amounts of sleep or to feel sick to my stomach. I'm often afraid I won't be able to measure up in school or that someone will discover how stupid I really am. I require strokes and feedback (in the form of good grades or a kind word from the teacher) in order to believe that I am intelligent and that I can do the work, and in order to propel me onward. In my more rational moments, I know I get good grades because I work hard and I deserve them. I also have some infrequent manic-type moments when I think I am just about the smartest student in the entire university. But I think it's a character flaw in me that I need to be goosed by outside forces in order to move toward excellence, that my need for teacher approval is my motivator instead of innate desire.

Your insecurity pushes you to be better and achieve more. Mine holds me back from achieving and keeps me mired in the status quo. Unless someone demands more of me, I will not put in the effort to give more. Yuck. Putting this on paper is forcing me to look at the ugly writhing entrails of myself.

Our letters have forced me to be more introspective too. As Martha Stewart says, "It's a good thing." (Don't you just hate that woman?)

I've been thinking a lot about what you wrote regarding identity issues resulting from adoption. As a nonadopted person, I think my identity was shaped through the genetic and environmental connection with my family, and that what I am comes down in a straight line from that connection. I also think that I didn't really become fully "me" until I was in my thirties—that the connecting line was more of an elastic line while I tested the parameters of my place on the family tree. Aside from having you, I did not stray too far from what I was destined to be—a middle-class married woman like my mother. My father wished that I would become a doctor, but given my genetics, my personality, whatever, his wish was never my dream. I wish I knew what factors prompt some people to be achievers and what makes me not one.

This topic of identity is so vast. I can't nail anything down. A thought moves in one direction, then sprouts more branches, and those turn in on themselves and eventually it's like Sleeping Beauty's castle: everything covered with thorny vines.

Anyway, I think maybe we all struggle to find our identities, but adoptees struggle much harder because you don't have a clear picture of where you came from. Your connecting line was broken and then tied somewhere else. Or maybe your parents gave you a whole new line. So now you have two lines of connection and you have to gauge the give and take between the genetic line and the environmental line in order to balance yourself. No matter how fluid your identity feels, I think it sounds better to be "flexible" than "inflexible," and the most important thing is that you are happy with what you feel inside. I firmly believe that you will never mutate into a lesbian-to-housewife-converting Christian Right proselytizer. You may, however, have to worry someday about capital gains taxes.

On now to the effects of our reunion on me. Really, Katie, I think reuniting with you has been amazingly positive for me. I have gained so much from having you back in my life again. I would say I am fully out of the closet now, and I can declare to the entire world that I am no longer ashamed. Telling more and more people is positively liberating. This must be what it felt like to you when you came out as a queer.

It is pure joy for me to be able to tell everyone about you. I have been happily telling practically everyone I meet about you: schoolmates, mothers of the kids' friends. Reactions have all been positive and sympathetic. People genuinely seem to share my joy. My friend Marie cried, she was so happy, and she thinks your parents would be delighted to meet me because I am such a lovely person.

Compared to six months ago, I feel much more secure in my relationship with you, especially since your visit earlier this month. Being able to have this relationship with you has perhaps made me more open with people in general. Maybe more willing to take risks with people—I have found myself starting conversations with strangers. Perhaps I am less aloof and reserved than I used to be.

I dislike the fact that you might be subject to "bastard moments." The shame was mine, not yours. And the key word here is *was*. There's no shame in having a terrific daughter like you.

Write pronto.

Love,

Ellen

February 1997

DATE: February 10, 1997
SUBJECT: A year of letters

Dear Ellen,

It was nice talking with you, Gus and Jack on the phone yesterday. I'm psyched about my visit to Chelmsford in March. My reservation is booked and paid for, so I'll see you on the seventh.

I appreciated your last letter, especially the part about your father. I hadn't known that he had been such a tyrant when he drank. The stuff about how you had to respond to him—"Yes father, it is I, Ellen"—made the hair on the back of my neck stand up. Do you think that growing up with him shaped the lives and personalities of the seven kids?

I had my novel writing class on Saturday, and I think it's going to be good. There are about fifteen of us, chosen from between thirty-five and forty applicants. I'm a little intimidated because it seems like the others already have so much more written than I do—they were saying things like, "Well, it's a story about this, and in the first section this happens, and then. . . ." I sat there thinking: Shit, I don't know what my story is about, I don't know how it begins, and to tell you the truth, I've got maybe twenty-five pages of draft, tops. I'm afraid to even say that I'm writing a novel—it just seems too huge and overwhelming. But I said none of this out loud.

The instructor warned us that the course may send us into

shellshock at first. "Being kind isn't going to help anyone," he said, explaining the atmosphere he wants to establish in the classroom. I wrote a single word in my notebook, "Oy." Oh well. Feeling scared and intimidated may provide the pressure I need to start producing more material. I also think his warning may have been overstated, because Saturday's group critique wasn't particularly harsh. One woman read a story she'd written, and afterward, everyone addressed what they saw as the piece's strengths and its weaknesses, with exactly the sorts of comments I'd like to receive for my own writing. I think I'll learn a lot. The instructor said that he doesn't just want us to write for our own pleasure, he wants every single one of his students to get published. I like that sort of motivation.

So much has happened since my last e-mail to you it's hard to know where to start. I told you on the phone about Theresa's baby, Jose, eight pounds, healthy. But I didn't tell you what's been going on with Matt.

His friend Jen has been using the Internet to search for his birthmother, and it looks like she found her. When I was in Boston this summer, I found his birthname, and from the marriage registry for Massachusetts, I got a list of women who might be his mother. Jen has been diligently going through all the possibilities, and she found the former sister-in-law of a woman who gave a son up for adoption around the time Matt was born. This sister-in-law, Pam, said that the woman, Alice, is superthin, with sleepy eyelids—just like Matt.

Matt wrote a quick letter to Alice asking if she is actually his birthmother, and he asked Pam to forward it for him (he doesn't have Alice's phone number or address). She should have it by now—Pam was going to deliver it at the end of last week—so now he can only wait.

His sense from talking to Pam is that Alice might be tough to connect with. She didn't open her Catholic Charities file to him, and she's got a solid record of broken relationships with her kids. She gave up a daughter for adoption before Matt, then gave up Matt, and then got pregnant again and married the father. They divorced within a couple of years and their daughter, who is my age, was raised largely by Pam, the sister-in-law. This info came from Pam, who didn't provide much more explanation.

Anyway, it looks like Matt's going to have a very different experience with this than I did. He already feels a lot of rejection about having been given up, and I think it's going to be tough for him if she doesn't want to have anything to do with him. He's been sick a lot over the past few months; his immune system is worn down from all the stress he's been under.

Did you know that today is the one-year anniversary of my first letter to you? Last year at this time I was polishing up those two pages, putting all my energy into whether the sentences were smooth and the details vivid, so that I didn't have to think about the enormity of what I was doing. But flashes of panic would grip me late at night, making me toss and turn in bed until I had to get up and start working things out in my journal.

Writing my first letter to you, I was terrified that you'd reject me. I loaded it with all the achievements I could fit—I got a scholarship to NYU, I have a master's degree, I teach at a university, I'm a performer. The first draft of the letter was even more brazenly self-promoting, but I edited out the more egregious stuff. Of course, I didn't let myself acknowledge these fears when I wrote to you, and I had a self-protection plan in place in case you rejected me.

Cara read the first letter before I mailed it, and she asked diplomatically if I was sure I wanted to come out as queer in our very first contact. "She needs to know that," I said, full of bravado. "She can't know me if she doesn't know that." This was true: If you were really going to know me, the real and complete me, if you were going to be a part of my life, you needed to know that I am queer.

But there was something else going on too. It wasn't just about getting to know me. Inside my head the reasoning had a harsh, defensive edge to it, something like: "If she can't deal with me being a queer, she can just fuck off."

I would have been shattered if you hadn't accepted me, but thinking of it this way gave me a way to reject you first, righteously, indignantly. I would have been able to say that you couldn't handle me being a queer, or a fire-eating Lesbian Avenger, or a producer of speculum puppet shows; rather than that you just didn't want me in your life. It was like the agreements between my friends and me during high school: If any of us heard that someone else's boyfriend was planning to break up with her, we would inform her immediately so that she could break up with him first. That way it wouldn't hurt so bad.

Sending off that first letter, I was also terrified of the unknown, terrified of who you'd be and what you'd want from me. This was the flip side of the fear of rejection, the fear that you'd want more from me than I wanted to give. I worried that you'd be a needy psychopath who started calling me all the time, maybe even stalking me. I was in the middle of moving when I sent that first letter off, so I really did need to give you my work address instead of my home one, but that felt like a fortunate coincidence, in case you showed up in San Francisco, at my doorstep. You probably noticed that I didn't give you my phone number.

It feels wonderful to look back on these fears from the vantage point of the present, secure in the knowledge that they were unwarranted. Instead of rejecting me because I was a Lesbian Avenger, you asked why dykes shave their heads and wanted clarification on butch-femme styles. And instead of overwhelming me with more intimacy than I could handle, you paid attention to the signals I was giving you and respected my needs, even when they were different from your own. We've been able to talk not just about our happiness, but also the pain and grief that come with adoption, and you've become more and more open about having me back in your life, something that makes me feel loved and secure.

I don't think things could have gone any better between us this year. Having you in my life again has given me so much, and I feel incredibly lucky.

I need to wrap up, but I wanted to send this out today to mark the first anniversary of our reunion.

I look forward to your next letter.

With much love,

Katie

Afterword

⸙

Ellen:

I feel so grounded and whole having Katie back in my life. It has been wonderful to relax together during a visit, while sharing a bottle of wine or watching a movie. I feel so much love and warmth and such a healing sense of comfort in having her near. Even as mundane a task as grocery shopping becomes fun as Katie dances through the aisles. In her, I feel I have found my best friend.

Since Katie entered my life again, the most ordinary things can foster happiness for me. For instance, during her first overnight visit Katie suggested that I should consider not blow-drying my hair. Ever since, I've appeared in public au naturel, relishing the fact that I no longer have to worry about humidity or being caught in a rainstorm, because dampness only enhances my wavy-haired beauty. I have also come to doubt the need for shaving my underarms and legs, although I am less willing to blatantly share this fact with the public. Who knows what other burdensome and time-consuming regimens I will eventually abandon under Katie's liberating influence?

We also have a running joke about my incompetence in the kitchen. Each time Katie visits, she justifiably complains about my kitchen: the lack of proper utensils, ingredients and appropriate pans, the accumulation of fire hazards on the countertop next to the stove, the missing cheese grater and so on. Last visit, she refused to make her famous chocolate chip and banana pancakes unless a new non-stick fry pan became available. Thanks to Katie, I now own three teflon pans in graduated sizes, which will probably stay in their current pristine state until her next stay.

I was thrilled when Katie invited me to visit her in San Francisco. One gloriously sunny day, we drove down to Santa Cruz, where we fed sea otters, pelicans and sea lions on the Bay. As we rode in Cara's truck and sniffed the California air, Katie apologized that her cat must have somehow mistaken the floormat for its litterbox. Later, while riding around with the windows open in Matt's car, which also smelled funny, we figured out that eucalyptus trees smell like cat pee. This smell will forever recall special memories.

During our first visits together I often felt compelled to touch and look at Katie. When she walked or sat near me, I had to hold myself back from placing my fingers on her. I had a compulsive need to reach her somehow, so that any distance between us would fall away. But twenty-seven years apart is an awful chasm to bridge.

The distance has not completely fallen away even now, after three years. There are times when our relationship feels as tentative and scary as it did when Katie first contacted me. I think that living on opposite sides of the country contributes to some of that distance: We don't get a chance to work things out face to face, and perhaps some of our issues don't get aired as they might if we were able to spend more time together. Somehow, it feels less safe to talk on the phone when you can't see one another's reactions.

There is also the inescapable fact that our relationship is founded on something that is much more difficult to overcome than geographical distance: I gave her away. I, her own mother, gave her away. It is devastating to me that Katie believes she is somehow responsible for having been given away six days after her birth. This sense of abandonment colors her self-perception and bleeds into the fabric of her life in pervasive ways, just as shame has permeated my life. I don't know how to comfort her when she talks about these feelings; it is terrible knowing that the very act I thought would ensure her happiness and a good life those many years ago is the cause of so much pain for her.

Also sad is realizing how much of a strain my coming back into Katie's life has put on her relationship with her mother. I regret that I am the catalyst for damaging their closeness, and I feel sorrow that Katie's joy in reuniting with me is tempered by the difficulty of walking a tightrope between her two families. I first understood just how difficult it was going to be for all of us when John and I met Katie's parents, David and Mary, in a restaurant in April 1997. Katie handled the arrangements long distance. There were protracted negotiations about when we could meet, and it almost felt like a border struggle between two neighboring countries, with Katie in the role of Henry Kissinger. I wavered between terrified panic and cool detachment, as I considered how her parents would receive me. At one point I was brave enough to think that I could handle it on my own, but I finally decided that I needed John's support to cope. He is so naturally gregarious and likable, I figured there was less chance of my falling flat on my face with him there.

My primary interest was to initiate a cordial relationship in the hope that all of us could somehow begin to merge into one big, happy family. I wanted to like them and for them to like me. I wanted them to feel good about Katie's having contacted me. I wanted all of their fears to dissipate. I fantasized about the possibility of their becoming like foster grandparents to Jack and Gus, and about being able to call on Mary's wisdom as a teacher. I hoped we could establish some common ground, and I thought that because we had so much in common (Katie), we would succeed.

Fantasies seldom become reality, however. Although our foursome may have been viewed by other tables as cordial and pleasant, with hugs all around, smiles and laughter, the reality was quite different: Meeting Katie's parents was a thoroughly wrenching experience.

During a lull in the conversation (and there were *many* that we worked hard to fill), Mary asked, "So, do you have any questions for us?" I immediately thought, "Katie has told me everything I need to know. Nope, no questions." Then my head buzzed with worries that I might venture into off-limits areas, that I might inadvertently reveal more than I was supposed to know. I considered thanking Mary for doing such a good job raising Katie, but then I worried that she would see my thanks as the worst sort of effrontery. I had no right to thank her. I had no rights at all. I felt like an intruder. I was afraid she'd think that I thought now it was my turn to take over the mother role in Katie's life.

After the meeting, I felt muddled, muddied and very depressed. I had come face to face with the fact that David and Mary are her parents—and I am not. In the bliss of my reunion with Katie, I had focused only on the present. Meeting the Herns and hearing about Katie's childhood trophies and accomplishments put me back in touch with an overwhelming sense of loss. I never got to do art projects with her or take her to museums. I never got to cover the refrigerator with her drawings. I never got to comfort her and rub her back as she threw up into the toilet. I never got to do any of the gazillion things a mother does for her child. So how could I *be* her mother?

Aftershocks from this meeting put a strain on my relationship with Katie, as she struggled to negotiate the emotions generated in both her parents and me. We had some tense telephone conversations in which I tried to get feedback about her parents' reactions to me. There were also a few constipated e-mails before I was finally able to recognize what had been making me feel so bad.

A conversation that occurred during my visit to San Francisco about a month later spurred more open communication between Katie and me regarding the meeting with her parents. At lunch one day Katie's friend, Emily, told us that when her birthmother, Cinnamon, and her adoptive mother met for the first time, the adoptive mother *thanked* Cinnamon for Emily's birth. I looked at Emily incredulously and said, "I can't imagine Katie's mother ever thanking me."

After that, Katie and I talked more frankly about the threat my entering her life represented for her parents. We were able to get everything out in the open. When Katie and I talk openly about the difficult issues, relief washes over me and I'm on top of the world. But when something crops up that we attempt to skirt around, my sense of balance is thrown off kilter and it is difficult to focus on anything else. I want to get inside Katie's brain to find out what she is thinking. And I feel so dense sometimes when I don't intuitively know what has upset her. There are times when I feel totally inadequate in offering her comfort. I want her to feel happy and loved, but I know I often spur unhappiness and insecurity in her.

I don't want Katie to be afraid of hurting my feelings. I know how wary she feels sometimes about expressing her true emotions, because I'm the same way. I tend to avoid confrontations and have to fight off insecurities to speak my mind. I think it will be great when we are secure enough in our relationship to safely yet vehemently disagree. I would love to have the typical mother-daughter relationship where I make a lame attempt to opine about some aspect of her life and she tells me to butt out. But a relationship like that only comes after years of being together, and we will have to work toward that easiness with each other.

As difficult as Katie's and my relationship can be, Jack and Gus have had no problems integrating her into their lives. They are thrilled to have another playmate when she visits. She gets right into the thick of things with them: drawing, sculpting, game playing and making a mess for me to clean up, just like they do. They have eagerly accepted her and look forward to squeezing out time with her. They vie for her attention, yelling, "Katie, look at this!" and "Katie, watch me!" Gus lurks outside her closed door every morning because he can't wait for her to wake up to play. Jack is more subtle in his desire for concentrated Katie-time, trying to lure her attention with interesting games. He also willingly participates in activities that usually hold little attraction for him, like making things out of clay.

Gus delights in Katie's admiration and encouragement of his artistic efforts, particularly because he respects and admires her talent too. He usually loads her up with drawings to hang on her refrigerator. He was especially proud when I told him that Katie's brother, Matt, had lined his stairwell with some of Gus's space alien pictures. It's great that Katie and Gus share this interest.

During one of Katie's visits, the boys introduced her to a computer game that required skill in estimating angles of trajectory and pitch to send explosive bananas flying through city skies to destroy King Kong. They were all screaming with laughter as they blew up buildings and each other's gorillas. As I watched the three of them playing, I was filled with contentment and happiness at having all my children together. And I saw that a vicious competitive streak was fully realized in each of them.

Jack and Gus often compete with each other, arguing over computer time, video games, parental attention, who is the better ball player, and so on. It seems only natural that they can be slightly proprietary about the time Katie and I spend together. For example, in May 1997 when I visited Katie, the fact that I was going to be in San Francisco during Jack's tenth birthday was hard for him to accept. I felt very guilty about leaving, but I had no choice in scheduling my visit between school semesters. Both boys wished that they could come along, but finances precluded a family trip.

I talked to them by phone at least twice a day while in San Francisco, and I made sure to buy Jack some extra special things. I felt so guilty that I bought him his first model rocket, an item he had been clamoring for, but that I had been hesitant to purchase. He has since said that although a model rocket was a great present, he would have preferred that I had stayed home with him to celebrate. He still likes to use this incident as another example of my playing favorites. Jack was put out, because for the first time in his life his birthday was secondary to me. He knows he is well loved; he just enjoys having the leverage that guilt produces.

The rest of my family has lovingly taken to Katie as well. In May 1998 we all attended a seventy-fifth birthday party for my Aunt Joey. It was Katie's first chance to meet all the McGarrys and for them to meet her. She was understandably nervous, but I knew she would feel fine once the introductions were over. My brothers and sisters have never pointed the finger of shame at me about being an unwed mother, and I knew they would welcome Katie. They were dying to meet her. I have always looked forward to family get-togethers because they make me feel more connected, more secure in the world, but this one I especially welcomed. I hoped Katie would feel that connection too.

Once the party was under way, I introduced her to my aunt, uncle, brothers, sisters, nieces, nephews and cousins, saying, "This is my daughter, Katie." I felt the greatest happiness to reintegrate her into my family. It was pure joy to see all the smiling faces. Katie said later that the tension she had initially felt just melted with the family's warmth. She won them all over with her sparkling wit and personality, and I was proud to have her take her rightful place as the oldest cousin in the McGarry clan. As we sat at a table with John, Jack and Gus, I filled Katie in on family gossip; it was like she had always been a part of these gatherings.

Shame was definitely not a part of that family reunion. But I *have* had to grapple with my shame at times during these past couple of years. When I think about having my experience nakedly displayed in this book, for example, I get "whatwillotherpeoplethink!" panic. In the beginning, I was very tentative about telling people about the book. When I told one of my English professors, she wanted to know more, but sensing my reserve, she held back from any pointed questions. I explained that it was a book about an adoption reunion and did not get any more specific. Since then, I have told practically the entire English department. I've suffixed my announcement of being published with forthright information about my status as a birthmother. Reactions have generally been favorable; English professors seem to be incredibly thrilled when one of their students writes something that someone else is willing to pay for.

These past three years have shown me that the initial stages of a reunion between a birthparent and a child are like courtship. At first, Katie and I were almost infatuated with each other. We lusted for revealing bits of information about each other, hardly able to stand the pauses in our snail-mail exchanges. Our first six months of letters were incredibly exhilarating for me. I wanted to pour my heart out to her and hold nothing back. It was easy to be open and honest, because any risk was mitigated by the fact that if we failed to bond, I knew that I had given it my very best effort. I had lost so much by being separated from her, I could cope with loss again.

After we met face to face, I was filled with the most incredible joy. Yet Katie became overwhelmed, torn by conflicting emotion and guilt about her parents' feelings of betrayal. She was paralyzed and frightened as she grappled with confusion about her identity. I misinterpreted her silence, thinking that somehow, when she met me in person, she had found me lacking and not worth caring about. I feared I would lose her again

When Katie was finally able to open up again, I felt totally inadequate. I wanted to help her. I wanted to ease her pain. I wanted to provide the "cure" for everything she was suffering. But there is no cure. Only the hard, often painful work of being open and honest with each other.

Working on this book with Katie has tested our relationship. We've had some bugs to work out, like the allocation of responsibility for manuscript preparation and editing. And issues of guilt and trust have resurfaced. That we've been able to work out these kinks is testament to the strength of our bond. In sharing our reunion correspondence with others, I hope readers can experience even a small measure of our joy. I would like to see all adopted children and birthparents find the integration that reunions can bring. In the process, I hope they are able to find love, groundedness and serenity.

Katie:

As I read back over this correspondence, now more than three years after I held my breath and mailed off my first letter to Ellen, I am struck by how fragile our reconnection initially felt. Desperate to do everything right so that I wouldn't lose her again, I was on my very best behavior. In my letter dated March 18, I wrote "I appreciate" three times in one paragraph. In June, as we geared up for my trip back to Massachusetts, we wrote to each other almost every day. At one point that month, when Ellen said that reading about my search for her had made her feel vulnerable and raw, we exchanged four panicky e-mails in a single day, then two more the next day.

Ellen and I remained nervous with each other well beyond the first year of our reunion. The first time I went to Chelmsford for an overnight stay, all four Carlsons were waiting at the airport to greet me: Ellen, John, Jack and Gus. The house was stocked with vegetables and homemade brownies, the lawn was freshly mowed and the downstairs playroom was so tidy it looked like a children's museum. I had insomnia for the entire trip, straining under my uncertain role as both family member and guest. I ended up wandering around the darkened downstairs until three or four in the morning, snooping in all the medicine cabinets for Sominex or Tylenol PM and feeling like an intruder. I thought about driving to an all-night grocery store, but I didn't have a car or a house key.

Part of me was bracing for an experience like the summer after my trip to Massachusetts, when I met Ellen for the first time since 1969. I was terrified that somewhere inside me, lurking just out of sight, was an impossible flood of grief that would knock me out of commission for months.

But over the past couple of years, as I've visited Ellen, and she's visited me and I've visited her again, things have started to feel much more normal. The nervous breakdown I've been guarding against hasn't come. We're comfortable enough to simply talk on the phone, rather than spend hours crafting cautious letters to each other, and my Sunday-best manners have dropped away. When we were preparing this manuscript for publication, Ellen would sometimes become obsessive-compulsive, checking and rechecking to make sure I was doing my share of the work: "Have you finished yet? Time is running short, you know." Two years ago I would have apologized and stayed up all night, my mind cycling around the worry that our relationship was about to crack apart. But now I respond like any daughter whose mother is hounding her: "I'm *doing* it, for Christ's sake. Get off my back."

It still worries me when we disagree or argue, but each time it worries me less. My stomach still gets fluttery when I head off for a visit to Chelmsford, but I don't have insomnia anymore. And though the Carlson home will probably never feel like *my* home, the awkwardness of being a guest has faded. During my last visit my welcoming party included only Ellen, toys littered the playroom floor, and the kitchen was bare until Ellen and I went to the grocery store the next day. Little by little, it feels like I'm becoming a regular member of the family. I'm hoping that one day, before too long, I'll see a ring of soap scum around her tub.

When I received my first letter from Ellen and saw the photo of Gus and Jack that she had included, I wondered why she had sent it. I didn't feel related to them, and although I wasn't exactly conscious of it, I felt a little itch of jealousy that she'd kept them but given me away. Those feelings began shifting during the first year of our letters, and now I'm fully established in my role as big sister—commiserating with Jack about the mean-spiritedness of junior high school, putting Gus in headlocks and wrestling him to the ground, telling Jack that the reason his frog jumped out of his tank and died was the voodoo spell I had cast. I even had the big Coming Out talk with them, which I'd long avoided. I dreaded the thought of sitting my new little brothers down at the kitchen table: *Boys, I have something important to tell you. I'm a homosexual. How does that make you feel?*

The moment came this spring, while Gus, Jack and I were drawing in the kitchen. Jack was laboring with his tongue out over a pencil sketch of Iron Man, and Gus was telling me about a mail-in contest that asked kids to vote for who they liked better, the Beatles or the Spice Girls. He said he couldn't believe anyone could ever vote for the Spice Girls, and I told him I was quite fond of them myself.

"Why do you like them?" Gus demanded.

"Because their music is fun, and they're cute."

"You think they're cute?" he said, looking up from his cartoon. "But you're a *woman*. And they're women."

"Yup," I shrugged. "I like women."

Gus wrinkled his nose and cocked his head to the side. Jack kept drawing, but I could tell his ears had pricked up. I could feel my heart thudding in my neck.

"People are different," I said, waving away Gus's reaction. "I like men and women both."

Still not looking up, Jack put in his two cents: "It's no big deal."

For the next day or so, I felt self-conscious and monitored them for any changes toward me. But after a three-way jousting match with foam swords and pillows, I relaxed. Their reactions were so mild that Ellen wasn't sure they had even understood what I told them. She asked them about it after I had flown back to the Bay

Area and found that although Gus still considered it odd for a "girl to like a girl," they were both unfazed.

Another significant part of my reunion with Ellen has been reuniting with the extended family I lost in 1969. My sense of connection to them has been the slowest to reawaken, and I still find myself referring to the family as *Ellen's* relatives—Ellen's aunt, Ellen's sisters and brothers. I guess this is normal, because we've never exchanged Christmas presents or joked together about family black sheep. I didn't have cookouts with them for the Fourth of July. I had no memories of them or any sense of shared history.

In May 1998 I attended a seventy-fifth birthday party for Ellen's Aunt Joey—my great aunt—and the entire McGarry clan was there, more than sixty people in all. Of course, I was a wreck beforehand. I worried that I'd feel like a circus act, the long-lost relative who'd been sent away at birth to live among strangers. I worried that the family would politely pretend that nothing was unusual about my presence. And at the same time, I worried that people *would* acknowledge the significance of this and that it would make me fall apart. Mostly, I worried that I'd fall apart.

Having Ellen with me helped. She didn't try to talk me out of my nerves or minimize what I was going through; she just acknowledged my feelings and arranged to drive us there early, in a separate car, so that I could case the joint for an hour before. The party was held in a function room at a hotel, a setting so benign it was surreal—round tables with tablecloths, platters of cold cuts and a big Bat Mitzvah next door. I inspected the nearby hallways and restrooms for a place where I could duck away if I needed to.

Then we sat down in the lobby with me facing the doorway, and the relatives began arriving in clusters. Ellen's first cousin and his kids, her sister Barbara with her daughter, her youngest brother John with his wife and brood of children. As they entered, I scanned each face for resemblance, and when I didn't see any, my insides would sink with disappointment. But when it *was* there—when I saw my eyes, or the shape of my face or the curve of my teeth—my body reacted instinctively to the recognition. My hand would lift off the armrest and I'd find myself pointing at these strangers, my family.

When we moved into the room, Gus introduced me to the pack of cousins he was running with: "That's my sister Katie. You've never met her before. She lives in San Francisco. She's a vegetarian." The kids paused to look at me, then resumed chasing each other in circles and hiding under tables. Ellen was in charge of introducing me to the adults, so she took my hand and led me from one group to another. "This is my daughter, Katie," she'd say, and we'd spend a little time chatting. Then, moving on to the next group, she'd say it again: "This is my daughter, Katie." And each time she said it, I felt like the sentence was a piece of thread mending the twenty-seven-year gash between us.

I talked about salmon fishing with Ellen's brother Jed, psychology with her cousin John, and book publishing with her other cousin Martha. But my favorite conversations were with the people who felt comfortable enough to acknowledge my birth and separation from the family. When I shook his hand, Ann's son Donny—my first cousin—held my hand in both of his and told me how wonderful it was to finally meet me. Ellen's brother Stephen told me that even though my birth was kept a secret, he had figured it out. Ellen's youngest brother, John, said the same thing, confessing that once, as he nosed around through Ellen's belongings, he had found a bottle of prenatal vitamins. And Ann's husband, Don, greeted me by holding his hands a foot apart and saying, "I haven't seen you since you were this big." I thought he was teasing, so I said, "You never saw me." But Don shook his head and said, "I did. I was at the hospital after you were born."

My brother's experience of finding his birthfamily has been very different from mine. In the final letter included in the collection, I mentioned that Matt might have located his birthmother, a woman named Alice. He sent her a letter through Pam, Alice's sister-in-law, to whom he had spoken on the phone. In that letter, he wrote, "In the event that this letter has found its way into the correct hands, I hope that you contact me. I am curious and want to know you. I have hoped for many years that you really do exist. If you want, I would like to share some of my life experiences and hope that we can become friends."

When six weeks passed without a response, Matt intuitively knew he had found the right woman. He contacted an adoption search agency, and they quickly located her current address and phone number. But they warned him against calling her out of the blue. Matt held off for forty-five minutes and then picked up the phone. Alice answered, and he tried to make her feel comfortable, to let her know that he'd try to respect her need for space. After an awkward silence, he asked her point blank if she was his mother.

"You know the answer to that," she replied. Then her emotions unraveled. "You can't do this. There was a contract. You'll ruin other people's lives if you continue this." He was lucky, she said. He already had everything he needed. He wasn't part of her family. "I don't want to talk to you. Don't ever call here again."

But a few days later, Matt called again. Now that she'd had some time to think about it, had anything changed for her?

"No," she said. "Don't call me again."

The next year involved long, painful waiting periods, as Matt hoped that the phone would ring or that he'd receive a letter. Every few months he would call. He couldn't help himself. But Alice never relented. Before long, she wouldn't even tell him not to call, she'd simply hang up as soon as she heard his voice.

When I think about what happened to my brother, I feel a palpable sense of relief. I have been incredibly lucky to receive so much love and acceptance from Ellen and the rest of the family. It could have gone so differently. At the same time, our reunion has been hard for me in a lot of ways. I go about my daily life with a competent exterior—writing, teaching, obeying traffic laws—but underneath I still have the ragged, torn-open feeling I described in one of my letters to Ellen. I can usually ignore it, but when I let myself feel it, the center of my chest physically contracts, and I'm filled with a sadness so pervasive and long-standing, it seems part of my cells.

I still hate the phrase "the primal wound," but I no longer doubt that it exists. In 1969, after nine months with Ellen—nine months inside her very body—I lost her completely. I never heard her voice again, never felt her touch, or saw her face. Never smelled her skin or received comfort from her. It's as if a part of myself was ripped away, leaving a gaping hole in my center. And I was six days old when it happened. Newborn babies can't do anything for themselves. They can't feed themselves, they can hardly see, they're completely bewildered by the world around them. The sheer act of living outside the womb is so exhausting, they sleep all the time. And yet, at six days old, I had to survive the loss of my mother.

How could a newborn baby survive something so annihilating?

I did it by shutting down. I clung to the adoptive parents who took me in, and I cut myself off from what had come before. No despair. No anger. I survived. But the despair and anger didn't go away; they just burrowed deep inside my body, like twenty-pound weights I couldn't put down. I was so shut down that I didn't notice I was carrying them.

Until I reunited with Ellen.

Since then, all the buried feelings have been leaking to the surface. Despair came first, a little at a time over the course of our letters, then in a crashing wave after the first time I saw her again. More than three years later, it's still coming and it's still enormous, spilling from that hollow space in my chest. I suspect that if I could just, once and for all, experience the grief—really mourn the losses I suffered—I'd be free. But right now, that's still too terrifying.

Anger was a little slower to arrive. For a long time, I talked myself out of being angry. I can see it in some of my letters to Ellen: So much good resulted from my adoption, I told myself, how could I *possibly* be angry? But the truth is, I am. It's a terrible thing to separate an infant from her mother, regardless of the good that might eventually emerge. I can't keep pretending that it isn't.

Now much of my anger flows toward Ellen's parents—and here it's intentional that I not call them my grandparents. Before Ellen and I began writing to each other, I harbored a small hope that reuniting with her would mean I would also find a grandfather and grandmother. Both of my adoptive grandfathers had died before I was a toddler, and though my grandmothers lived until I was in college, I hadn't been close to either of them. I was disappointed to learn in Ellen's early letters that her parents had died before I could meet them.

But ever since I learned the story of my birth—and the role that Ellen's parents played in my being given away—my feelings toward them have bordered on hatred. I can rationally understand the position they were in, but my insides harden whenever I see their photographs, especially photos of Ellen's mother. I was her first grandchild. She had bonded with seven children of her own. Somewhere beneath their denial, she and Ellen's father must have known how damaging it would be to send me away. But they cared more about what the neighbors might think.

I'm also angry about the way adoption was handled back then, with a system founded on the ludicrous notion that you could take away a child's mother and simply substitute someone else, no harm done, without the child even noticing. I'm angry that my adoptive parents weren't counseled to understand the enormous losses my brother, sister and I had suffered. Angry that no one told them that the beautiful babies they'd been waiting for would need to grieve and might eventually seek out their birthparents. Angry that no one warned them not to take it personally.

And this last piece has been the hardest to admit: deep down, I'm angry at Ellen. She was twenty years old when she had me. An adult. She could have made a different choice.

The hardest thing about reuniting with Ellen has been its impact on my relationship with my adoptive mother. As I reread my e-mail from three years ago describing how I had finally told my parents about finding Ellen, I get a wave of sadness, knowing what I do now and seeing how hopeful I was then. My mother had asked good questions. She had acknowledged that I must have felt a big void in not knowing where I came from. She wanted to know if Ellen could draw. She didn't seem threatened. I thought that every-thing would be fine. Looking back, I wonder if I really believed that or just wanted to.

My letters to Ellen don't convey the full strain that my reunion with her placed on my relationship with my parents, my mother in particular. At the time I felt that even writing about it would be a betrayal, so I spoke in generalities and tried to protect them. But during that trip to Massachusetts, when Ellen and I met for the first time since my birth, there was enormous pressure on me not to have a relationship with her.

The pressure started the night I returned to my parents' house after my first day with Ellen. I had spent nine hours with her, first at a restaurant and then at her house with Gus, Jack and John. She gave me flowers. I looked at her photo albums, and she looked at mine. I played video games with the boys. Ellen showed me the pencil marks on the wall where they chart Gus and Jack's height, and told me to stand against there so she could add me to the records—Katie, 6/96, 5'6". I stayed for dinner and they gave me an early birthday party with cake and presents. It was all wonderful, and it was all completely overwhelming. I left loaded down with brownies and Gus's drawings. I forgot my flowers.

Then I got into my father's car and drove an hour and fifteen minutes to my parents' house. I barely remember the drive except that it was dark and the oncoming headlights seemed fuzzy, and I was worried that Ellen would think I wasn't grateful for the flowers. When I walked in their back door, my mother and father were waiting in the living room, the most formal room in the house, literally on the edges of their seats. They didn't appear to be breathing.

"How was it?" they wanted to know.

"It was good," I said, perching on the piano bench. "Yeah, it was nice."

I only remember snatches of the conversation after that. My father asked if what my mother had told him was true—had this woman really called the house looking for me years before? It's true, I told him, remembering how loved that had made me feel.

"Isn't that amazing?" I said.

"That's got to be illegal," he replied.

My mother informed me that she wasn't at all threatened by Ellen, then followed up with the warning: "Just make sure she never calls here." She also demanded that I never visit Ellen unless I visited them too.

"Why would I ever want to?" I asked, bewildered that she would even imagine something like that. I came back for long visits all the time, way more than my brother or sister.

The next morning, while I was still in my pajamas, my father sat down for a talk at the kitchen table. My mother, he told me, was not handling this well at all. So he was going to ask me something, not a very big thing, really, and he hoped I could do it. When I went for my second visit with Ellen the next day, couldn't I cut it short by a little? "Just, you know, come back sooner. It's not that big of a deal. You don't need to spend *that* long with her, right?"

I blinked and tried to find my bearings amid the fury and guilt roiling inside me. I hadn't seen my birthmother in twenty-seven years, and he was begrudging me a few *hours?* I told my father that I was sorry this was so painful, but that I didn't think it was fair to ask me that. He backed off, but the experience stayed with me and was a big part of the meltdown I had when I returned to San Francisco after that trip.

To this day, part of me still feels like a traitor to my parents, to my adoptive mom in particular. In the beginning, I spent a lot of time trying to reassure my mom that my reuniting with Ellen didn't mean I loved *her* any less. On the day of my second visit to Chelmsford, I had a bouquet of flowers delivered to my mom with a card that read, "No one could ever replace you." I tried to talk to her about my experience, to help her understand why I needed to connect with my birthmother. I wrote my mom letters about how important she is to me. But somehow, she couldn't hear me. Whenever I would mention the reunion or my feelings about being adopted, her whole body would go stiff, and her head would pull back as if I were about to strike her.

In my most utopian fantasy for how this will all turn out, there's a blending of the McGarry-Carlson family and the Herns. I imagine the backyard cookouts of my childhood, only this time the yard is filled with people from my adoptive *and* biological families. My father is at the grill joking with Jack about my tofu wieners. Gus is showing my mom his cartoons. John is chatting with Joe and Fran from across the street, and Ellen is sitting in a lawnchair beside my Auntie Kath. My brother's birthmother is there too, and both of his biological sisters. And my sister, Theresa, with her whole family. I look out and see all the people I love together, the rift inside me healed. And then I trounce everyone in a croquet tournament.

For now, though, things are painfully unresolved. My dad has been able to talk with me about my reunion with Ellen, and our relationship has grown and deepened. But there is an enormous distance between me and my mom. We haven't been able to talk about what's happening, so we haven't been able to move forward. I've made several trips to Chelmsford without even telling my parents I was in the state. I am having a clandestine affair with my birthfamily.

Or rather, with my *maternal* birthfamily. I haven't tried to contact my biological father, though I did go to a public library in Massachusetts to find his high school yearbook. I could see myself in his senior photograph and in his team picture on the varsity basketball page. The basketball photo was more flattering, and I noticed that I felt something like relief, as if I had somehow become better looking through that second image.

I have grainy copies of both photographs somewhere in my apartment. I also have a slip of paper with what I think is his current address, but so far all I've done is repeatedly misplace it. I'm not sure what's stopping me. I want to meet him. The last time I was in the town where he lives—buying Junior Mints at the local drugstore—I fantasized that someone would recognize me. I imagined that the cashier or a fellow shopper might see me and stop, confused: *She looks just like Doug's kids.* Then I realized that one of Doug's kids might *be* the cashier. Doug might even be there himself, waiting for a prescription. I looked hopefully at the faces around me and then left, disappointed.

Maybe the fear of rejection is holding me back. Ellen had opened the Catholic Charities file to me, but Doug never did, and I'm not eager to repeat my brother's experience. Or maybe I'm afraid reuniting with my biological father will cause problems in my relationship with Ellen. Or with my adoptive dad. I don't know. But I remember the hope I felt in that drugstore, and my dismay that I'd found only two photographs of him in the yearbook.

As hard as this reunion has sometimes been, it has also been profoundly healing. Before writing my letters to Ellen, I had never been able to really share my grief with anyone. I had spent my life pantomiming what I thought was mental health: always being in control, denying all unacceptable emotions, happy and positive all the livelong day. And it had kept me in a state of emotional limbo. I hadn't been fully living my life.

During the last three years I've started to understand what author Rachel Naomi Remen meant when she wrote, "It is actually difficult to edit life. Especially in regard to feelings. Not being open to anger or sadness usually means being unable to be open to love and joy. The emotions seem to operate on an all-or-nothing switch." At this point, although I wouldn't describe myself as quite *open* to anger or sadness, we're at least acquaintances. I recognize them when we pass on the street.

In return, my life has started to open up as well. When students come into my office, frustrated or upset about their writing, I am more compassionate. I can even sit calmly with them when they cry, instead of wishing they'd stop mistaking me for a therapist. My friendships are closer. And I've started noticing flowers—bright pink bougainvilleas, roses, rhododendrons, and all kinds of beautiful, anonymous bursts of color I'd never noticed before. They seem to be everywhere I go this spring.

Somehow, too, the sense of tenuousness I described in my letters to Ellen has receded. I no longer need two boxes of tampons under the sink, and last year, at age twenty-nine, I finally bought my first car. I had fantasized about having a car since graduate school. Seven years of bumming rides from other people and taking public transportation. Between the bus, the train and my own two feet, I spent two and a half hours commuting to and from work each day. But my existence didn't feel secure enough to commit to a car. Monthly payments. Insurance. Gas. Maintenance. Tolls. Parking tickets. If I lost my job, the car would be like a boulder strapped to my ankle, pulling me down to the bottom of the river.

Then last August I bought a beautiful, almost-new Nissan Sentra with power everything, and my commute shrank to twenty minutes each way. At first I imagined that the car would be stolen at any minute. Or smashed by a hit-and-run driver. Or that a rock would fly into my windshield on the freeway and send me crashing to my death.

But now I zoom along the freeways, basking in the beauty of the Bay and the golden California hills and the clear, shining light that makes me fill my lungs with oxygen. I don't worry about getting a flat tire, or driving off the Bay Bridge, because I know how to change a tire and I'm not prone to sudden, uncontrollable swerving. Instead, I rest my arm on the open window and appreciate the warm, liquid satisfaction of driving my own car. When I coast over a hill or lean into a curve, my body is released from the posture it had been locked in for so many years: the clench of bracing against the worst case scenario. And I feel, in these moments, fully alive.

Bibliography

Adopted Child. A monthly newsletter published since 1981 by Lois R. Melina. Moscow, ID. (888) 882-1794.

Brodzinsky, David M., Marshall D. Schechter and Robin Marantz Henig. *Being Adopted: The Lifelong Search for Self.* New York: Doubleday, 1992.

Brown, Rita Mae. *Rubyfruit Jungle.* New York: Bantam Books, 1973.

Didion, Joan. "Why I Write," *New York Times Magazine,* December 5, 1976.

Frey, James N. *How to Write a Damn Good Novel.* New York: St. Martin's Press, 1987.

Lamott, Anne. *Bird by Bird: Some Instructions on Writing and Life.* New York: Pantheon Books, 1994.

Lifton, Betty Jean. *Journey of the Adopted Self: A Quest for Wholeness.* New York: Basic Books, 1994.

Lifton, Betty Jean. *Lost and Found: The Adoption Experience.* New York: Dial Press, 1979.

Remen, Rachel Naomi. *Kitchen Table Wisdom: Stories That Heal.* New York: Riverhead Books, 1996.

Schaefer, Carol. *The Other Mother: A Woman's Love for the Child She Gave up for Adoption.* New York: Soho Press, 1991.

Strauss, Jean. *Birthright: The Guide to Search and Reunion for Adoptees, Birthparents, and Adoptive Parents.* New York: Penguin Books, 1994.

Verrier, Nancy Newton. *The Primal Wound: Understanding the Adopted Child.* Baltimore, MD: Gateway Press, 1993.

Wells, Sue. *Within Me, Without Me: Adoption: Open and Shut Case?* London: Scarlet Press, 1994.

Resource Organizations

The Adoption Connection, 11 Peabody Square, Peabody, MA 01960. Susan Drake, Director. (978) 532-1261.

Adoptee Liberty Movement Association (ALMA), P. O. Box 727, Radio City Station, New York, NY 10101-0727. (212) 581-1568.

Concerned United Birthparents (CUB), P. O. Box 396, Cambridge, MA 02238. (978) 342-8196. National Headquarters: 2000 Walker Street, Des Moines, IA 50317. (800) 822-2777.

About the Authors

Katie Hern teaches writing at John F. Kennedy University in Northern California and has written for numerous publications. She lives in Oakland, where she is currently at work on her first novel.

Ellen McGarry Carlson, a homemaker and college student, lives in Chelmsford, Massachusetts.

Selected Titles from Seal Press

Adiós, Barbie: Young Women Write About Body Image and Identity edited by Ophira Edut. $14.95, 1-58005-016-6. Essays filled with honesty and humor by women who have chosen to ignore, subvert or redefine the dominant beauty standard.

The Adoption Reader: Birthmothers, Adoptive Mothers and Adopted Daughters Tell Their Stories, edited by Susan Wadia-Ells. $16.95, 1-878067-65-6. With eloquence and conviction, more than thirty birthmothers, adoptive mothers and adopted daughters explore the many faces of adoption

Dharma Girl: A Road Trip Across the American Generations by Chelsea Cain. $12.00, 1-878067-84-2. Written to the unmistakable beat of the road, this memoir chronicles the twenty-four-year-old author's homecoming to the commune in Iowa where she grew up with her counterculture parents.

Dutiful Daughters: Caring for Our Parents as They Grow Old edited by Jean Gould. $16.95, 1-58005-026-3. A compassionate collection of stories by women who have taken on the role of "dutiful daughter" with uncommon—and often unexpected—results.

The Lesbian Parenting Book: A Guide to Creating Families and Raising Children by Merilee Clunis and G. Dorsey Green. $18.95, 1-878067-68-0. This practical and readable book covers a wide range of parenting topics as well as issues specifically relevant to lesbian families. Information on each child development stage is also provided.

The Single Mother's Companion: Essays and Stories by Women, edited by Marsha Leslie. $12.95, 1-878067-56-7. In their own words, the single mothers in this landmark collection explore both the joys and the difficult realities of raising children alone. Contributors include Barbara Kingsolver, Anne Lamott, Linda Hogan, Julia A. Boyd and Senator Carol Moseley-Braun.

Wild Child: Girlhoods in the Counterculture edited by Chelsea Cain. $16.00, 1-58008-031-X. In this collection of essays, the daughters of the hippie generation speak for themselves about growing up in the counterculture.

Seal Press publishes many books of fiction and nonfiction by women writers. If you are unable to obtain a Seal Press title from a bookstore or would like a free catalog of our books, please order from us directly by calling 800-754-0271. Visit our website at www.sealpress.com.